POWER REVEALED

POWER REVEALED

The Message of Luke–Acts: Then and Now

Robert P. Vande Kappelle

WIPF & STOCK · Eugene, Oregon

POWER REVEALED
The Message of Luke–Acts: Then and Now

Copyright © 2019 Robert P. Vande Kappelle. All rights reserved. Except for brief quotations in critical publications or reviews, no part of this book may be reproduced in any manner without prior written permission from the publisher. Write: Permissions, Wipf and Stock Publishers, 199 W. 8th Ave., Suite 3, Eugene, OR 97401.

Wipf & Stock
An Imprint of Wipf and Stock Publishers
199 W. 8th Ave., Suite 3
Eugene, OR 97401

www.wipfandstock.com

PAPERBACK ISBN: 978-1-7252-5375-9
HARDCOVER ISBN: 978-1-7252-5376-6
EBOOK ISBN: 978-1-7252-5377-3

Unless otherwise noted, Bible quotations are from the New Revised Standard Version of the Bible, copyright © 1989 by the Division of Christian Education of the National Council of the Churches of Christ in the United States of America. Used by permission.

Manufactured in the U.S.A.   OCTOBER 28, 2019

You will receive *power* when the Holy Spirit has come upon you; and you will be my witnesses . . . to the ends of the earth.

—Acts 1:8

With great *power* the apostles gave their testimony
to the resurrection of the Lord Jesus,
and great grace was upon them all.

—Acts 4:33

Contents

Preface | ix

Unit I—Preliminary Topics | 1

    Chapter 1   Understanding History | 3

    Chapter 2   Understanding Scripture | 16

    Chapter 3   Understanding Luke–Acts | 31

Unit II—Introductory Topics | 51

    Chapter 4   Luke's Literary Task | 53

    Chapter 5   Luke's Liturgical Task | 70

    Chapter 6   Luke's Historical Task | 83

    Chapter 7   Luke's Theological Task | 98

Unit III—Exegetical Topics | 115

    Chapter 8   The Infancy Narrative (Luke 1:1—2:52) | 117

    Chapter 9   Jesus' Galilean Ministry (Luke 3:1—9:50) | 135

    Chapter 10   Luke's Travel Narrative (Luke 9:51—19:27) | 149

    Chapter 11   Jesus' Passion, Resurrection, and Ascension (Luke 19:28—24:53) | 168

    Chapter 12   The Christian Mission in Jerusalem (Acts 1:1—6:7) | 182

    Chapter 13   The Christian Mission in Judea, Samaria, and Syria (Acts 6:8—12:24) | 197

    Chapter 14   The Christian Mission in Asia Minor and Europe (Acts 12:25—28:31) | 215

Epilogue | 237

Appendix A   *Lukan Christology* | 239
Appendix B   *Lukan Soteriology* | 247
Bibliography | 253
Index | 257

Preface

HAVING RECENTLY COMPLETED BOOKS on spirituality, church history, and theology, I return to my first love—scripture—adding this volume on Luke–Acts to my "Then and Now" series on biblical topics such as the book of Revelation (*Hope Revealed*, 2013), the Gospel of John (*Truth Revealed*, 2014), the biblical wisdom literature (*Wisdom Revealed*, 2014), and Paul's letter to the Romans (*Grace Revealed*, 2017), in addition to my study on the Bible as a whole (*Securing Life*, 2016).

Why Luke–Acts? Because this two-part story, separated in the biblical canon but hyphenated in 1927 by Lukan scholar Henry Cadbury to highlight the historic unity of the two books, constitutes over one quarter of the New Testament, making its author the first and most important early Christian historian and together with Paul and John one of early Christianity's greatest theologians (German biblical scholar Ernst Käsemann called Luke "the greatest New Testament theologian"). Taken together, the two roughly equivalent narratives constitute the largest works in the New Testament, and together, they represent the foremost literary contribution by a single author. Furthermore, Luke's skills as author and historiographer, when judged by first-century standards, are of the highest order. A gifted literary artist, capable of writing an elegant style of Greek, he produced a Gospel justly described by the celebrated nineteenth-century French writer Ernst Renan as "the most beautiful book in the world." A gifted storyteller, Luke includes some of the most memorable passages in the Gospels, such as the parables of the Good Samaritan and the Prodigal Son. Described by Dante as "the scribe of the gentleness of Christ," Luke more than any other evangelist (gospel writer) has given the world a Jesus to love.[1] Luke's Gospel, unique in its perspective and creative in its rendering of Jesus' life and

---

1. Brown, *Introduction to the New Testament*, 267.

teachings, is worthy of prolonged and independent study, as is the book of Acts, the only book in the New Testament canon dealing with the history of the church and early Christianity.

Spiritual Power

The notion of power is foundational to Luke, as it is to Western civilization. Modern Americans seem fixated on power, consuming "power drinks, power eggs, and power crunch bars," using "power tools" to fix things and "power rackets" to play tennis. Our children have "power wheels" and "power ranger" toys, and senior citizens take "power naps." However, Americans also prize power because it represents core values such as vitality, success, individuality, influence, authority, and self-determination. Such values, however, are not what Luke had in mind when he spoke of spiritual power. Living in a Greco-Roman world, early followers of Jesus experienced religious prejudice and social discrimination from all sides, Jewish and Roman alike. Driven by the need to provide guidance and assurance to followers of a crucified Messiah, Luke's narrative focuses on notions of divine power, assuring believers of God's overarching plan for human history and of God's providential care for beleaguered believers.

The theme of power appears early in Luke's Gospel, with the birth of John the Baptist, seen as the forerunner of Jesus: "Even before his birth he [John the Baptist] will be filled with the Holy Spirit. He will turn many of the people of Israel to the Lord their God. With the spirit and *power* of Elijah he [John] will go before him [Jesus], to turn the hearts of parents to their children, and the disobedient to the wisdom of the righteous, to make ready a people prepared for the Lord" (Luke 1:15–17). Later in Luke's introductory chapter, the angel Gabriel tells Mary that this same divine power will be present in the conception of her child, Jesus: "The Holy Spirit will come upon you, and the *power* of the Most High will overshadow you; therefore the child to be born will be holy; he will be called Son of God" (Luke 1:35). This same Spirit will drive Jesus into the wilderness, where he will be empowered to resist temptation. After that, "filled with the *power* of the Spirit" (Luke 4:14), Jesus enters into the Galilean phase of his ministry, equipped to defeat evil. Throughout his ministry, the Jews are amazed at Jesus' power (see 4:36; 5:17), which he imparts to his disciples (9:1; 24:49).

Luke stresses the role of the Holy Spirit, both in the life of Jesus and in the life of the early church. Significantly, from the start of his mission, Jesus' mission is based on Spirit empowerment, "The Spirit of the Lord is upon me" (4:18), while Acts begins with Jesus' promise that the disciples would also receive the power of the Holy Spirit, which would guide the early church's life and its expansion from the center of the Jewish world to the heart of the Roman world: "But you will receive *power* when the Holy Spirit has come upon you; and you will be my witnesses in Jerusalem, in all Judea and Samaria, and to the ends of the earth" (Acts 1:8; see also 4:33). Luke describes the fulfillment of that promise in Acts 2, the so-called birth of the church on Pentecost.[2]

As we shall see, Pentecost, for Luke, is a paradigmatic episode that, in parallel with Jesus' reception of the Spirit, signals conferral of power for and the beginning of the church's mission and witness to the ends of the earth (see Acts 2:33). As we see in Acts and in the letters of Paul, the early church was charismatic, its work dominated by the experience of the Holy Spirit. Church members believed the Holy Spirit was the only organizing force they needed. This understanding of Christian fellowship became central for Paul and quite likely for other apostles as well.

The typical picture of a local church in the New Testament is of groups of Christians acting together in a spirit of mutual love and friendship. Central to community life was an understanding that believers had been endowed with spiritual gifts such as "speaking in tongues," faith healing, and other demonstrations of divine power. Such charismatic activity described the early church. Early Christians viewed the Spirit as the "organizing principle" of church life, and all participated in corporate worship. Spiritual gifts were admired in apostolic churches and widely manifest in the first century. A classic Pauline passage dealing with "spiritual gifts," particularly their misuse, is found in 1 Corinthians 12. Because Paul is concerned with unity in his churches, he introduces the topic with a call to Christian humility, an important manifestation of the transformation that should characterize the believer. However, Paul is concerned that believers not take an overly individualistic approach to spirituality. He wants believers to recognize that transformation of character is demonstrated in relationships with one another.

Paul's premise in 1 Corinthians 12 is that God gives to every believer a spiritual ability to perform for the common good, to encourage and build up the church, which he calls the body of Christ. In Corinthians 12:8–10 Paul lists nine spiritual gifts: wisdom, knowledge, faith, healing, working miracles, prophecy, discernment of spirits, speaking in tongues (known as glossolalia), and interpretation of tongues. Such gifts, called "sign gifts," are

---

2. In my earlier book, *The New Creation*, I trace the birth of the church—defined as the mystical and invisible "people of God"—to God's covenant with Abraham (see Gen. 12:1–3), rather than to the events of Pentecost. Since that definition is not germane in this context, I will not pursue it here.

granted to individuals for the common good. They can be divided into three groups:

- Declarative gifts (power of speaking). Gifts of communication include prophecy, the ability to distinguish between true and false prophecy, speaking in tongues, and the ability to interpret speaking in tongues.
- Dynamic gifts (power of doing). Gifts of practical ministry include faith (the precondition for miracles), healing, and miracles.
- Discerning gifts (power of knowing). Gifts of pedagogy include wisdom and knowledge.

Another list, called "service gifts," appears in 1 Corinthians 12:28: apostles, prophets, teachers, workers of miracles, healers, assistants, leaders, speakers in tongues. These support gifts are granted to individuals for church ministry. For Paul, the bottom line is this: every Christian ought to consider his/her gift(s) as a ministry of service to others. That is the biblical understanding of power, whether human or divine.

Despite Luke's focus on Peter and Paul in Acts, the main protagonist is not any of the apostles but rather the Holy Spirit, who is mentioned fifty-seven times. If Luke is the Gospel of Jesus, Acts is the Gospel of the Spirit. Thus, one might say that in Luke we have the story of the work and presence of the Spirit in Jesus, whereas in Acts we have the story of the work and presence of Jesus through the Spirit. As Luke makes clear, the same power at work in Jesus is at work in the early church, for it is the same Spirit. Ultimately, this understanding of divine power answers our initial question. Why study Luke–Acts? Because the Spirit at work then is also at work today.[3]

Lukan studies today constitute one of the New Testament's most vibrant areas of scholarly study. Commentaries on the Third Gospel and/or on the book of Acts number in the hundreds, as do special studies on specific Lukan topics. Some of these volumes are technical, literary, and theological in nature, while others are more practical and devotional. The ultimate goal of all biblical study, however, whether historical, literary, theological, or exegetical, is to connect readers of scripture with the inspirational source, the Triune God. As long as that relationship remains central, the books of Luke–Acts promise a fruitful field of study for years to come.

---

3. The role of the Holy Spirit in Luke–Acts is elaborated further in chapters 6 and 7 below.

Overview

Broadly speaking, scholars have introduced three major approaches to Luke, developing perspectives on Luke as historian, literary artist, and theologian (these topics are addressed in chapters 1–5 below). One area of debate concerns the Jewish background of Luke–Acts, and the accuracy of the traditional profile of Luke as a Gentile convert to Christianity. Another trend in recent scholarship is a heightened interest in Luke's portrait of Jesus (i.e. Luke's christology). Scholars are working hard to define more clearly Luke's understanding of Jesus and, in so doing, reexamining Luke's views on salvation and the plan of God. Whatever value Luke's writings may have as history, most scholars today are more interested in the contributions they make to theology. Viewed as a capable and original theologian, Luke's interpretation of early traditions played a major role in the development of Christianity.

Another area of scholarly importance is the question of Luke's purpose in composing his two-volume work. Answers range from Christianity's relationship to Judaism and the secular world to sectarian influences. Underlying this question lies the assumption that Luke does not "do theology" in a vacuum, but rather is responding theologically to genuine concerns of real people. Interest in Luke's social context is indicated by a marked increase of studies on his treatment of social and political issues. Of course, Luke is concerned with such matters insofar as they affect his own community, but many scholars believe his interest in questions of peace, equality, and social justice transcends particular application. As Lukan studies indicate, social and political categories may be as important for understanding Luke as traditional theological ones.

Another important development in Lukan studies has been the diversification of literary approaches, using literary criticism to examine the genre, sources, plot, themes, character development, and artistry of Luke's writings. For example, a few decades ago it was widely assumed that the "Synoptic problem" had been solved, and that any study of Luke's Gospel could proceed from the fact that Luke had used Mark and "Q" (a supposed "sayings" source, now lost, said to be used independently by Matthew and Luke in the construction of their Gospels) as sources. The debate on this topic has been re-opened. One group of scholars, led by Michael Goulder and John Drury, contends that Luke's parallels with Matthew can be accounted for by a direct dependence solely on that Gospel, rather than upon the hypothetical "Q" document. Goulder and Drury explain Luke's editing of Matthew in terms of lectionary needs and contemporary literary practices. They believe Luke produced his Gospel as a "midrash" (a Jewish practice of imaginatively retelling scripture for the purpose of homiletical interpretation) on Matthew and Mark, with frequent reference to the Old Testament, rendering the existence of "Q" unnecessary. For example, Drury argued that Luke's entire "travel narrative" (Luke 10–19) was modeled on Deuteronomy.

Chapters 6 and 7 are devoted to Luke's purpose, which brings us to what are unquestionably the major theological issues in Lukan studies: theology, christology, pneumatology, ecclesiology, and sociology, including such topics as eschatology and salvation history. These matters are still of interest today, forming the core of Lukan studies. The future of such studies will undoubtedly see a significant increase in contributions from women theologians, third-world scholars, and other scholarly minorities, and these will bring surprising new insights.

Despite scholarly focus on intellectual, controversial, and technical issues and concerns, the heart of Lukan studies, as of biblical study in general, remains exegesis, namely, expositing the biblical text for practical, pastoral, and spiritual needs. For that reason, unit III (chapters 8–14) explores select exegetical studies from the Gospel of Luke and the book of Acts.

Distinctive Features

My goal in writing this book is to produce a volume on Luke–Acts that addresses the interests and needs of a general Christian audience, providing guidelines for understanding the message of this ancient work and its application to twenty-first-century readers. *Power Revealed* is not an exegetical commentary, for it does not offer verse-by-verse analysis of the text. Neither is it a textual study, in which a scholar makes a case for a preferred reading. Instead, it offers perspective on specific introductory, theological, and exegetical topics that arise from a reading of the biblical text. My intent is to proceed from general to specific, from understanding to text to application.

Whether you are reading this book individually or with a group, I recommend that you keep a journal, noting insights and questions from readings. The journal will also be used to record the weekly homework assignment. Designed as a study guide for individual and group use, each chapter includes various features helpful for study:

1. summary or outline of the chapter
2. homework assignment
3. learning objectives (only chapters 1–7)

In addition to a journal, participants in group study should also bring to class a Bible as well as a copy of *Power Revealed*. Group leaders are encouraged to add or substitute their own priorities or methodologies. Upon concluding each chapter or session, readers and participants will profit by asking the question, "What is the primary insight I (we) gained from this chapter or session?"

UNIT I

Preliminary Topics

CHAPTER 1

Understanding History

Summary: Chapter 1 explores the topic of historiography, particularly, how to study ancient history. The task of historians is always constrained by the nature and availability of sources. Because the past cannot be experienced or known directly, historians utilize ancient sources, themselves preserved pieces of memory. In this respect, second-hand primary sources such as the Gospel of Luke and the book of Acts must be examined with regard to reliability and bias, for all historical records, whether from antiquity or modernity, are heavily layered and necessarily biased.

As the biblical record indicates, history unfolds according to a discernible pattern—order, disorder, and reorder. This archetypal pattern, evident in scripture and throughout church history, is also paradigmatic for life, history, and reality in general. When compared with other Gospel accounts and with other historians of antiquity, Luke's writings, accurate and reliable by ancient standards, represent nuanced and biased historical accounts, recorded not simply for their own sake but also for their theological and sociological significance regarding the meaning of history and the future of humanity.

Assignment: Read the Preface and Introduction of *Power Revealed*. If you have time, read the Gospel of Luke in its entirety. Even if you have read this Gospel before, it is helpful to refresh your memory and have an overall sense of Luke's first book before studying the introductory topics in chapters 3 through 7 of *Power Revealed*, so the sooner you start, the better. Likewise, the assignment for Chapter 2 asks you to read the book of Acts in its entirety. Answer the following questions, writing the answers in your journal. [If you are in a study group, be prepared to share your views with others in the class.] 1. Explain and assess the merits of the author's statement that "historical accounts by nature always have a fictional character." 2. In your estimation, should Luke be evaluated as a modern historian, that is, by current standards of historiography, or as a historian of his age? Explain your answer.

Learning Objectives: After completing this chapter, participants will be able to:

1. Appreciate and explain the differences between the remedial and creative functions of historiography.
2. Acknowledge the distinction between first- and second-hand primary sources.
3. Understand the role bias plays in the historical process.
4. Provide examples of the order-disorder-reorder paradigm in biblical and church history.
5. Acknowledge and assess the threefold role of scripture.
6. Assess Luke's role as historian, theologian, and social analyst.

Before we examine Luke–Acts directly, including introductory topics such as authorship, date, audience, unity, structure, and purpose, we explore two related disciplines, namely, historiography and hermeneutics, or, more specifically, how to study ancient history and how to interpret scripture. Readers of my books will find historiography an essentially new concern, whereas hermeneutics[1] is one I address in my biblical commentaries. We begin with historiography.

When we speak of history, what do we mean? If we are thinking solely of the past, or of something that happened factually in the past, we need to keep in mind that while the study of history has a remedial function—assessing evidence to correct errors and misconceptions—it also has a creative function.

Modern thinkers often define history as an objective reporting of facts. However, the notion of scholarly objectivity is fallacious, as shown by scholars such as Paul Ricoeur, who stress that all history is written in response to subjective interests of historians. According to William Willimon, "without such subjective interests, historiography would be nothing more than a jumble of unrelated data without meaning. Whoever looks for

---

1. The topic of biblical interpretation is discussed at length in chapter 2 below.

nothing in history finds nothing."[2] Because the past cannot be experienced or known directly, the study of history cannot simply be descriptive. Rather, history is more adequately understood as a constructive activity in the present carried out by historians. Historians take preserved pieces of memory from human events and experiences in the past and subject them to critical analysis. In the case of biblical history, they ask, for example, whether writings are first-hand primary sources, such as the undisputed letters of Paul, or whether they are second-hand primary sources, such as the Acts of the Apostles. Historians ask other critical questions about sources, such as their geographical location, date, reliability, and bias. Then, on the basis of this examination, they try to construct a narrative concerning the events to which the sources bear witness.

By necessity, historians speculate concerning the evidence and the limits of their information, supplying elements such as sequence, motivation, and cause. Because historians cannot construct a narrative without using devices of fiction, historical accounts by nature always have a fictional character. As a constructive activity carried out in the present with bits of memory from the past, history is inherently limited in its way of knowing reality. While it has to do with human events, even defining the character of events and their boundaries involves guesswork and decision. When historians and people in general speak definitively of recent events such as World War II or the Depression, they know that such categories are artificial boundaries drawn—for purpose of analysis—within the constant flux of human experience. How far greater the uncertainty when we speak of events from antiquity!

Historical accounts are also necessarily revisionist, both because new information regularly becomes available and because historical perspectives constantly change. For example, consider how differently historians might evaluate Abraham Lincoln's presidency, whether from temporal proximity or distance to that event, or from Northern or Southern perspectives. Political leaders, often excoriated in the short term, are frequently viewed more positively with the passage of time. While evidence may not have changed, subsequent events often provide differing perspectives.

The task of the historian is, above all, constrained by the nature and availability of sources, themselves ultimately memory units representing what someone may have said or done in the past. What someone said or wrote had to be perceived, recorded, preserved, edited, translated, published, and read. Every step of that process required interpretation. Additionally, each person in that process had a distinct point of view. Perception

---

2. Willimon, *Acts*, 7.

shaped writing, and assessment as to the value of what was written determined preservation. Furthermore, original sources might have been lost or destroyed, requiring reconstruction. Finally, the modern historian—or in the case of this book, the author—also speaks from a distinct perspective and with specific bias. None of this can be avoided. What appears in this or any book or news story, whether about antiquity or modernity, is of necessity biased and heavily layered.

The Trajectory of History: Uncommon Beginnings and Unfinished Endings

The following illustration, taken from a group Bible study, reveals insights into people's perspectives and biases, as well as lessons about history gained by the study of scripture.

The week after Easter, nine participants gathered in a rural Pennsylvania church for the weekly workshop on personal growth and spiritual transformation. Ray, the group's most conservative member, was leading, and I was present as a guest. The members were studying church history, concluding their review of the Old Testament by examining three episodes in Israel's history: the Davidic kingdom, the prophetic period, and the Babylonian exile.

Ray's relaxed leadership style, antithetical to his dogmatic theological stance, stimulated an open and wide ranging conversation. As a result, an unplanned topic emerged—the role of scripture in twenty-first-century life. Mary Lou got the discussion started, noting that she had recently heard a television commentator state that the role of religion in contemporary society was declining dramatically. Was this correct, we questioned, and if so, what were the implications? These questions and concerns returned us to the topic of what the Bible teaches about the trajectory of history. Should people of faith be hopeful or pessimistic about the future?

As the biblical record indicates, history seems to unfold according to a discernable pattern: creation (stability), chaos (instability), and re-creation, or, as contemporary thinker Richard Rohr puts it, order, disorder, and reorder.[3] As the following examples illustrate, this paradigm occurs repeatedly in scriptural and historical writings, beginning in Genesis and continuing throughout church history.

- *Pattern of creation.* God transforms darkness into light, bringing order out of chaos. Adam and Eve's disobedience results in expulsion,

3. Rohr, *Universal Christ*, 243–48.

fratricide, wandering, and futility of labor, but also in forgiveness, new beginnings, and the start of human civilization.

- *Pattern of the flood.* Human disbelief and disobedience result in banishment and desolation, but also in redemption and re-creation. Noah becomes a second Adam, and humanity starts anew.
- *Pattern of the exodus.* The Israelites are enslaved for four hundred years, but God hears their cries and brings deliverance. Moses becomes a third Adam, at least for Israelites, a pioneer who leads the people to a new start in the Promised Land.
- *Pattern of the judges.* While occupying and subjugating the Promised Land, the tribes of Israel compromise their identity as God's chosen servants. However, through punishment and repentance they experience deliverance. This cycle of disobedience, repentance, and deliverance is repeated seven times in the book of Judges. In times of darkness and insecurity, the judges institute social stability by helping the people live up to the ideals of loyalty, trust, and covenant faithfulness.
- *Pattern of the monarchy.* Surrounded by powerful empires, the tribes of Israel seek survival and the stability of nationhood through a dynastic monarchy. Saul, the first king, is a failure, but David becomes a new Moses by defeating Goliath, the Philistine colossus, by establishing a royal covenant in the city of Jerusalem, and by establishing an ideal reign in the kingdom of Judah.
- *Pattern of the exile.* The destruction of Jerusalem by Babylon in the sixth century BCE brings an end to political, social, and religious life in Judah. In exile, the people of Judah are reconstituted around the Torah. Using the typology of the exodus, the prophet known as Second Isaiah ignites the hope of the people, assuring them of imminent deliverance from captivity. Cyrus of Persia emerges as God's "messiah" (see Isa. 45:1–3), liberating the Jews from captivity and permitting repatriation.
- *Pattern of restoration.* The period following return from exile (known as the Second Temple period), challenges the modest Jewish community, overpowered by Persian, Egyptian, Greek, and Roman cultural influences. A new Goliath, the Syrian ruler Antiochus Epiphanes, attempts to undermine Jewish uniqueness through forcible Hellenization. Unsuccessful in paganizing the Jewish community, his efforts incite the Maccabean revolt, under the leadership of Judas Maccabeus, and eventually lead to Jewish independence under native Hasmonean rulers.

- *Pattern of the new covenant.* Conquered by Rome, the Jewish people struggle to maintain their cultural and spiritual identity. In the first century CE (designated the fullness of time by Paul; see Gal. 4:4), God establishes a new covenant with humanity, sending Jesus to be the firstborn of God's new humanity, the mediator of a new covenant (Heb. 8). Called the Son of David, through his life, death, and resurrection Jesus demonstrates his role as the second or last Adam (see 1 Cor. 15:45, 47).

- *Pattern of the New Israel.* Following the destruction of Jerusalem by Rome in 70 CE, the Jesus movement separates from the Jewish synagogue to become God's new creation, God's New Israel (see Gal. 6:5–16).

- *Pattern of Christendom.* The pattern of creation–chaos–recreation, established in scripture, continues throughout church history, as exemplified in Christianity's struggle with official imperial persecution in the second and third centuries and the ascendance of Constantine to imperial power at the start of the fourth century, paving the way for Christendom.

- *Pattern of Christianity's expansion to Europe.* Preceding and following the fall of the Roman Empire, the growing Christian movement builds on the efforts of courageous missionaries such as Ulfilas, Patrick, Columba, Augustine of Canterbury, Boniface, Cyril, and Methodius.

- *Pattern of Christianity's struggle with internal corruption.* As Christianity establishes itself in the known world, dissension and decay in the late medieval period lead to the emergence of reformers John Wycliffe and John Hus in the fourteenth and fifteenth centuries and later to the reforming efforts of Martin Luther, John Calvin, and Ignatius Loyola.

- *Pattern of Christianity's struggle with modernism and secularism.* The modern period is spearheaded by revitalizing movements such as pietism, evangelicalism, and ecumenism; by the efforts of individuals such as mathematician Blaise Pascal, social reformer Count von Zinzendorf, and revivalist preachers John Wesley, Jonathan Edwards, and George Whitefield; and by the emergence of religious societies and voluntary parachurch organizations that mobilize movements such as the great awakenings in America and the great global missionary and social efforts of the nineteenth and twentieth centuries.

The preceding examples, documented in scripture or inspired by the biblical narrative, all attest to the threefold role of scripture:

- *to remind* believers of their common identity as servants of the living God
- *to warn* believers of the consequences of compromise and loss of vision
- *to inspire hope* in the God who loves humanity unconditionally, for whom nothing is impossible, and who controls the present by dwelling simultaneously in the past, present, and future.

As Christianity maintains, the heart of scripture is Jesus Christ. Scripture, like history, points to Christ, is fulfilled in him, flows from him, and is guided by the pattern he establishes for reality: life–death–resurrection.

As our study group discovered that rainy post-Easter night, the role of scripture is to remind us that when we feel discouraged, frustrated, or overwhelmed, God is in charge and has a hopeful plan. As Holocaust survivor Corrie ten Boom, reminds us: There is no darkness from which God cannot produce light, no pit so deep that God's love cannot plumb its depths, and no situation so hopeless that God's grace cannot transform. In fact, as scripture, history, and nature demonstrate, darkness precedes dawn. When things seem hopeless, bleak, and desperate, God always provides a vision, a passage, or a deliverer.

At one point in our discussion, Marybeth asked the group whether global warming might be God's wakeup call to our generation. That comment elicited a varied response from those gathered. Ray wondered whether global warming was real. "Of course it is," Jess replied, "for which science is supplying undeniable evidence, such as unstable weather patterns, increasingly violent storms, seal-level rising, and glacier loss."

Acknowledging that global warming might be real, Jim pondered the effects human response might have on the end game, at best perhaps only forestalling the inevitable. Convinced by the scientific evidence, he breathed a sigh of relief, thankful he would not live to witness global warning's worst effects. Marybeth wondered whether these might be the "last days."

Questioning what we could do in the face of profound environmental change, we pondered the lessons of scripture. In the past, during times of trouble, God always provided an alternative. Couldn't God inspire a new vision, produce a new prophet, or simply remind us again of the divine paradigm revealed in Jesus, that from darkness comes life, and that death is but a prelude to resurrection and new creation? Believing that faith could move mountains, the first Christians, proceeded to move mountains, with God's help. Could we trust God like that again?

As Robert Schuller exhorted in his "Possibility Thinker's Creed,"

When faced with a mountain, I will not quit!

> I will keep on striving until I climb over,
> Find a pass through, tunnel underneath,
> Or simply stay and turn the mountain into a gold mine, with God's help.

In his seminars on human development, author William Bridges[4] claims that successful transitions go through a three-stage process, which he labels ending, lostness, and beginning. Ending, the first stage of every successful transition, is followed by a period of confusion and distress, which he describes as "emptiness"; without endings and critical times of emptiness, there can be no genuine newness, no healthy beginnings. Such a pattern may be found in nature, with its succession of fall, winter, and spring. That pattern, Bridges argues, must be followed if transitions are to be therapeutic and complete. Despite this natural model, we humans often avoid transitions, for they require adaptation and change.

Healthy transitions start with endings, and how we recognize endings, says Bridges, is the key to beginning anew. Affirming God's presence in life's in-between times, in the wintry emptiness that separates endings from beginnings, contributes immeasurably towards beneficial new starts. That legacy, perhaps scripture's greatest, is God's way to remind, warn, and inspire hope in all people of faith.

This perspective, clearly demonstrated in Luke's writings, helps explain why he begins and ends his Gospel and the book of Acts as he does, with uncommon beginnings and unfinished endings. Luke's focus is on beginnings, not endings, for what humans see as endings are but beginnings in God's sight.

Luke as Historian

Scholars repeatedly point to the abilities of Luke as theologian and narrator, but leave open the disputed question of his role as historian. In the past, scholars and general readers viewed Luke's Gospel and the book of Acts as a history of Christian origins, considering Luke's work a vast storehouse of information for reconstructing what happened in the lives of Jesus and his earliest followers. Modern times, however, have introduced a refinement of critical methodologies for conducting historical research, and Luke the historian has fallen on hard times. However, since he starts his two-volume work by talking about composing an accurate account based on rigorous questioning of original eyewitness (Luke 1:1–3), by any standard the question of history is appropriate.

---

4. Bridges, *Transitions*.

Even a cursory comparison of Luke's Gospel with other Gospel accounts reveals how creative these authors were with their tradition. Yet, no matter how much liberty Luke may have taken with regard to traditions about Jesus, we wonder how much he knew about early Christianity, and how accurately he portrayed the Jerusalem church and the spread of Christianity. On these topics, estimates range widely. Leaving the details to specialized study, it is obvious that the accounts in Acts, like those in Luke's Gospel, are highly selective chronologically and geographically. While the events recorded in Acts cover a time span of about thirty years, the incidents narrated in that span of time are few. For example, by concentrating on the Jerusalem Christians and the transition to Antioch, Acts does not tell us when and how the followers of Jesus spread to Damascus (9:2). The author reports Paul's travels to the west, but nothing about the spread of Christianity to eastern Syria or North Africa, or even about the initial evangelizing of Rome itself. Thus even if everything he reports were judged historically accurate, his account is sketchy at best.

There is no doubt that Luke romanticizes the early Christian picture at Jerusalem in terms of the rapidity and numbers of conversions, the saintliness of life, the generosity in giving up possessions, and the single-mindedness of believers. Does Luke display bias? No doubt! Notable examples from the book of Acts include (1) Luke's stress on harmony and unity among Christian leaders, and (2) his emphasis on the continuity between Israel and the church. While Acts reports some elements of dissidence and disagreement in the church, when we contrast Acts with what we learn from Paul's letters about these controversies, it is clear that Acts is overly optimistic. The early Christian movement, in Luke's view, was a harmonious movement initiated by Christ and led by the Holy Spirit. In addition, Luke views the church as an expansion of Judaism, not as a new creation having broken decisively with Judaism. Acts necessarily smooths over a rough course of events.

As for provable errors, the most obvious are in Palestinian history. Whether Gamaliel advocated tolerance toward the early followers of Jesus, his speech is undoubtedly a Lukan creation (Acts 5:34–39). Furthermore, Luke 2:2, combined with 1:5, is inaccurate about the date of the census of Quirinius, and there is a similar inaccuracy in Acts 5:37 about the revolt of Judas the Galilean directed against the census.[5] However, such minor inaccuracies do not mean that we can dismiss the general historicity of Acts'

---

5. There are anachronisms in Gamaliel's speech, such as the chronology between Theudas's revolt and "after him Judas the Galilean." If this Sanhedrin session took place around 36 CE, Theudas's revolt had not yet taken place and Judas's revolt had taken place thirty years before.

portrayal of early Christianity, any more than inaccuracies in Josephus and the discrepancies between his *Antiquities* and *War* entitle us to dismiss his general historicity.

Another obstacle modern readers face is the cavalier way in which Luke's narrative reports a predilection for the supernatural, recounting tales of fantastic miracles and adventures of good and evil spirits, of exorcisms and healings by Jesus and his followers. The antisupernaturalistic bias of modernity aside, Luke's uncritical use of oral and written sources calls into question his competence as historian. In addition, there are discrepancies between his account of the Jerusalem Council in Acts 15 and the account given in Galatians 2:1–10 by Paul, who actually attended the conference. Furthermore, Luke's knowledge of Palestinian geography seems inadequate at times, leading one prominent scholar to remark, "Jesus' route cannot be reconstructed on any map and, in any case, Luke did not possess one."[6]

In *Luke: Historian and Theologian*, conservative scholar I. H. Marshall notes that modern skeptics may be overly hasty in their assessment of Luke's abilities. The apparent discrepancies concerning the Jerusalem Council, for example, can be resolved if the account in Galatians is read as referring to a different, earlier meeting (see Acts 11:30). Similarly, many of the so-called geographical inaccuracies stem from a failure to recognize that Luke uses terms differently than we do today. For example, it is possible that he is not always consistent in his use of the term "Judea." Sometimes he uses the term in a narrow sense, as a reference to a particular region, while at other times he also seems to have a broader sense in mind, referring to all of Palestine. Luke is a theologian, Marshall agrees, but he is also a historian.

Luke's interest, admittedly, is not simply in recording history for its own sake, but in interpreting its significance for human salvation. In addition, Luke seems to believe that the truth is available primarily as narrative, regularly hidden from direct explanation or easy accessibility. We can expect surprises in religious history because meaning is ambiguous. More than one interpretation can be offered for events in the life of Jesus or in the early church, for no single explanation can do justice to the truth of Christ, his birth, life, death, and resurrection, or to the church's birth, life, and mission. The account in Luke–Acts is strange, inscrutable, and altogether beyond the bounds of the imagination. No flat, prosaic explanation can do justice to the truth of Jesus' life and message, or to the truth of the church's origin, meaning, and message.[7] These mysteries can only be conveyed through metaphor, story, and by inspired imagination, commitment, trust, and faithful witness.

---

6. Conzelmann, *Theology of St. Luke*, 63, n. 6.
7. Willimon, *Acts*, 29.

Given that Luke was not an eyewitness of what he narrates and that he is highly selective, the author of Acts gets fairly good grades for historical accuracy. Long ago, the British scholars J. B. Lightfoot and W. M. Ramsay pointed to the extraordinary accuracy of Acts' knowledge of the widely differing titles of municipal and imperial officials in the various towns visited (see 13:12; 17:6; 18:12; 19:31, 35). Overall, the book is also accurate about the boundaries and alignments of districts and provinces in the middle of the first century. As New Testament scholar Raymond Brown demonstrates, much of what Acts tells us correlates well with what we can determine from Paul's letters.[8]

In evaluating Luke, it is doubtful whether writing history was his intent. Luke wrote to proclaim, to persuade, and to interpret, not to preserve records for posterity. It is also worth remembering that this author never called his Gospel a gospel, and never calls his Acts a history. He thought of both as "narrative" ("orderly account"; see Luke 1:3). In Acts, as in Luke, the narrative he recounts is primarily intended to give believers assurance (Luke 1:4), to strengthen them spiritually and intellectually with theological insight. Therefore, whatever history these books preserve is put to the service of theology and pastoral exhortation. Luke is primarily a theologian, not a historian. As theologian, his concern appears primarily practical and pastoral, not speculative or theoretical.

In antiquity, there were two ways to write history, a Greek (and more modern) way of thinking, which focused on what actually happened, and a Hebraic (and more ancient) way of thinking, more concerned with what events meant. To the Hebrews, history was "the mighty acts of God," and God was Lord of history, whose character and purpose could be known only through divine acts: "I am the Lord your God, who brought you out of the land of Egypt" (Exod. 20:2). Historical events were seen against a background of faith, and history and theology tended to become inseparably intertwined. Unlike modern historiography, concerned more with "what" and "when" questions, Luke's historiography focused on "why" and "who."

As a historian and theologian, Luke often mixed history and theology. This is not to suggest that he mixed fact and fantasy. It is to affirm, rather, that the history of a people, a nation, and a religious community cannot be understood apart from a consideration of the transcendental forces embedded in that history. As we discover in Acts, there are instances where some of Luke's details appear embellished, questionable, or even wrong. Furthermore, much of biblical language is marked by hyperbole. Such

---

8. Brown, *Introduction to the New Testament*, 424.

overstatement, mixed with irony and wit, is the hallmark of memorable writers and speakers. Like Jesus, Luke was a gifted storyteller.

When evaluating Luke as historian, the reader should remember that Luke was writing history in the same manner as other historians of antiquity. Ultimately, his method of writing history does not allow any easy answer to the modern historian's question, "What actually happened?" Luke certainly believed he was dealing with real events, but, like great historians, he was more concerned with finding patterns and meaning in human experience. As we have seen, all historiography is interpretation, and the best historians raise questions about the meaning of history and the future of humanity, questions for which, as historians, they can provide no ultimate answers. The answers belong to the realm of theology, and it is into this realm of metahistory that Luke and the other New Testament writers lead us. Whether we like it or not, when it comes to scripture, we must be content to live with a measure of uncertainty as to where fact ends and interpretation begins.

In recent years, the topic that has sparked the greatest interest in Lukan scholarship has been the evangelist's views on political and social issues. In part, this may be due to the rise of liberation theology, the development of feminist hermeneutics, and the increased appreciation for the work of scholars in the third world. In another sense, however, the tendency to understand Luke through his political views is not new, for it has long been recognized that his Gospel displays an extraordinary awareness of the world in which it was written. Luke's historical notes (1:5; 2:1–2; 3:1–2) indicate that he intends to tie the significance of the events he reports to their social context. The book of Acts features numerous accounts that prove he is aware of the benefits and hazards that political connections can pose to the church. It is no surprise that as early as the nineteenth century, political motivations were considered important for an understanding of Luke's project. This approach was advanced in the mid-1950s by influential British scholars Henry Cadbury and Hans Conzelmann,[9] who wrote persuasively that Luke's writings had an apologetic intent, namely, to make clear that despite Jesus' crucifixion at the hands of Roman authorities, the founder of the early Christian movement and his followers posed no political threat to Roman rule.

Despite its influence, Conzelmann's thesis has been challenged and even rejected by numerous scholars, particularly by Richard Cassidy, who in his book *Jesus, Politics, and Society* argues that Luke's Gospel was never intended as a political apologetic or as an attempt to make peace with the existing social order. For one thing, the words and deeds of Jesus reported

---

9. Conzelmann, *Theology of St. Luke*; Cadbury, *Making of Luke–Acts*, 299–316.

by Luke are of such revolutionary consequence that no one who reads them would ever be convinced that he was politically harmless. As Cassidy notes, Jesus advocated a new society, one based on service and humility rather than on traditional power structures (Luke 22:24–27). He opposed injustice, spoke out against oppression, advocated nonviolence, affirmed new roles for women, condemned the rich, and praised those who give away their possessions. Luke presents Jesus as one who refuses to defer to authorities. He calls Herod a "fox" (13:31–33) and speaks of Pilate's atrocities (13:1–3). He defies the Jewish Sanhedrin (22:67–70) and repudiates Gentile rulers (22:24–27). In the final analysis, Cassidy concludes, Pilate and Herod were wrong in pronouncing Jesus innocent. According to Luke, Jesus ultimately posed more of a threat to the existing social order than they could ever have imagined.

In conclusion, Luke should be evaluated not as a modern historian but as a historian of his time. In this respect, he includes items in his works that are typical of the writings of the historians of his period. Both Luke and Acts begin with formal literary prologues (Luke 1:1–4; Acts 1:1–5) that can be compared with the prefaces of classical historical and literary writers such as Herodotus, Hippocrates, Josephus, Polybius, and Thucydides. Moreover, Luke repeatedly provides chronological information that declares his intention to set the events he narrates in the context of Greco-Roman and Palestinian history. This manner of writing makes Luke a good historian, representative of his age.

Viewed by the standards of the first century, Luke was not so much taking liberties with the events he sought to narrate as he was following the conventions of history writing of his day. Luke's writings show that he was a cultured, relatively sophisticated citizen of his world. He is aware of cultural patterns from a variety of geographical regions. He also shows familiarity with political, military, and social structures and institutions. Because he assumes a sophisticated audience with his finely nuanced narrative, Luke was no mere provincial, but rather a cosmopolitan believer who styled his narrative through appreciation for subtlety.

Because he writes to inform as well as reassure his audience of God's plan in Jesus Christ, readers reaching the end of Luke's "second account" will both know the events of the origins of Jesus and the church and realize that the salvific activity of Jesus is an ongoing reality.

CHAPTER 2

Understanding Scripture

Summary: Chapter 2 explores the topic of Christian scripture, focusing on its origin, nature, and status as standard of authority for belief and practice. Explaining the similarities and differences between "scripture" and "tradition," the text describes the process that led to the development of the Christian canon. Noting four distinct "ways of being religious" in early Christianity, the narrative describes three valid ways of reading scripture, acknowledging the merits of historical-metaphorical approaches over literalist ways to read and interpret the Bible.

Assignment: Read chapter 2 of *Power Revealed*. If you have time, read the book of Acts in its entirety. Even if you have read Acts before, it is helpful to refresh your memory and have an overall sense of Luke–Acts before studying the introductory topics in chapters 3 through 7 of *Power Revealed*, so the sooner you start, the better. Answer the following questions, writing the answers in your journal. [If you are in a study group, be prepared to share your views with others in the class.] 1. Of the four ways of "being religious" in early Christianity, which one best describes your preferred or dominant form of spirituality? Explain your answer. 2. Do you read scripture primarily for information, formation, or transformation? Explain your answer. 3. If you consider yourself a theological conservative, how does this perspective influence the way you read and interpret scripture? If you consider yourself a theological moderate or liberal, how does this outlook influence the way you read and interpret scripture?

Learning Objectives: After completing this chapter, participants will be able to:

1. Understand the process that led to the formation of the Christian canon.
2. Explain the similarities and differences between "scripture" and "tradition."
3. Explain the difference between reading scripture literally and historically-metaphorically, and why the latter is preferred.
4. Understand and explain four distinct ways of being religious found in ancient Greco-Roman culture and how these modes found expression in early Christianity.
5. Explain the difference between reading scripture historically, metaphorically, and sacramentally.

Most religious communities have a list of scriptures considered binding or authoritative. Such a collection is called a "canon," a concept derived from a Greek word meaning "measuring device" or "ruler." As applied to religious literature, it refers to the rule or standard of authority for belief and practice. Arriving at a definitive canon or binding list of scriptures involves judging the authenticity, doctrinal soundness, and communal acceptance of texts. While Jews and Christians have a "closed" canon, meaning that no books may be added or deleted from that official collection of writings, this does not mean that their religious communities always agree about which books they include in their respective canons, the form of those books, or the order in which those books occur.

By the start of the first century CE, when Christianity emerged, most Jews subscribed to the special authority of the Torah. Not all accepted the authority of the Prophets (for example the Sadducees did not), but most mainline Jews, including the Pharisees, certainly did. Jesus quoted from some of these books, as did Paul and other New Testament authors, so we can assume that all accepted them as authoritative. The third part, the Writings, was not yet completed in the first century, but one of its major components, the book of Psalms, was already in use in synagogue worship. Indeed, this book was so important that the third part of the Jewish canon could be referred to simply as "the Psalms." This usage is found in Luke's Gospel, from the late first century, which refers to "the Law of Moses, the Prophets, and the Psalms" (Luke 24:44).

It is no surprise that a faith firmly anchored in the sacred texts of its parent religion would develop scriptures of its own. Christians did develop their own scriptures, but not immediately. The first generation proclaimed its message almost exclusively by word of mouth and saw no pressing need to assemble its own sacred tradition, since it expected Christ to return shortly. As the expected return of Christ was delayed, and as the number of believers continued to expand, the need for written documents became manifest. With the passing of the first generation of Christians, the need arose to preserve those crucial stories and lessons that had given shape to their community; continuity and order were at stake.

Near the end of the first century, Christians were citing Jesus' words and calling them "scripture" (see 1 Tim. 5:18). Furthermore, some of Jesus' followers, such as the apostle Paul, understood themselves to be authoritative spokespersons for the truth (Gal. 1:8–12). Paul's letters, written occasionally to specific congregations and individuals, were reverently saved and shared with Christians in other places. Shortly thereafter they began to assume the authority of scripture, at least among some Christians (2 Pet. 3:16). In fact, Paul's authority was becoming so significant that documents written by others were being ascribed to him (see 2 Thess. 2:2; also the Pastoral Epistles and disputed letters like Hebrews, which some Bibles attribute to Paul). In the next century a host of additional gospels, epistles, and apocalypses appeared, vying for authenticity. The author of Luke's Gospel openly admits that "many writers" had preceded him in the attempt to "draw up an account of the things that have happened among us" (Luke 1:1).

By the third century, more than twenty gospels were in circulation, all claiming, like the *Gospel of Peter* or the *Gospel of Philip*, apostolic derivation. Notable among them was the *Gospel of Thomas*, consisting exclusively of isolated saying attributed to Jesus. The abundance of gospels was due mostly to the growth of Gnostic sects within Christianity, especially in the second century. The vast majority of Gnostics were "dualists," believing that human beings were spiritual entities trapped in an evil material world, and that they could be freed, or saved, only through secret knowledge. They shared in common a tendency to produce texts that claimed to distill new revelation. It is no coincidence that the first lists of scripture began to appear among orthodox scholars and theologians shortly after the emergence of Gnostic sects.

The process that led to the formation of the Christian canon is complex but fascinating. The four Gospels now found in the New Testament, together with the other canonical writings, may have been produced by diverse, even antithetical communities, but all were viewed to be sufficiently orthodox to make the final cut. However, during the second, third, and fourth centuries, Christians continued to debate the acceptability of certain writings. The arguments centered on three criteria:

- *Apostolicity*: the book in question had to have derived from the initial community of Jesus and his disciples.
- *Orthodoxy*; the book in question had to be valued as inspired and revelatory, that is, as derived directly from God and hence harmonious with the rest of the New Testament.
- *Catholicity*; the book in question had to be accepted and used by a wide range of communities, especially those considered authoritative or apostolic.

At first, a local church would have only a few apostolic letters and perhaps one or two Gospels. During the course of the second century most churches came to possess and acknowledge a canon that included the present four Gospels, the Acts, thirteen letters attributed to Paul, 1 Peter, and 1 John. Seven books still lacked general recognition: Hebrews, James, 2 Peter, 2 and 3 John, Jude, and Revelation. On the other hand, certain Christian writings, such as the first letter of Clement, the letter of Barnabas, the *Shepherd* of Hermas, and the *Didache*, were accepted as authoritative by several ecclesiastical writers, though rejected by the majority.

Paradoxically, Marcion, the second-century heretical Christian preacher, was responsible for the first canon of the New Testament. Unable to reconcile the Old Testament's portrayal of God as violent and vengeful with the New Testament's portrayal of God as good and loving, he created a restrictive canon that excluded all of the Old Testament and any Christian literature that had Jewish overtones. Marcion's teaching prompted a hearing before other clergy in Rome that resulted in his condemnation. Soon afterward, other church leaders began to form their own canons or lists of approved books. The most famous of these is the Muratorian Canon, dated to the church at Rome circa 190. It included the four Gospels, the Acts of the Apostles, thirteen letters attributed to Paul, Jude, and 1 and 2 John, as well some books that were later excluded, including the *Apocalypse of Peter* and the *Wisdom of Solomon*. What is unusual about the latter is that despite being a Jewish work, written prior to the birth of Christianity (in the first century BCE), it was listed as a Christian text.

Strangely, the development of a definitive canon of scripture took orthodox Christians nearly four centuries to complete. The earliest surviving list to include all twenty-seven books now known as the New Testament is from the year 367, appearing in an Easter letter written by Athanasius, bishop of Alexandria, to congregations in the eastern section of the church. In the west, the twenty-seven books of the New Testament were accepted at the subsequent councils of Hippo (393) and Carthage (397).

Scripture and Tradition

A strong connection exists between "scripture" and "tradition," terms of special significance for scholars and others who think historically. It is helpful to start with a definition of scripture. By scripture we mean a book or a collection of books preserved by religious communities as authoritative sources of teaching or worship. The main point to remember about scriptures is that they are historical objects crafted in human cultures. The texts are preserved by human memory and recorded in human languages, even if they are believed to have come to humans by revelation. Scriptures enjoy special prestige as "holy" or "sacred" texts only because human communities have at some point agreed to treat them in certain ways. Any text regarded as scripture came to be so because a community, formally or informally, so decided. The process that led to authoritative designation is called "canonical," meaning "rule of authority." This decision to accept a text as canonical is often a source of conflict, as different segments of a larger community might dispute whether a particular writing is truly authoritative for all members. Thus it often happens that a text considered as scripture in one community is simply a book in another.

The decision to regard a text as scripture often brings into play the term "tradition." Most simply, tradition means "that which has been handed down from the past." Tradition sustains a book in the life of a religious community long enough for it to acquire the status of scripture. Relatively few examples of writings penned by a known author have attained scriptural authority in that person's own lifetime. Once a traditional literary work becomes scripture, it is usually preserved in a fixed text not to be modified or emended. Scripture and tradition, to summarize, are intertwined realities. Scripture is the collective term for literary traditions that enjoy the veneration of a specific community. A "canon," or closed collection of scripture, is thereby a tradition, passed on as a unique and unchangeable record of communal memory, belief, and discipline.

During the period between 200 BCE and 100 CE, various types of religious literature not found in the Jewish canon or in the New Testament emerged. Collectively, these works are sometimes labeled Intertestamental Literature because, for the most part, they came into existence between the times in which the Old and New Testaments were written. The expression "Old Testament," widely used for the Hebrew Bible, is a Christian designation. For the Jewish community, there is only one "Testament" or "Covenant," namely, the Hebrew Bible. Today the Jewish people refer to their scriptures as Tanakh, an acronym made up of the initial consonants of the three major divisions of the Hebrew Bible: Torah (Law), Nebiim (Prophets), and Ketubim (Writings).

The Hebrew Bible is fundamentally the same as the Christian Old Testament, although the arrangement differs. To understand the Hebrew Bible, we can imagine three concentric circles: "The inner circle, the Torah, presents the basic story of the people and includes laws to guide them in living. The next circle, the Prophets, is a critical commentary on the life of the people to whom the Torah is given. The outer circle, the Writings, is a diverse and open-ended collection that broadens out from Israel's worship and festal celebration to wisdom reflection."[1] While the Christian Old Testament begins with the five books of Torah, it then departs from the Hebrew Bible in order and, in certain cases, in content. These differences are largely accounted for by the fact that many early Christians were Greek-speaking, meaning that they read or heard the Hebrew Bible read in Greek, particularly in the translation called the Septuagint, begun in the third century BC in Alexandria Egypt. This translation places the prophetic writings last, while the Hebrew Bible concludes with the Writings (ending with 1 and 2 Chronicles). Moreover, the Septuagint includes works not part of the Hebrew Bible, though these works were originally highly regarded in Jewish circles, for they were written by Jews for Hellenized Jewish audiences.

Interpreting Scripture: The Historical-Metaphorical Method

Literature invites interpretation; significant literature demands it. This is particularly true of scripture, its truth claims fraught with meaning and therefore open to investigation. There is no such thing as a noninterpretive reading of the Bible. Reading the stories of creation or the stories of Jesus' birth literally involves an interpretive decision equally as much as does the decision to read them metaphorically. When we speak of meaning in relation to a biblical text, five levels come to mind: (1) what the Spirit of God intended and intends; (2) what the human author intended (this concern should be important to all readers, conservative, moderate, and liberal alike); (3) how biblical scholars and theologians interpret a particular passage or verse (their views, both ancient and modern, are readily available in commentaries, handbooks, Study Bibles, and other interpretive aids. Those interested in breadth of insight should consult works from across the denominational and theological spectrum); (4) how leaders in one's church or denomination interpret a particular passage or verse; and finally, (5) what

---

1. Anderson, *Old Testament*, 3.

the text means to you. This final level, while indispensable, should not be arrived at quickly. Without the corrective of the other levels, this approach to the Bible can result in as many meanings as it has readers. This postmodern approach, based on the belief that "the meaning of a text is what it means to me," lacks hermeneutical validity.

We who read the Bible need assistance, a method to help us discern how to hear and value its various voices. When we read scripture, we encounter historical, linguistic, social, and cultural gaps between the ancient and modern worlds, barriers we must overcome if we are to understanding the original meaning of the text. In addition, each of us approaches the text with some preunderstanding of the subject. Those who read the Bible only from the perspective of their immediate personal circumstances, who forget that the passage was originally written for someone else, can easily misunderstand what the text says.

Four Ways of "Being Christian"

During the second century the books that comprise the New Testament began to impact the emerging Christian community as a whole. From among a broad range of sources including letters, gospels, collections of saying of Jesus, acts of various apostles, manuals, homilies, and apocalypses, Christian leaders began to decide which were canonical, meaning which were essential for Christians to read and revere. Four Gospels were selected (Matthew, Mark, Luke, and John) as well as letters attributed to Paul, James, Peter, John and other early Christian leaders; the book of Acts (a historical perspective on the early church associated with Luke); and the book of Revelation. These writings were produced by Christians in different social, cultural, and geographical settings, representing diverse expressions of Christian living, ethical values, social organization, perspectives of Christ, sacramental practices, and leadership styles. It might come as a surprise to think of such diversity in early Christianity, but scholars agree that diversity was greater in early Christianity than in contemporary Christianity. While it is customary to assume that Christianity began as a unified and cohesive entity, this was not the case. Diversity in Christianity preceded the uniformity of later generations.

In his lectures on church history, eminent New Testament scholar Luke Timothy Johnson notes that in the early centuries of Christianity four distinct "ways of being religious" found in Greco-Roman culture emerged within a Christianity that was increasing Gentile in its population and culture. The first way, by far the dominant way of being religious among pagans, was the "Way of Participation in Divine Benefits." In early Christianity, this mode is found in those phenomena that emphasize the presence of the divine power in everyday life, such as in healings, prophecies, and other displays of divine power known as "signs and wonders" (see Acts 4:30).

In the early days of the church, before there was a New Testament or even Gospels, people learned about Jesus and God's alternative kingdom from wandering prophets and teachers who moved from village to village spreading the good news. Some of these evangelists might have had a direct encounter with Jesus, numbering among his actual disciples and therefore valued as apostolic eyewitnesses. Others might have known Jesus indirectly, perhaps having had limited contact with him, while the majority probably had only a visionary experience of Jesus that fueled their passion.

Most of the early believers were probably *visionary Christians*. Before there were written Gospels, people relied upon orally communicated information for their knowledge of Jesus and the Christian life. Certainly some of the tradition concerning Jesus, including words spoken in his name, were authentic, but many deeds and words attributed to Jesus actually came from local leaders and wandering prophets, who spoke in Jesus' name and with his authority because they were believed to have Jesus' Spirit within them. Their words came directly from Jesus but in a different way, not from the historical figure, but from the divine inspiration begun by his presence and maintained charismatically. Ultimately it was believed that all the teachings came from God, through Jesus, through the Spirit, to the believers, and to the world.

Yet another group was attracted to Jesus and the Christian movement through the filter of healing. In an age when medicine was expensive and unreliable, people interpreted miraculous healing as a sign of God's presence, or, at least, as sign of an intervening divine power. Common people in particular were persuaded by healing miracles. The Jewish lens correlated healing with the prophetic tradition. Likewise, Greeks and Romans had traditions about the god Asclepius who could heal the sick, so when people heard the stories of miracles by Jesus and his followers, some became *healing Christians*, interpreting miracles within their own cultural frame.

A second way of being religious can be called the "Way of Stabilizing the World." This approach to the divine may be viewed as the supply side of the first way of being religious, in that it supports participation and benefits by providing the financial means for festivals, feasts, and other sacred rituals and practices. Insisting on a link between authentic religion and society, the religious sensibility of these *communal Christians* is represented by the emergence of an organized hierarchy within early Christianity, in figures of local authority such as elders and deacons as well as in apostles, teachers, and bishops, whose authority and ministry were universal.

A third way of being religious is the "Way of Transcending the World," or perhaps even escaping the world. It was found in dualistic traditions such as Platonic and Gnostic traditions. It appears among Christians like the Thessalonians to whom Paul wrote or like the Asian Christians to whom John of Patmos wrote the book of Revelation. These *apocalyptic Christians*, who assumed they were living in the end-times, when Jesus would return from the sky and bring judgment to the world, eagerly awaited the final apocalypse that would cause evil to end and bring God's kingdom into physical reality.

The fourth way of being religious, the "Way of Moral Transformation," was exemplified by philosophical schools such as the Pythagoreans and Epicureans, who offered an organized form of life, a community life that provided sound teaching, sound practice, and the opportunity to live in a community of moral integrity. They, together with Stoic philosophers, focused on the cultivation of virtue and on the dispositions and behavior of individuals and societies. This way emphasized the connection between right thinking and right acting.

While "participation in benefits" dominates the narratives of the Gospels, Acts, and the epistolary literature as a whole, the New Testament writers are united in their efforts to shape their readers into a community of character. The letter of James stresses the need for having "the deeds of faith" rather than mere belief, and the Gospels of Matthew and Luke note the words of moral instruction given by Jesus, above all in the Sermon on the Mount (Matt. 5–7) and the Sermon on the Plain (Luke 6). The kingdom of God, proclaimed by Jesus, requires a change of moral outlook and behavior. Not everyone heard in the same manner the story about Jesus and God's rule, however. Others, perhaps more philosophically or ethically inclined, may have expected a new wisdom from above, through a sage carrying God's wisdom for a new age. These *wisdom Christians*, building on the Israelite Wisdom tradition found in Proverbs and in deuterocanonical works such as Sirach or the Wisdom of Solomon, were particularly attracted to the parables and discourses of Jesus and of later Christian sages who interpreted Jesus as the Wisdom of God. In this early period, some participants had a school-like concern, focusing on the wisdom sayings of Jesus and elaborating them with accounts that were applicable to different circumstances. These pedagogical Christians valued the process of elaborating sayings as instrumental in educating the young as well as in making converts and perpetuating tradition.

Interestingly, all four approaches, emphasizing charismatic/prophetic, communal, apocalyptic, and wisdom traditions, can be found in the Gospels, though each gospel community favors one over the others. Like these early Christians, each Gospel writer saw in the tradition a new way to live, organized around a different way of understanding Jesus as representative of God's new world order. By the beginning of the second century two organizational models predominated in conventional Christian orthodoxy: (1) apostolic authority, representing the Pauline/Petrine tradition and supported by the Synoptic tradition and the book of Acts, and (2) charismatic authority, represented by the Johannine literature, which refers back to the earlier mode of church organization and revelation, with diverse leaders and modes of revelation, while retaining some of the Synoptic tradition. The two traditions, divergent in many ways, would eventually coalesce, as evidenced by their presence in the Christian canon.

Reading Scripture: Three Approaches

People read the Bible for many reasons: literarily (as great literature), philosophically (as a guide for moral and reflective thought), theologically (as a compendium of truth), or devotionally (as a resource for meditation and a source of comfort). Despite the Bible's widespread scriptural use, most devout people read it only occasionally, and superficially. How people read it is perhaps more important than why they read it. For those who wish to engage with scripture seriously and in depth, I recommend that you find a method of study that works for you, whether individually or with others, and commit to it. Of many valid ways of reading scripture, the following are recommended:

- Reading for *information* – to learn as much as possible about the setting of the authors and their primary audience in order to discover the original meaning of a particular passage of scripture and its potential application.
- Reading for *formation* – to establish one's identity, values, and beliefs in order to live meaningfully, joyously, and securely.
- Reading for *transformation* – to provide resources for developing soul-centrically rather than egocentrically, aligning more deeply with one's powers of nurturing and creating, presence and wonder.

Of course, it is quite possible for these approaches to overlap, due to the complexity of our intellectual, theological, and spiritual needs. It is equally possible that biblical passages convey messages appropriate to our varied abilities and needs. Scripture is multivalent, meaning that its message allows for multiple interpretations. While one text might strike terror in the heart of an unrepentant person, the same passage might exhort devout believers to greater faithfulness and even greater freedom. When you read Luke–Acts, particularly in a group setting, keep in mind the possibility that biblical passages contain multiple messages, depending on one's needs, temperament, and spiritual journey. Scripture, like a good smorgasbord, provides healthy options for different appetites. And you don't always have to eat the same food; sometimes a change of diet can be helpful.

As Paul showed in 1 Corinthians, the important thing is to keep growing spiritually. Paul's concern with the Corinthians was that they were in a state of spiritual immaturity, unable to eat solid food. It takes time—and conscious effort—to grow spiritually, from egocentrism to soulcentrism. How people hear and read scripture (eat spiritually) reflects their spiritual maturity.

Perhaps you have heard it said that the modern age has problems with authority in general, and with the authority of scripture in particular. However, according to an important and oft-quoted passage found in 2 Timothy 3:16, the Bible should not be considered as an authority in the modern sense of the word; in other words, the Bible does not exist for its own sake. Note that 2 Timothy 3:16 does not say, "All scripture is inspired by God and is *authoritative*." It says that all scripture is inspired and *useful*—useful to teach, rebuke, correct, instruct, and equip us for our mission as the people of God. For too long we have read the Bible as if it were God's encyclopedia, God's rule book, God's answer book, God's scientific text, God's easy-steps instruction book, God's little book of morals for all occasions. In Jesus' day, the only people who would have had anything close to these expectations of the Bible would have been the scribes and Pharisees. And Jesus certainly disapproved of their attitudes and methodology regarding scripture.

While the Hebraic scriptures (the Old Testament) provide codes of behavior and belief that can be systematized into groups of tens or twelves, the canonical writings of Christianity intentionally fail to do so, even for religious matters. To the question, "What does the New Testament teach on X or Y?" the proper answer seems, "What did you read last in the New Testament?" The New Testament is not a collection of books that provides a system of law for personal or public behavior, but rather a way of life based on discernment and wisdom, subjecting morality under fuzzy topics such as "love," "mercy," and "forgiveness."

When you let go of the Bible as God's answer book, you get it back as something so much better. It becomes the family story—the story of the people who have been called by the one true God to be his agents in the world, to be his servants to the rest of the world. So I suggest we stop reading the Bible as a "modern" answer book. But that doesn't mean we should discard it. Just the opposite! When we let it go as a modern answer book, we get to rediscover it for what it really is: an ancient book of incredible spiritual value for us, a kind of universal and cosmic history, a book that tells us who we are and what story we find ourselves in so that we know what to do and how to live. Of course, the Bible is even more than a book of wisdom and wisdom development. It is a book that calls together and helps create a community, a community that is a catalyst for God's work in our world.

In his intriguing fable, *A New Kind of Christian*, Brian McLaren criticizes modern liberals and conservatives alike for reading the Bible in very modern ways. Modern conservatives treat the Bible as if it were a modern book. They are used to reading modern history texts, modern encyclopedias, modern science articles, and modern legal codes, and so they assume that the Bible will yield its resources if they approach it like one of those texts. However, none of those categories even existed when the Bible was written. Sure, there was history, but not with all of the modern trimmings like a concern for factual accuracy, corroborating evidence, or absolute objectivity. There was law, but surely not a one-to-one correspondence between ancient Near Eastern concepts of law and our modern concept. The conservatives seem somewhat blind to these kinds of differences. Modern liberals seem to make a corresponding mistake. Acknowledging that the Bible is a different kind of text from our modern texts, they still judge it by modern standards. If something doesn't fit in with a modern Western mindset that reveres objectivity, science, democracy, individualism, and the like, they dismiss it as primitive and irrelevant.[2]

There is a third option: instead of reading the Bible, what if you let the Bible read you? If that sounds a bit ethereal, perhaps even mystical, think of it this way. Think of a scientist preparing to dissect a frog, or think of a detective at a crime scene. How would you describe their attitude or approach? Now think of a teenage girl meeting a boy at the mall. Surely her attitude differs from the scientist's or the detective's. Her approach wouldn't be so analytical or objective. And there would be some fun in it, a sense of personal investment, a feeling of adventure. In one sense, there's less caution, less holding back. Yet in another way, there is holding back, because she wants to make her move and then leave room for him to respond. This approach is less aggressive, less controlling, and more relational. We need to

---

2. McLaren, *A New Kind of Christian*, 55–56.

approach the Bible that way; we need to flirt with it, romance it—or possibly let its message romance us.³

Our modern age has predisposed us to only a limited range of postures with the Bible, like the objective analysis of a scientist or like forensic science, always trying to prove something. It's all about conquering the text, reducing it to something explainable by our preconceptions, turning it into moralisms, principles, outlines, conclusions, or proofs. What would happen if we approached the text less aggressively but even more energetically and passionately? What would happen if we honestly listened to the story and put ourselves under its spell, so to speak, not using it to get all of our questions about God answered but instead trusting it to pose questions about us. What would happen if we simply trusted ourselves to it—the way we fall in love, or fall asleep?

Christianity is centered in the Bible. Of course, it is ultimately centered in God, but it is the God of whom the Bible speaks and to whom it points. God may be known in other ways and through other religions, but to be Christian is to be centered in the God of the Bible. This is not a mark of Christian exclusion, but of Christian identity. The Bible is for Christians their sacred scripture, their sacred story. ⁴

Yet the Bible has become a stumbling block for many. In the last half century, many Christians have left the church because of the Bible. More precisely, they left because the traditional literal way of interpreting the Bible, with its emphasis on biblical infallibility, historical factuality, and moral and doctrinal absolutes, became intolerable. In his writings, biblical scholar Marcus Borg provides an alternative to biblical literalism. Utilizing three adjectives—*historical*, *metaphorical*, and *sacramental*—he describes how scripture, creeds, and other normative Christian teachings should be understood.⁵

1. To speak of *the Bible as a historical product* is to see that it is a human product, not a divine product. Not "absolute truth" but relatively and culturally conditioned, the Bible uses the language and concepts of the cultures in which it took shape. It tells us how our spiritual ancestors saw things, not how God sees things. The Bible is not verbally inspired, since the emphasis is not upon words inspired by God but on people moved by their experience of God.

For modern Christians, describing the Bible as sacred scripture and therefore as "holy" is to value the historical process known as canonization.

---

3. Ibid., 56–57.
4. Borg, *Heart of Christianity*, 43.
5. Ibid., 43–60.

The documents that make up the Bible were not "sacred" when they were written, but over time were declared sacred, meaning that they became the most important documents for that community, providing its foundation and shaping its identity.

2. Much of the language of the Bible is metaphorical: one third of the Old Testament is poetry or semi-poetical literature. To speak of *the Bible as metaphor* is to emphasize that this language should not be interpreted literally. Metaphor does not mean that the Bible is not true, but rather that it is not primarily concerned with facticity. The Bible does contain history, but even when a text contains historical memory, its meaning is more than (not less than) literal. For example, although the exile in Babylon in the sixth century BCE really happened, the way the story is told gives it a more than historical meaning. It became a metaphorical narrative of exile and return, providing images of the human condition and its remedy. In other cases, as the Genesis stories of creation, there may be little or no historical factuality. Though these stories are not literally factual, they are profoundly true.

Because the Gospels combine memory and metaphor, some of these accounts, when literalized, become literally incredible. The story of Jesus walking on water illustrates the point. A literal reading of the story emphasizes the spectacular event as a sign of Jesus's identity, "proof" that he was divine. A metaphorical reading of this story yields a different meaning. It seems to be a way of saying: "Here in a nutshell is what the story of Jesus is about."

Historically speaking, the Gospel accounts do not begin with what Jesus said and did before his death. Christianity begins with the experience of Jesus after his death by his followers. They write of him as one resurrected from the dead and exalted to God's presence. Accounts of his birth and transfiguration, of his feeding the multitudes, restoring sight to the blind, turning water into wine, raising the dead, and walking on the water, all are resurrection stories! The Gospel accounts are all told from the perspective of resurrection, of victory over death. The evangelists are not writing about an ordinary human, but rather about one who is already viewed as Lord, Messiah, and preexistent Christ.

A metaphorical reading of the Gospels provides rich meaning for Christians in all times and places; a literal reading misses all of this, emphasizing belief in the miraculous elements rather than on its meaning for a life of faith. Metaphorical language is *a way of seeing*. To apply this to the Bible means that in addition to its metaphorical language and metaphorical narratives, the Bible as a whole may be thought of as a "giant" metaphor.

"Thus the point is not to believe in the Bible—but to see our lives with God through it."[6]

3. To speak of *the Bible as sacrament* is to say that it mediates the sacred. If a sacrament is a physical vehicle or vessel for the Spirit, the Bible is sacrament in the sense that it is a visible human product whereby God becomes present to us.

For modern Christians, "the Bible—human in origin, sacred in status and function—is both metaphor and sacrament. As metaphor, it is a way of seeing—a way of seeing God and our life with God. As sacrament, it is a way that God speaks to us and comes to us."[7] The Bible is a two-way bridge, a path to the divine and a way to connect to our deepest self. Like a backboard in the game of basketball, scripture is a means to an end, not an end in itself.

---

6. Ibid., 57.
7. Ibid., 59.

CHAPTER 3

Understanding Luke–Acts

Summary: Chapter 3 examines matters of authorship, audience, and date, addressing questions about Luke, whether he was ethnically Gentile or Jewish, whether he traveled occasionally with Paul, whether he was with Paul during his imprisonment in Caesarea and Rome, and whether the author of Luke–Acts was a physician, and if so, the relevance of his profession to his writings. Other topics include Luke's intent as author, an issue raised by the conclusion of Acts. Did Luke intend on writing a trilogy, and if so, might this intent have been fulfilled in the Pastoral Epistles, attributed to Paul or to a Pauline collaborator? Envisioning a predominantly Gentile rather than a Jewish audience, Luke–Acts was written late in the first century, likely addressed to a mixed group of Jewish and Gentile Christians in Greece and Asia Minor associated with the Pauline mission.

The chapter concludes by examining the plot and structure of Luke's Gospel and the book of Acts, asking whether these books should be read as a continuous narrative or canonically, as distinct and separate units of scripture. The first approach focuses on thematic motifs in the Lukan corpus, the second on theological contributions each volume makes to biblical theology.

Assignment: Read chapter 3 of *Power Revealed*. [If you have not finished reading Luke–Acts in its entirety, do so as soon as possible.] Answer the following questions, writing the answers in your journal. [If you are in a study group, be prepared to share your views with others in the class.] 1. As you ponder the issue of Luke–Acts authorship, how convincing do you find the

traditional view that this material was written by "Luke the beloved physician," the occasional companion of the apostle Paul? Explain your answer.
2. Having read the book of Acts, what questions does this book raise about early Christianity? What lessons does it provide for your own life and faith?

Learning Objectives: After completing this chapter, participants will be able to:

1. Demonstrate an understanding of Luke as author of Luke–Acts, providing details concerning his religious background, occupation, literary production, relation to Paul, and his overall role in early Christianity.

2. Clarify matters concerning the audience and date of Luke–Acts, including the possible identity of someone named "Theophilus" in Luke 1:3 and Acts 1:1.

3. Demonstrate familiarity with the plot and structure of Luke's Gospel and of the book of Acts.

4. Explain the differences between reading Luke–Acts literarily and canonically.

Having spoken of Luke as the author of Luke–Acts, we need to clarify matters of authorship, audience, and date. Who was Luke, to whom was he writing, and when did he write? These issues are of some significance, for they influence our understanding of Luke, the purpose for which he wrote, and his theological, ecclesiastical, and sociological perspectives. Was the author an eyewitness of the events he records, or a later writer? If later, how accurate are his narrative, perspective, and the information he records?

Author

We begin with two obvious assertions. First, though Luke–Acts is attributed to Luke, each work is anonymous, for nowhere in the text of the Gospel or Acts is the author mentioned by name. Secondly, as the prologue of these books indicate (Luke 1:1–4; Acts 1:1–5), both are dedicated to a cultured Greek reader named Theophilus. Why, then, do we speak of Luke as author? Who was he, and who was Theophilus? Let us address these questions in order.

Church tradition attributes the Third Gospel to Luke the physician, a companion of Paul who according to 2 Timothy 4:11 remained faithful to him even during his imprisonment. While the derivation of the tradition concerning Lukan authorship is uncertain, we know that by the end of the second century documents appear connecting Luke–Acts with this individual. The tradition for Lukan authorship is widespread: Irenaeus in Gaul (c. 185), Tertullian (c. 207) in North Africa, and the Muratorian Canon (c. 200) in Italy. However, this attribution no doubt represents an early Christian inference taken from biblical passages such as Colossians 4:14, 2 Timothy 4:11, and Philemon 24. These passages do speak of someone named Luke as Paul's companion, but can we be certain that this individual was the author of Luke–Acts? Additional support undoubtedly comes from passages in Acts, where the author uses the pronoun "we," switching abruptly from the third person to the first person plural (16:10–17; 20:5–15; 21:1–18; 27:1—28:16). Are these passages authentic, or could they simply be the author's way of pulling "us" readers into the "we" experience, substituting literary device for historical source? While these references undoubtedly create a dramatic sense of being with Paul, they do not require direct partnership with Paul or even participation in his travels. Nevertheless, the sporadic nature of the "we" feature in Acts suggests that the author was relying on some type of diary, either his own or that of a minor figure who traveled occasionally with Paul.[1]

In discussing our author's association with Paul, we should note that persuasive arguments have been adduced against associating Luke with Paul. Perhaps the greatest argument against such relationship is the claim that Luke shows little or no knowledge of Paul's epistles, little understanding of his distinctive theology, and only slight appreciation for Pauline concerns such as justification by faith and freedom from the law.

Scholars who cannot reconcile the picture of Paul in Acts with the picture revealed in Paul's own letters have proposed that the author somehow got the diary of a true companion of Paul and introduced segments of it at appropriate moments to enhance the narrative with realism and thus with greater credibility. However, the "we" sections are written in a style indistinguishable from that of the rest of the book. If we suppose that the author was using as one of his sources a diary written by another individual, we must add that he rewrote it so thoroughly as to eliminate all traces of its original style and yet so carelessly that he did not always remember to make the change from first to third person. The simpler solution is that the author was using his own diary, allowing the first person to stand in order to indicate places where he had been an eyewitness.

---

1. The topic of the "we" passages is addressed more fully at the end of chapter 4 below, at the conclusion of the segment on Luke's "use of sources."

Close analysis of the grammar, syntax, and vocabulary found in the "we" passages in comparison to those factors in the rest of Acts shows that they are consistent with the style and vocabulary in the rest of Acts. Surely the most reasonable explanation is that Luke was present for a limited time with Paul during the second missionary journey and more extensively during the third. Assuming that Luke was a companion of Paul at this time, we notice that the "we" references appear first in Troas (16:11; about 50 CE, during Paul's second missionary journey). According to Acts 20:6-7, this is where Paul stayed for a week on his third missionary journey (about 58 CE, at the end of Paul's third missionary journey). In that first sequence of "we" passages, Paul and his companions went from Troas to Philippi, where the "we" usage has its final reference at 16:16, before Paul and Silas are incarcerated. If Luke is referring to himself, he is not claiming to have been with Paul at Thessalonica, Athens, Corinth, or back to Antioch. The "we" passages resume precisely at Philippi (20:5-6), with another week's stay in Troas. Could Philippi or Troas have been the home of the author of Luke–Acts? After the occasion recorded in Acts 20:7-12, Luke remains with Paul for the balance of the events recorded in Acts.[2]

Unfortunately, the matter of Luke's relationship with Paul and whether he traveled occasionally with Paul during his ministry remains unclear. If Luke did travel with Paul, his lack of acquaintance with Paul's life and letters or with central aspects of his theology would be understandable if he wrote decades after Paul's death, if he simplified and reordered information (as he did in the Gospel when he took material from Mark and Matthew), or if as a true theologian he thought some of Paul's emphases were no longer appropriate.

If we cannot know whether our author was Paul's companion, was he a physician? In the past, most everyone thought the language of the Third Gospel confirmed this to be true. Comparing Luke's Gospel with the others, readers noted that the Third Gospel emphasizes the equality of all humanity, viewing Jews and Gentiles alike as beneficiaries of God's salvation (see 3:6). Likewise, to a greater extent than other Gospels, Luke elevates the status of the poor (see 14:12-14), despised Samaritans[3] (only Luke includes the

---

2. If this view has any validity, then it reveals that Luke was not with Paul during the major part of his missionary activity, or during the period when Paul's most important letters were being written. It would also mean that Luke would not have been with Paul when the latter was formulating the essence of his thinking or facing such crises as the Judaizing problem, the struggle with factions in Corinth, or the eschatological questions that arose in Thessalonica. This would explain why there is such a difference between the Paul of Acts and the Paul of Paul's letters.

3. From the perspective of pious Jews, the Samaritans were a stereotypical group of outcasts. Nevertheless, Samaritans are shown in a positive light in each instance where

parable of the Good Samaritan, 10:29–37, and the account of the Samaritan leper, the only one of ten who returns to thank Jesus for having healed him, 17:4–19), and of other disadvantaged groups in society. In addition, Luke's Gospel heightens the role of women (narrating the birth of Jesus from the women's point of view and focusing more on Jesus' friendship with Mary and Martha than any other Gospel writer). While such emphases speaks volumes about the author's mindset, do they imply he is a physician? Perhaps indirectly, for a doctor would certainly be concerned with women, children, the poor, and outcasts in society.

Furthermore, readers detect three places in Luke's Gospel that show awareness of medical features, such as the diagnosis given of Peter's mother-in-law's fever in 4:38, the extent of the leper's disease in 5:12, and a comparative reading of 8:43 with Matthew 9:20 and Mark 5:26, where the author, dependent upon Mark, changes Mark's "grew worse" to "no one could cure her." Presumably, such a change is one a doctor might make, cringing at the thought that someone could spent all they had on the care of physicians, only to get worse.

Scholars no longer find such information relevant to the question of the author's profession. Ancient medicine was not nearly as technical in antiquity as it is today, and numerous writers outside the medical profession are known to have used expressions similar to those found in the Third Gospel. The author's redaction at 8:43 is no longer viewed as conclusive evidence that he here defends the medical profession, but rather as another example of Luke's literary custom of abbreviating and softening Markan and Matthean judgments. In this particular case, Luke is simply affirming a central theme by highlighting the woman's desperate situation: no one was able to heal her. Of course, this assessment does not disqualify the author of Luke–Acts from being a doctor. Furthermore, there is clear evidence from Greek epitaphs of peripatetic doctors who traveled around the Mediterranean world practicing their trade, and Luke may well have been one of them.

In summary, the anonymity of the two-volume work must be respected. Furthermore, we cannot ignore the tradition that Luke–Acts derived from Luke, a physician and companion of Paul, for there seems no reason why anyone in the ancient church would create this testimony, making a relatively obscure figure the author of this work. While it is not impossible that a doctor wrote Luke or that a minor figure who had traveled with Paul for parts of his ministry wrote Acts, neither feature influences

---

they appear in Luke's Gospel.

the interpretation of the text. For easy reference, however, we will follow conventional practice, using the name Luke throughout this study.

Another matter of debate regards the ethnicity and religious upbringing of Luke, whether he was a Gentile or Jewish convert to Christianity. While the majority of scholars today believe Luke was a Gentile, a growing number believe he was ethnically Jewish, following the views of the Norwegian scholar Jacob Jervell, who argued in his 1972 book *Luke and the People of God* that a correct interpretation of Luke's work depends on the "Jewishness" of Luke–Acts, which includes the Jewish identity of both Luke and his community. In this light, some scholars, primarily Continental European authors, have advanced proposals that Luke may have had Pharisaic origins and possibly even been a Jewish priest prior to his conversion, finding autobiographical reminiscence in passages such as Acts 6:7, 13:43, and 21:20.[4]

If Luke were ethnically Jewish, that could explain many aspects of Luke's writings, such as his knowledge of the Jewish scriptures; of the theology and promises of God found in those scriptures; the midrashic character of his Gospel (biblical history as interpreted in light of Jewish rabbinical tradition); and his close links with the history of the people of Israel. However, it cannot explain Luke's mistake about purification in Luke 2:22 ("their" wrongly implies the purification of the father), a blunder impossible for one who grew up in a Jewish family. Furthermore, his biblical quotations are regularly from the Septuagint, rather than from the Hebrew Bible. The reason is clear: there is no evidence that Luke knew Hebrew. While having its positive points, Jervell's position has drawn much criticism, notably from the American exegete Joseph Fitzmyer, who favors the traditional view that Luke was Gentile by birth and wrote for a predominantly Gentile Christian audience.

According to the testimony of the *Anti-Marcionite Prologue to the Gospel of Luke*, a document commonly dated to the late second-century but by some scholars to the fourth century, Luke was Syrian by birth, a Gentile native of the city of Antioch. The knowledge of the church at Antioch exhibited in Acts 11:19—15:41 has been advanced as support for the tradition that Luke was an Antiochene. Many think that the Eucharistic formula in 1 Corinthians 11:23–25, which Paul says he received from tradition, came from the practice of the church at Antioch, from which Paul had been sent on his missionary journeys. Luke's form of the formula in Luke 22:19–20 is not derived from Mark and is close to that of Paul, and thus could show contact with the Antioch church. The better assumption, however, is to

---

4. This thesis is advanced by Salvatore Principe and Rick Strelan; see Chrupcala, *Everyone Will See*, 14–21.

CHAPTER 3—UNDERSTANDING LUKE–ACTS   37

understand Paul as Luke's source for his information on Antioch. If Luke was from Antioch, we would expect the "we" section of Acts to begin at this juncture and not in Acts 16.[5]

This connection of Luke with Antioch does not tell us, however, whether Luke remained in Antioch, and whether his audience is Antiochene. Furthermore, if Matthew was written for the church at Antioch, as is commonly held, it would be doubtful that Luke was addressed to the same church. The Lukan and Matthean Gospels differs in many ways from one another, and the possibility that two such dissimilar infancy narratives could have been shaped in the same area and intended for the same people is highly unlikely.

We do not know where Luke resided or what Christian community he might have joined. Hypotheses regarding Antioch, Caesarea, and Ephesus are informed guesses. As we noted regarding the "we" passages, there is nothing there to associate Luke with Antioch, but much to associate him with Troas or Philippi. Later pious tradition placed Luke's death in the Greek region of Boeotia and burial in the city of Thebes, his bones transferred to Constantinople in 357 and from there relocated to Padua in Italy, where they remain.

Was Luke Jewish by birth and hence Jewish Christian? The way that Colossians 4:11 is phrased, namely, that all those listed before that verse are of the circumcision (meaning Jews by birth), suggests that Luke, who is listed in 4:14, is not a Jew. This reference has traditionally led commentators to conclude that Luke was a Gentile, and hence the only non-Jewish writer of the New Testament. However, the phrase "of the circumcision" could also be used to speak of Hellenized Jews, a further way to differentiate between those Christians who strictly observed the rituals of Judaism and those who did not.

In the fourth century, speculation led church fathers such as Epiphanius and John Chrysostom to include Luke among the disciples of Jesus, whether one of the seventy sent forth by Jesus (Luke 10:1–24), the disciple of Emmaus of whom the name is not mentioned (Luke 24:13–35), the "brother" of whom Paul speaks in 2 Corinthians 8:18, or Lucius (a variant of the name "Luke") of Cyrene who evangelized the Gentiles of Antioch (Acts 13:1; see also Rom. 16:21, where Lucius is named among Paul's co-workers).[6] Such identifications, however, are highly improbable if Luke is a third-generation Christian, as he seems to indicate in his prologue (Luke

---

5. We are right to be suspicious of the "we" found in the Western text of Acts 11:28. See Metzger, *Textual Commentary*, 391.

6. In his lengthy article, "Identification of Luke," John Wenham revisits the patristic sources that refer to the identity of the author of Luke–Acts.

1:1–4).[7] Also significant in this regard is the testimony of Tertullian almost two centuries earlier, who distinguished Luke from apostolic eyewitnesses.

Of the four evangelists, Luke demonstrates the best use of the Greek language, easily utilizing numerous styles, varying from Septuagintal to classical to colloquial. In Acts he exhibits a knowledge of the rhetorical conventions of Greek historians and some knowledge of Greek literature and thought. This ability in Greek has caused many to posit that he was a Gentile convert to Christianity.

Thankfully, a solution that does justice to both sides of the issue is found in Acts. There, Luke distinguishes three categories of Gentiles present across synagogues of the Roman Empire: (1) *the proselytes*, that is, circumcised converts to Judaism[8] (2:10; 6:5; 13:43); (2) *the "God-fearers,"* that is, devout pagan adherents to the synagogue despite not being circumcised (10:2, 7, 22, 35; 13:16, 43, 50; 16:14; 17:4, 17; 18:7); and (3) *the pagans*, idolaters and enemies of God and Israel. Of the three, Luke was most likely a God-fearer, which explains his intent to show the continuity between converted Jews and Gentiles, both united by a common faith in Jesus Christ. It also explains his presentation of the centurion Cornelius (Acts 10–11) as a model to imitate for those wishing to become members of Luke's Christian community.

Further evidence that Luke–Acts is the work of a Gentile who had become a proselyte or God-fearer comes from the way the author of Acts envisions the church's mission. While in Acts the mission to the pagans appears to be a failure (14:8–20; 17:16–34), this outcome is different for the mission directed to devout Jews and God-fearers, which is successful (see 13:43; 17:4, 10–12).

The ending of Acts—dated to the early 60s, with Paul awaiting trial and the future of the Christian movement far from certain—raises an interesting question. Why does Acts stop at that point? Did Luke intend to write a trilogy, leaving a third and concluding volume unwritten, or did he feel his conclusion in Acts fulfilled his literary and historical purpose? (Because this latter idea bears merit, it is addressed more fully in chapter 4, under Luke's literary purpose.) If Luke did intend to write a third volume, did he

---

7. Regarding this point, see the discussion in chapter 4 below.

8. Some scholars question whether by "proselyte" Luke really meant circumcised converts to Judaism, since the Septuagint regularly uses that term to render the Hebrew *gēr*, which means foreigner or alien. Such people might participate in Israelite worship, but they could not be called "converts" in the sense of those who embraced Judaism and all its rituals, including circumcision. When Luke uses the term "proselyte," is he being consistent? If so, is he using the term in a technical sense or simply equating proselytes with God-fearers? The answer is uncertain, as the translation in Acts 13:26 indicates.

accomplish his intention by penning material pseudepigraphically (in this case, under Paul's name)? In the past, occasional support emerged for Lukan authorship of the book of Hebrews, traditionally attributed to Paul but now to an anonymous writer. If not Hebrews, could Luke's concluding material constitute the Pastoral Epistles (1 and 2 Timothy and Titus)? The Pastorals, once attributed to Paul but now to an unknown disciple of Paul, more likely were penned by someone like Luke, a sympathetic commentator on the Pauline heritage who attempted to strengthen local church organization by weaving information about Titus and Timothy into a compatible though fictional account.

Furthermore, certain features of the Pastorals (style, terminology, the nature of the false teaching, the view of women in the church, church structure and leadership, theology, christology, and Pauline biographical information) point to authorship other than Paul, and to a date later than Paul's undisputed letters.

As many have noted, in atmosphere and vocabulary the Pastorals appear close to Luke–Acts, to the point that some have thought that the same person wrote them.[9] Historical parallels, such as the reference to Paul's sufferings at Antioch, Iconium, and Lystra, echo the journey of Paul recounted in Acts 13:14—14:20 and in 2 Timothy 3:11. The same can be said of Paul's farewell address found in 2 Timothy 3:10—4:8 and Acts 20:18–35. A further connecting tie appears between Acts, which ends with Paul imprisoned in Rome, and the Pastorals, which declare Luke as Paul's sole companion at the end: "Only Luke is with me" (2 Tim. 4:11). Because the style and vocabulary of the Pastorals differ notably from Paul's known usage, and because the atmosphere and context point to the late first or early second century, we need another candidate for authorship, and it cannot be Titus or Timothy, occasional co-authors with Paul, since they are the presumed recipients of this correspondence.

To account for the incongruities between these epistles and Paul's undisputed letters, scholars have introduced the "fragment theory," postulating that the Pastorals may have been compiled from fragments of genuine Pauline letters. Such a view, while explaining seemingly vivid biographical elements such as those found in 2 Timothy 4:9–21, introduces further difficulties, such as why such fragments survived independently, merely as scraps of personal information with no theological or pastoral context. Furthermore, if the Pastorals are the creation of a pseudepigrapher, why did this person choose as his pattern letters addressed to individuals rather

---

9. Supportive data appear in Brown, *Introduction*, 666. See J. D. Quinn in Talbert, *Perspectives on Luke–Acts*, 62–75.

than the more common pattern of letters addressed to communities? While the "fragment" thesis has had relatively little following, a better explanation is the hypothesis that Paul told a colleague what themes he wished covered and handed over to that individual the actual work of composing the three letters (for occasions in undisputed letters when Paul utilized secretarial service, see Romans 16:22, 1 Corinthians 16:21, and Galatians 6:11–18). If a colleague composed the Pastorals under such editorial circumstances, could it have been Luke?[10]

Ultimately, however, when we think of Luke's identity, what is important is not his background or upbringing so much as his conversion to Jesus Christ. It is this point—that Luke is a Christian—with which we close the discussion of authorship. Whether Luke was a Gentile Christian, as most believe, or a Jewish Christian, as some contend, is secondary to the unanimous agreement among scholars that the author of the Third Gospel and the Acts of the Apostles was a Christian. This insight is significant because it is as a Christian that Luke approaches the Jesus tradition, which he used to create the Gospel and the early Christian story that underlies the book of Acts.

Audience and Date

Traditions about Luke's place of birth or residence do not tell us where or to whom he wrote Luke–Acts, although the tradition that Luke was a companion of Paul raises the likelihood that Luke addressed his books to churches descended from the Pauline mission. The concentration in the last half of Acts on Paul's career makes it likely that the addressees were somehow connected with that apostle's proclamation of the gospel message. Occasionally a Roman audience has been suggested because Acts ends there, but Rome in the finale of Acts is primarily symbolic as the center of the Gentile world. In addition, if Mark were written to Rome, as most scholars maintain, would another Gospel have been needed there?

It is obvious from a number of features in Luke–Acts that the author envisages a Gentile rather than a Jewish reading public. Thus, the Third Gospel makes comparatively few quotations from the Old Testament. For the same reason Luke seldom appeals to the argument from prophecy.

---

10. Knight, *Pastorals*, thinks Paul may have used Luke as secretary in writing the Pastorals. John Drane agrees, suggesting that Luke may have written them after Paul's death, using rough drafts of genuinely Pauline material as a starting point, *Introducing the New Testament*, 365. In view of parallels in style, vocabulary, and thought, some scholars believe Luke may also have written Colossians, Witherington, *Acts*, 170, n. 25.

These would have been foreign and unconvincing to non-Jews. Likewise, instead of using the Jewish word "rabbi," Luke is the only New Testament author who substitutes the classical Greek equivalent, a word meaning "master" (Luke 5:5; 8:24, 45; 9:33, 49; 17:33). Unlike Matthew, who traces Jesus' lineage from Abraham, Luke carries Jesus' genealogy beyond Abraham to Adam (Luke 3:23–38). Furthermore, Luke drops Markan Aramaic expressions and place-names as well as sectarian Jewish references such as Herodians as if his audience would not have understood them, substituting terminology more intelligible to people of Greek background. Thus, if there were Jewish Christians among the addressees, they probably did not speak Aramaic.

All this would make sense if Luke–Acts were addressed to a predominantly Gentile area evangelized directly or indirectly by the Pauline mission. Of course, that description could fit many places. Interestingly, the ancient *Anti-Marcionite Prologue to the Gospel of Luke* locates the Lukan audience in Greece ("in the regions of Achaea"), in an area clearly associated with the Pauline mission. Notice that this suggestion concerning locale speaks of an area, for rather than thinking of Luke's intended audience as a single house-church or even as inhabiting one city, perhaps we should think of Luke's congregation as a mixed group of Jewish and Gentile Christians spread over a large region. Support for this early tradition that Luke wrote from and to an area of Greece might be found in Acts 16:9–10, which portrays Paul's movement from Asia Minor to Macedonia (Greece) as dictated by divine revelation.

The *Anti-Marcionite Prologue* provides two additional features of interest. It tells us that Luke was eighty-four at the time of his death, and that he wrote after Matthew and Mark. That Luke used Mark and Matthew is plausible from internal evidence (see chapter 4 below). If Mark wrote around 70, when Romans were destroying Jerusalem and early Christians were separating from Judaism, and Matthew wrote around 80 from Antioch in Syria, when the Jewish world was in turmoil, a date earlier than 80–85 for Luke's Gospel is unlikely.

Although some scholars date Luke–Acts to the second century, such a view seems implausible, as the following points indicate: (1) the Gospel's symbolic interest in Jerusalem as a Christian center does not match the outlook of second-century Christian literature; (2) for Asia Minor and specifically for Ephesus, the writer of Acts seems to known only a church structure of elders (Acts 14:23; 20:17); Acts provides no sign of the developed pattern of having one bishop in each church, attested by Ignatius for that area in the decade prior to 110; (3) also, the writer of Acts shows no knowledge of the letters of Paul, which were collected by the early second century. With this in mind, the best dates for Luke's Gospel are 80–85 and 85–90 for Acts. By that time, the temple had been destroyed, the Jewish religious rites that centered on the temple could no longer be performed, and the church, severed from any connection with the synagogue, was becoming more exclusively Gentile in nature. Such features are supported by internal Lukan evidence.

Our discussion of Luke's audience cannot overlook his prologue, where we learn that Luke wrote his two-volume work for someone named "Theophilus" (Luke 1:3; Acts 1:1). The name, meaning "lover of God," could refer to a wealthy patron who provided funds that enabled Luke to write and publish his account. As an affluent Greek and probable convert to Christianity, he would have desired a useful narrative to confirm his support for a maligned religion in the face of mounting confusions and challenges. In light of Luke's address ("most excellent"), some interpret Theophilus to have been a specific individual of social prominence, possibly a Roman or Jewish official,[11] although the name could also be used symbolically for Christian readers in general. Whatever their ethnic and religious background, Luke is dealing with an audience of believers in Christ, who like Apollos "had been instructed in the Way of the Lord" (Acts 18:25; cf. Luke 1:4) but who find the transition from one symbolic world to another difficult, particularly in light of mounting social, political, and economic challenge.

While Luke's mixed audience represented Gentile converts, God-fearers, and Jewish Christian converts, all were united by a common faith in Jesus Christ. To underscore unity in the church, Luke demonstrated continuity between Jews and Gentiles, not the replacement of one group by another. As Paul makes clear in Romans 11:25–26, continuity has been God's plan all along: "I want you to understand this mystery: a hardening has come upon part of Israel, until the full number of the Gentiles has come

---

11. In "Theophilus," Richard H. Anderson identifies Theophilus with the son of Annas (the Jewish High Priest at the passion of Jesus; see John 18:13, 24; cf. Luke 3:2; Acts 4:6), who held the office of High Priest in the years 37–41, as attested by the first-century Jewish historian Josephus. This view, however, is dubious, given the tension between Jews and Christians in the ninth decade of the first century. A more likely view is that Theophilus was a sympathetic Roman official or a confessing Christian. Tradition has identified him with Titus Flavius Clemens, cousin of Emperor Domitian and father of Domitian's adopted heir, whose wife Domitilla was a Christian, and who, having forfeited the emperor's favor during the year of his consulship, was executed on a charge of "atheism." Religion in Rome was largely a matter of public ceremony, and non-conformity with official worship of Rome's gods was considered treason, for which the penalty was death. The policy adopted by Rome was that foreign religions, though illegal, might be tolerated, provided they did not cause a breach of the peace or interfere with the official cult. The use of a pseudonym by Luke may have been to protect such an official from association with an illegal religion and therefore from the perils of persecution.

in. And so all Israel will be saved." For both Paul and Luke, the coming of Christ constitutes the fulfillment of prophecy; the church is the renewed or eschatological people of Israel. And it is through this church that God's salvation becomes available to humanity. The future of the gospel, however, lies not with Judaism but with the Gentiles, as the closing lines of Acts (28:25–28) indicate: "let it be known to you then that this salvation of God has been sent to the Gentiles; they will listen." The ending of Acts, featuring Gentile receptivity of the gospel, seems to describe the situation a generation or so after Paul, when Luke wrote Luke–Acts.

Luke's perspective, which no doubt reflects the view of his community, is that God is not partisan, meaning that God makes no distinction between Jews and Gentiles. However, Luke's interest is more pragmatic than theological. While fundamental Jewish beliefs and moral commitments are basic to all Christians, the customs of the Jews need not be those of the Gentiles. As Luke's community seems to assume, the Gentiles have their own type of piety, and it is as adequate as that of the Jews. In the final analysis, however, being a Jew or a Gentile brings no advantage; both must rely for salvation exclusively on Christ (Acts 15:11).

Plot and Structure

It seems obvious that Luke intended his work to be read as a single book in two volumes. The church's mission to the world is integral to the gospel, and the ascension is not the end of one story and Pentecost the beginning of another, but both are the climax of a single series of events, the hinge linking the death and resurrection of Jesus to the fulfillment that this climax inaugurates.

A central concern of Luke's two-volume narrative is legitimation; how Israel's hopes for salvation can be realized in a community composed increasingly of Gentiles, with Jews dividing in response to its message, and how Israel's Messiah—and Jesus' followers—can make sense of Christ's scandalous death by crucifixion. Luke shows how these surprising developments represent the working out of the divine purpose for Israel and the nations.

Luke's Gospel

Luke gives distinctive shape to a story others told before him, reworking Mark's narrative of Jesus' ministry and weaving it with other sources (written and oral): birth stories, teachings of Jesus (many shared with Matthew), and resurrection appearances.

The plot of Luke is simple. Conceived, empowered, and guided by the Holy Spirit, Jesus both embodies the Way to God and makes provision for others to follow in it, thereby fulfilling the divine plan. While the focus is on Jesus, his story is set against the background of the divine plan. In addition to presenting Jesus' work in Galilee and his last week at Jerusalem, Luke includes special infancy material, an expanded episode of Jesus' final journey to Jerusalem, and unique material regarding the resurrection and post-resurrection appearances of Jesus. In his travel section (9:51—19:27), Luke preserves many of the most beloved of Jesus' parables, such as the Good Samaritan, the Prodigal Son, the Unjust Judge, and the Pharisee and the Tax Collector.

The universal mission of Jesus is emphasized (1) by tracing his genealogy to Adam; (2) by including references that commend Samaritans, members of a despised race; (3) by indicating that women have a new place of importance among the followers of Jesus; and (4) by promising that Gentiles would have an opportunity to accept the gospel.

The structure of Luke can be outlined as follows:

1. Preface (1:1–4)
2. Beginnings (1:5—4:13)
    A. Birth Narratives and Childhood of John and Jesus (1:5—2:52)
    B. Preparation for the Ministry of Jesus (3:1—4:13)
3. Galilean Ministry of Jesus (4:14—9:50)
4. Jesus' Journey to Jerusalem (9:51—19:27)
5. Jesus' Final Days (19:28—23:56)
    A. Teaching Ministry in Jerusalem (19:28—21:38)
    B. The Passion of Jesus (22:1—23:56)
6. The Resurrection Ministry of Jesus (24:1–53)

The Book of Acts

The plot of Acts is equally straightforward. Empowered by the Holy Spirit, the followers of Jesus bear an unstoppable, universal witness to Jesus by word and deed, thereby fulfilling the divine plan. In Acts, the focus is on the church, set against the background of the divine plan. Despite its title, "The

Acts of the Apostles," Acts does not tell the story of all the apostles. Only some are mentioned, and the book has most to say about Peter (the focal figure of chapters 1–12) and Paul (the focal figure of 13–28), together with selected incidents from the lives of such early Christian leaders as Philip, John, James the brother of Jesus, and Stephen.

Focusing on the spread of the new religion to lands around the northeastern Mediterranean world, Luke prepared a remarkably well-ordered account. Instead of providing merely a chronicle of events and a list of converts, Luke arranged his material around growth and expansion, namely, the spread of Christianity from Jerusalem to Rome. Like any historical narrative, Acts is selective in what it includes, so we would be mistaken to imagine that this book gives "the history of the early church." Its focus is oriented around the missional agenda set forth by Jesus in 1:8: "you will be my witnesses in Jerusalem, in all Judea and Samaria, and to the ends of the earth."

Christian expansion, as narrated in the book of Acts, resulted in a twofold shift: geographically, the center of the church gravitated from Jerusalem to Rome; ethnically, the church's identity shifted from Jewish Christians to predominantly Gentile Christians. According to Acts, the church expanded because it fulfilled faithfully its two tasks in society: to evangelize, that is, to serve as Christ's witnesses "to the ends of the earth" (Acts 1:8; see also Matthew's Great Commission in 28:19–20), and to live by the ethics of love and mercy that Jesus had taught.

In an orderly way, Luke traces the story of the Christian movement from Jerusalem to Rome. Within these two termini, and spanning a period of about a third of a century, Luke arranges his material in what has been described as six "panels," each concluding with a comment that summarizes the success attained. In this respect, the structure of Acts may be outlined as follows:

1. Preface (1:1–14)
2. First Panel: Early episodes in the Jerusalem church (1:15—6:7)
3. Second Panel: Extension of the church through Palestine (6:8—9:31)
4. Third Panel: Extension of the church to Antioch (9:32—12:24)
5. Fourth Panel: Extension of the church to Asia Minor (12:25—16:5)
6. Fifth Panel: Extension of the church to Europe (16:6—19:20)
7. Sixth Panel: Extension of the church to Rome (19:21—28:31)

Reading Luke–Acts Canonically[12]

For the most part, scholarly approaches to Luke–Acts start with questions of authorship, date, audience, and sources. These are important matters for understanding context, purpose, and structure. Approached in this manner, Luke's Gospel is seen as the start of a two-part work, and Acts as the second volume of a continuous narrative. This narrative is shaped by the author's pastoral intentions, composed with ancient literary, rhetorical, and historiographical conventions, and informed by theological convictions designed to serve the Christian formation of his immediate audience and perhaps the church at large. However, reading these books canonically requires more than an analysis of their social world, literary artistry, and theological perspective. Concentrating solely on these features runs the risk of freezing the meaning of Luke–Acts in an ancient world far removed from that of current readers.

Those who formed the church's canon for future generations evidently did not think it necessary or even profitable to read Luke and Acts together. More likely, the pre-canonical Acts circulated apart from Luke's Gospel, with different collections of letters, both Pauline and other epistles, termed "general" or "catholic."[13] For this reason, by the time the canonical process had concluded a few centuries later, the Third Gospel and Acts had their own individual function within the biblical canon.

The question we ask here is not, "Why did Luke write Acts or his Gospel?" but "What are the church's reasons for reading these as scripture?" As early Christians noted, each Gospel presents the story of Jesus in a different way. Each Gospel contains a different structure, develops different themes, addresses a different audience, and portrays the person of Jesus in its own unique way. At first a local church would have only a few apostolic letters and perhaps one or two Gospels. During the course of the second century most churches came to possess and acknowledge a canon that included the present four Gospels, Acts, the letters of Paul, and several of the General Epistles. By the late second century, when a host of other gospels appeared, all claiming apostolic derivation but obviously of heterodox (Gnostic) origin, bishop Irenaeus of Lyons (130–200) argued for a canon of four Gospels. In his central work, *Against Heresies*, a lengthy apologetic work in five books written around 185 CE, he denounced Christian groups that used only one Gospel or that embraced the texts of newer gospels. Using the analogy of the four corners of the earth and the four winds, he built upon the biblical

---

12. This segment is adapted from Wall, "Acts of the Apostles," 26–32.

13. By General or Catholic Epistles we mean non-Pauline canonical letters such as Hebrews and those attributed to Peter, James, and John.

image of four creatures before God's throne with four faces, that of a lion, an ox, a human, and an eagle (see Rev. 4:6–10, Ez. 1:5, 10).[14] Viewing these as equivalent to the "four-formed" gospel, Irenaeus was ultimately successful in declaring that the four Gospels collectively, and only exclusively these four, contained the truth. He also supported reading each Gospel in light of the others.

Regarding Acts, the implications of reading this work as scripture, that is, canonically, are significant, for canonical context highlights different literary relationships within the New Testament. For example, evaluating the canonical context of Acts, its location after the four Gospels and before the two collections of letters, marks the reader's approach to the New Testament. According to this arrangement, the fourfold gospel (and not simply Luke's Gospel) is perceived as prerequisite reading for the study of Acts, and the study of Acts under the Gospel's light is prerequisite reading for the study of the letters that follow.

The canonical relationships forged by the canonical process are also valuable when assessing the distinctive importance of the theology of Luke's Gospel and Acts within the New Testament. No longer do we focus exclusively on the thematic interests of these works in terms of their congruence with one another. Rather, we can examine the theological contribution each makes to biblical theology in general. Put differently, the interpreter is now urged to imagine what a biblical witness to God might lack apart from the Third Gospel, and apart from Acts; also, to consider what distorted idea of the church's faith, its religious or social identity, or of its vocation in the world might result if either of these books were not included; furthermore, what misreading of the Pauline or catholic letters might result if the interpreter failed to prepare by first reading the story of the apostles in Acts. What is at stake here is not so much the historical accuracy of Luke's portrait of Jesus and the apostles, or even the importance of his credibility within earliest Christianity—even though these are greatly debated by scholars—but rather what do the Jesus of Luke's Gospel or the Paul of Acts have to say about Christian worship, faith, and life?

Reading Acts as scripture introduces new layers of meaning for contemporary issues, such as the relevance of the Ethiopian eunuch's story (8:26–40) for reflecting on the relationship between the church and its homosexual membership, or the example of Priscilla in chapter 18 as a role model for prophetic ministry in congregations that once were reluctant to encourage women in ministry. The vivid portraits of shared possessions

---

14. Readers should avoid associating the four creatures with the four evangelists, as many have done, for such association is entirely fanciful.

("the community of goods") or snapshots of Paul's relations with Rome can also challenge today's believers to a more prophetic understanding of church as counterculture.

If scripture is approached as a narrative written for and relevant to only its original audience, then current readers will find little of value for their own Christian formation. This may well have been a concern that guided the canonical process that produced the New Testament in its present form. For example, in its canonical setting, the book of Acts is detached from Luke's Gospel, which is not read as one of a set of four. If Acts is read in its current canonical placement rather than as the second volume of Luke–Acts, then the reader will naturally reflect upon its narrative as continuing the story of Jesus presented by the four Gospels. The reader's understanding of "all that Jesus did and taught from the beginning" (Acts 1:1) will be greatly expanded and enriched by a fourfold presentation.

The strategic placement of Acts between the Gospels and the letters suggests the transitional role it performs within the New Testament. The narrative of Acts continues and concludes the authorized biography of Jesus while introducing the Bible's readers to the apostolic writings that follow. Acts functions as a bridge connecting Gospels and letters in a logical relationship that mirrors the ultimate aim of the New Testament: to nurture Christian discipleship after the pattern of Jesus.

Perhaps the most important role Acts performs within the New Testament is to offer biographical introductions to the implied authors of the letters that follow. In canonical context, such biographies serve a theological purpose by orienting readers to the religious and moral authority of apostolic authors as trustworthy carriers of the word of God. While the historical accuracy of Luke's narrative of Paul and other leaders of earliest Christianity may be challenged, the rhetorical and ethical power of these figures confirms and commends the importance of their letters. The central issue is not whether Acts fails as a historical record but that it succeeds as a theological resource, contributing to the church's understanding of its vocation and identity in the world.

Given the similarities and dissimilarities in emphasis found when comparing the Pauline and Catholic Epistles may actually correspond to the manner by which Acts narrates the relations among Peter, John, James, and Paul and their respective missions. While Luke softens the disagreements between the leaders of earliest Christianity, what is often overlooked is that the church collected and eventually canonized letters often polemical and potentially divisive. Might it not be the case that the church recognized the importance of Acts in succeeding the Gospels and introducing the apostolic writings not so much to smooth their disagreeable edges as to embrace their diversity and provide interpretation? According to Acts, the church that claims continuity with the first apostles values a rich pluralism even as the apostles did, not without controversy and confusion.

What was achieved at the Jerusalem Council (Acts 15) is a kind of theological understanding rather than a theological consensus. The apostolic decree issued by this council (Acts 15:28–29) forms a pluralizing monotheism that in turn informs two distinct missions, Jewish and Gentile (see Gal. 2:7–10). While Acts points to the two collections of letters in a sectarian fashion (the Pauline letters reflect the more progressive gospel of a Gentile mission, while the Catholic Epistles reflect the more conservative gospel of a Jewish mission), Acts also forces us to interpret the letters ecclesiastically, that is, to expect such diversity to be useful in forming a single people of God. "The canonical approach presumes that the connection is complementary rather than adversarial. In this case, the Pauline church, which may be inclined to accommodate itself to the mainstream of the world in order to more effectively spread the gospel (see 1 Cor. 9:19–23), is reminded by the catholic witness that it must take care not to be corrupted by the values and behaviors of the world (see Jas. 1:27). That is, the synergism effected by the dominant theological commitments of Acts suggests that the diverse theologies ingredient in the biblical canon compose a dynamic, self-correcting system, preventing theological distortion."[15]

While scholars often debate matters such as sources, genre, and perspective—all important for doing exegesis (that is, for "reading out of scripture" the author's intention rather than "reading into scripture" our own agendas and bias)—the main question remains, What does the text mean to me, in my situation? Those who read the Bible faithfully discover its texts offering new meanings as they are read in changing circumstances and by people with different backgrounds, concerns, and questions. While this may be threatening for those who desire finality and closure, it is what makes the Bible essential. If meaning were something we could extract from a text in a final and definitive way, we would eventually be able to dispose of the text. However, that is not the case. The biblical text is always relevant because it presents new possibilities, raises new questions, and offers new insights.

At its core, the Bible, like Christianity, is a story. It is the story of God's dealings with humanity and with all of creation, particularly through Jesus Christ, and since then, by the power of the Holy Spirit. This means that as we read the gospel story, we cannot improve on that story by distilling from it abstract principles, theories, or doctrines. Thus commentary on those

---

15. Wall, "Acts of the Apostles," 32.

parts of scripture that, like the Gospels and Acts, are narrative must not seek to supersede the narrative, nor to turn it into abstract principles, but to relate it to the life and proclamation of the church and its members. This remains the goal of all reading and study of the Bible.

UNIT II

Introductory Topics

CHAPTER 4

Luke's Literary Task

Summary: Chapter 4 investigates Luke's artistic and literary approach and his use of sources. The preface to Luke and Acts provides hints of Luke's literary method. His work takes ancient Jewish and Hellenistic literary components and blends them into interesting genres imitating ancient biographical and historiographical models, including features of Hellenistic historiography such as speeches, generalizing summaries, mimesis (archaisms), and dramatic episodes, and Semitic features such as formal or allusive quotations of biblical passages and apologetic or narrative theological history. In addition, Luke achieves his practical, homiletic program by using patterns such as paired stories and examples involving male and female characters, parallel actions and experiences between Jesus and his followers, and by casting Jesus in the mold of biblical kings and prophets, a technique known as intertextuality.

Luke's use of sources consists of documents such as the Septuagint and earlier Gospels, eyewitness reports, and his own accounts, based on personal experience and careful investigation.

Assignment: Read chapter 4 of *Power Revealed*. [If you have not finished reading Luke–Acts in its entirety, do so as soon as possible.] Answer the following questions, writing the answers in your journal. [If you are in a study group, be prepared to share your views with others in the class.] 1. After reading this chapter, explain your understanding of gospel as a literary genre. In what respect can the Gospels be said to comprise a unique literary genre, and to what extent do they reflect the ancient biographical genre?

Explain the intent of such scholarly techniques as source, form, redaction, and narrative criticism, and what they contribute to your understanding of the Gospels as literary creations? 2. After reading this chapter, explain your understanding of the composition, reliability, and accuracy of the book of Acts.

Learning Objectives: After completing this chapter, participants will be able to:

1. Explain the purpose and function of Luke's literary prologues.

2. Explain the function and nature of the gospel as literary genre, demonstrating its similarity and dissimilarity from other biographical writings in antiquity.

3. Demonstrate an understanding of Hellenistic and Semitic compositional techniques evident in the book of Acts, providing examples of paired stories and parallel actions in Luke–Acts.

4. Demonstrate an understanding of Luke's use of sources, including documents, eyewitness reports, and diaries.

5. Explain the meaning of intertextuality, providing examples from the Hebrew scriptures (the Old Testament).

6. Explain and assess the merits of four scholarly approaches to gospel research, including source, form, redaction, and narrative criticism.

Whether in terms of style, grammar, vocabulary, communicative skill, or rhetorical strategy, scholars give Luke a high rating. Of New Testament writers, this author ranks among those who have a strong command of the Greek language and as one of the most literarily adept. Like all New Testament writers, Luke reflects the common (*koiné*) Greek vernacular of the first century, even as he displays his own peculiar style and patterns. However, in Luke–Acts we discern a more elegant style than that of the other evangelists, greater consciousness of temporal and spatial factors, and a broader perspective on Jesus Christ and the early Jesus movement.

In accordance with contemporary literary custom, Luke employs interlocking prologues for Luke and Acts, prologues that reveal a literarily and historically conscious writer. Indeed, providing historical synchronisms for the story's setting, the author relates the events of Jesus' life to the reigns of emperors, kings, governors, and Jewish authorities (Luke 1:3; 2:1–2; 3:1–2). For Luke, Christianity has taken its place on the stage of history, for it is a universal movement whose founder initiated Jewish and Gentile missions (Luke 9:1–6; 10:1–24; Acts 1:8).

Luke's Literary Task

Fortunately, we find hints of Luke's literary method in the preface to each volume (Luke 1:1–4; Acts 1:1–2), particularly in the prologue to his Gospel, intended as an introduction to the two-volume work: "Since *many* have undertaken to set down an orderly account of the events that have been fulfilled among us, just as they were handed on to us by those who from the beginning were *eyewitnesses* and servants of the word, *I too* decided, after investigating everything carefully from the very first, to write an orderly account for you, most excellent Theophilus, so that you may know the truth concerning the things about which you have been instructed" (Luke 1:1–4).

As his prologues indicate, Luke's literary intention is to write a reliable account of Christian origins. He will do so by writing two books, the first about the life and teachings of Jesus and the second about the origins of the church. The prologue mentions various issues concerning the composition of Luke and Acts. Writing from a pastoral perspective ("that you may know the truth"; the Greek word Luke uses here, *asphaleia*, means "security" or "assurance" about the things in which he has been instructed, not "truth," as most translations have it, which implies intellectual certainty), Luke indicates he will accomplish his intention by:

1. organizing his report sequentially ("orderly" account");
2. using various genres ("accounts"); and
3. utilizing many sources (see italicized terms above).

Although Luke may not originally have anticipated a companion volume to his Gospel, he clearly built upon it when composing Acts. While his Gospel reports what Jesus began to accomplish, Acts narrates what the resurrected Jesus continues to do and teach through his followers. Acts 1 builds on Jesus' post-resurrection appearances in Luke (24:13–32, 36–53), noting that Jesus appeared to his followers during forty days (Acts 1:3). The risen Lord's parting mandate in Acts 1:4–5, 8 that his apostles wait to "be baptized with the Holy Spirit" echoes Jesus' words in Luke (3:16; 24:47–49). Lest they be forgotten, Luke reprises the names of the apostles in Acts 1:13. They match the original list in Luke 6:13, with some minor exceptions, such as the absence of Judas Iscariot. The ascended Lord is no absentee figure. While Jesus may no longer be present physically, Acts shows Jesus' continued involvement in earthly affairs, albeit in Spirit (2:33; 7:55–56; 9:3–6; 16:17; 18:9–10; 22:17–21).

Literary Genres

When one compares Luke's writing with that of the other evangelists, one discerns a more elegant style, greater awareness of historical matters, and a broader perspective on the life of Jesus. The same holds true for Acts and its depiction of origins of the church. Further, Luke's work takes both Jewish and Hellenistic literary components and blends them into an interesting perspective on the new movement.

Attempting to determine *the* genre(s) of Luke and Acts is vexed by two issues: (1) the rich mix of poems/hymns, scriptural citations, aphorisms, parables, speeches, letters, miracle stories, martyr accounts, sea voyages, and other literary forms, complicates any single generic label; and (2) the unity question. However else they may be linked, must Luke and Acts represent the same genre? In some sense, both books can be called "narratives" in the broad sense, but ultimately, the designation is not very helpful.

Until recently, it was believed that the Gospels had no literary ancestors, being a unique genre of literature peculiar to Christianity, unwittingly invented by the first compiler of the gospel tradition, an early Christian named Mark. As a unique invention, combining history, theology, and literature, the gospel genre tells the story of the Son of God, focusing on the good news of God's redemptive plan for humanity as seen through the birth, ministry, passion, and triumphant resurrection from the dead. While many New Testament scholars still hold the view that the Gospels are unique, the genre having developed out of primitive Christian preaching and teaching and determined by the needs of evolving Christian communities, the gospel genre is now considered as analogous to certain types of biographical writings in antiquity.

Ancient biographies, for example, were often written by devoted disciples whose intent was to produce an instructive story of a model person's life. Frequently these biographies included extended teachings of the individual's philosophy, in addition to emphasizing the particular lifestyle the person modeled. The biographies related the particularities of the person's birth, emphasizing the presence of divine forces and agents attending the birth and the death of the person. The point of such biographies was not so much to inform as to model a way of life through the narrative, including social relationships for those choosing the holy person's way of life, connections to cultic centers and religious leaders, and even attitudes toward the emperor and Roman society. In other words, "the holy person became an exemplar of a whole set of social relationships consistent with the holy person's way of life."[1] The Gospels, like ancient biographies, were not simply written to inform audiences but were designed to evoke a response from the listener.

If the Gospels are related to the ancient biographical genre, as commonly held, a feature of all such ancient documents was a prologue or introduction, generally separate from the portrayal of the central character. In *What Are the Gospels?* Richard Burridge lists six features common to ancient biographies, including (1) a prologue, (2) focus on a particular individual, (3) the use of chronological, geographical, and topical categories to arrange the material, (4) the recording of deeds and words used to reveal a person's character, (5) a length of no more than 24,000 words and (6) a tone that is respectful or even reverential for the subject. Luke's Gospel conforms fully to this pattern. While containing twenty-four chapters, four less than Matthew, Luke's Gospel is the longest, with 19,482 words, compared to 18,346 for Matthew.

Those who insist on keeping Luke and Acts within the same generic camp often opt for some kind of ancient biographical narrative. Luke's Gospel, for example, is similar to Greco-Roman biography. The author borrows genre and content from Mark and extends the timeline backward and forward. Jesus' story is expanded backward to include resurrection appearances, and forward to include annunciation and birth stories. The virginal conception of Jesus indicates not a higher christology, as in Matthew, but rather meets the requirements of popular biography (see Luke 2:40, 52), wherein heroes are attributed divine origins, unusual births, or prophetical omens. Luke recasts Markan controversies and rewrites passages to make Jesus appear noble and innocent of wrongdoing (6:11). In other instances he models episodes after the Hellenistic symposium genre (7:36–50; 11:37–54; 14:1–24), including turning the Last Supper into a farewell address or testamentary banquet for Jesus' last instructions (22:14–38; see also Acts 20:17–38).

While scholars traditionally viewed Acts, like the Gospels, as a unique literary form, conforming to no existing pattern, it now seems likely, given the author's Greek background, that he builds on existing patterns, presenting his material in a way favorable to the Hellenistic world. In Acts, Luke appropriates models of historiography practiced by such contemporaries as Polybius, Tacitus, Livy, and Josephus. Such models involved numerous compositional techniques, including (1) the insertion of speeches and letters, (2) generalizing summaries, (3) mimesis or archaisms, that is, imitating

---

1. Valantasis, *The Gospels and Christian Life*, 37. For a detailed comparison between the Gospels and other ancient biographies, see Burridge, *What Are the Gospels?*

classical models through stylistic affectation of the past, and (4) the "dramatic-episode" style of presentation.

The centerpiece of most of the dramatic scenes found in Acts is a speech, whether a mission sermon (chapters 2 and 17), a prophetic indictment (chapter 7), a didactic commentary on the event at hand (chapters 10 and 15), or a formal apologia (defense) before public authorities (chapters 22 and 26). The popularity of speeches as historiographical devices is well documented in Hellenistic literature, notably in the works of the first century Jewish historian Josephus (this is also a regular feature of the deuterocanonical literature known as 1, 2, and 3 Maccabees). Their primary intent is to develop the book's theme(s). As is well known, the speeches in Luke–Acts are not verbatim, nor should they be read as recollections of actual addresses. The major public addresses, whether of Jesus (Luke 4:18–27), Peter (Acts 2:14–36; 3:12–26; 4:8–12; 11:5–18; 15:7–11), Stephen (7:2–53), James (15:13–21), or Paul (13:16–41; 17:22–31; 20:18–35; 21:40—22:41; 24:10–20; 26:1–23), while delivered "in character," all reflect characteristic Lukan language and interests. In modern parlance, Luke was the main speechwriter, or, in the case of speeches cast as forensic defenses, Luke functions as the apostles' lead attorney.

While the archaic flavor and Semitic idiom of the speeches to Jews in Acts can be taken as pointing to older tradition, they more likely pertain to writing techniques widely practiced in the postclassical culture, which relied on imitating classical models and stylistic affectation of the atmosphere of the venerated past. In the section of Acts dealing with the mission under the Twelve, just as in Luke's infancy narratives, the classical model is the Septuagint, the Bible of Greek-speaking Jews. Luke's mimesis, of course, is enhanced through formal or allusive quotation of biblical passages, but particularly by adaptation of their style and idiom for his own writing. With his mimicry of Septuagintal style and idiom, as with his archaizing sermonic material, Luke cultivates the impression of the church's beginning as a "sacred time," hallmarked by "sacred speech." [A clear modern example is the Book of Mormon, with its mimicry of King James' linguistic style and idiom.] Interestingly, Septuagintal mimicry is suspended after Acts 15, when the Twelve likewise exit Luke's stage, though it reappears in 20:18–35. Luke introduces the most literary style of Greek precisely where the occasion calls for it, such as 17:16–34, when Paul addresses the citizens of Athens, or in 24:1–23 and 26:2–29, when he delivers an appeal to important Roman officials.

Another feature of Hellenistic historiography is the generalizing summary, something Luke uses regularly to fill the gaps between freestanding episodes, a device he observed in Mark's composition of the Jesus tradition

(Mark 1:32–34, 39; 3:10–12). The major summaries of Acts occur in the first five chapters, where Luke's information was probably most fragmentary (2:24–47; 4:32–35; 5:11–16). Minor summaries, often only a single verse, occur at 1:14; 6:7; 9:31; 12:24; 16:5; 19:20; 28:30–31, mostly to sum up the success attained during each of the six "panels" or periods into which he arranges his material. These summaries are not mere stopgap devices, but rather are important compositional stratagems for sustaining the argument and the impression of a steady growth of the Christian movement, guided by God's Spirit.

The last feature involves the author's attempt to create vivid historical reality by concentrating on particular paradigmatic events while deemphasizing the chronological sequence between them. The clearest examples of these freestanding dramatic episodes in Acts are Pentecost (chapter 2), Stephen's martyrdom (chapters 6–7), the conversion of Cornelius (chapter 10), the Jerusalem Council (chapter 15), Paul's mission in Athens (17:16–34), and the trials of Paul (chapters 21–26). While some think that this method makes Luke more an edifying storyteller than a historian, Hellenistic historiography did not sacrifice truth to edification just because it singled out the typical, the exemplary, or the programmatic.

Some scholars, defending Luke's purpose as stated in his prologues, suggest "historical monograph" as an accurate category for his genre. Viewed from this perspective, both Lukan volumes, self-enclosed but interrelated, demonstrate the author's purpose as describing the entire process of salvation history, viewing the continuity of God's plan through the life of Jesus and the birth of the church to be the central feature of Luke–Acts. According to this "continuity thesis," Luke's intention is to demonstrate the full scope of the divine plan whereby the church proves to be the proper continuity of God's way with Israel. Given this understanding, more adequate literary designations for Luke–Acts are "biblical history" or "apologetic history."

Both volumes are dependent on the Old Testament, not merely for discrete models, motifs, and proof-texts, but like antecedent "historical" biblical writings (the books of Samuel–Kings, 1–2 Chronicles, Ezra–Nehemiah), they present theology via history. "Rather than a *Summa Theologica* or *Institutes of the Christian Religion*, Luke writes a narrative theological history of God's mission, meant to instruct in the character of God, to appeal for allegiance to God, and to inspire in God's service."[2] Representing an insider's attempt to establish the identity of a subgroup of people within the setting of the larger context, Luke–Acts also aims to define or defend the "Christian" community, an upstart, messianic Jewish sect attracting numerous Gentile

---

2. Spencer, *Luke and Acts*, 52–53.

converts—within a dominant pagan environment, among traditional Jews, and to Christians themselves. As such these writings can be classified "apologetic history." Although using Hellenistic techniques, Luke derived his understanding of history from biblical predecessors such as the Deuteronomic historian, with whom he shared a confessional stance regarding God's activity in human affairs.

Literary Features

In his book *Literary Patters, Theological Themes, and the Genre of Luke–Acts*, Charles Talbert likens Luke–Acts to the "cultic biographies" of the Greco-Roman world. In this literature, a narration of the life of the founder of a religious community is followed by stories of his successors and disciples. Moreover, the story is told in such a way that the apostles reproduce in their lives key events in the life of the earthly Jesus. The lifestyle of the new community is thus shown to be rooted in the career of Jesus.

Modern readers of Acts may suppose that they are reading history. However, Acts is so filled with miracles, visions, dreams, and novelistic events (such as Paul's sea journey in Acts 27:1—28:15) that even classical historians such as Thucydides or Plutarch might have questioned the veracity of its story as history. Talbert's view of Luke–Acts suggests that, like much of classical biography, it has a practical, homiletical purpose—to tell the story of Jesus and his followers in such a way that the values of the founder and his immediate successors might be emulated by others.

Luke accomplishes this intention uniquely, by the use of numerous broad patterns such as (1) paired stories and examples involving male and female characters, and (2) parallel actions and experiences between Jesus and his followers.

Male-Female Pairing

Luke often juxtaposes stories or statements involving male and female figures, mostly in material unique to his narratives.[3] Examples include:

- hymns of praise: Zechariah (Benedictus, Luke1:67–79) and Mary (Magnificat, Luke 1:46–55);
- victims healed by Jesus: Gerasene demoniac (Luke 8:26–39) and hemorrhaging woman, Lk. 8:40–56);

3. For a chart of twenty such pairings, see ibid., 42–43.

- contrasting helpers: active Samaritan, passive priest (Luke 10:30–37) and active Martha, passive Mary (Lk. 10:38–42);
- healings by Jesus on the sabbath: man with dropsy (Luke 14:1–6) and woman with bent back (Luke 13:10–17);
- finding lost things: shepherd finding lost sheep (Luke 15:3–7) and housekeeper finding lost coin (Luke 15:8–10);
- Spirit-filled prophets: sons and male slaves (Acts 2:17–18) and daughters and female slaves (Acts 2:17–18);
- dishonest contributors: Ananias (Acts 5:3–6) and Sapphira (Acts 5:7–10);
- victims restored by Peter: Aeneas in Lydda (Acts 9:32–35) and Tabitha in Joppa (Acts 9:36–43);
- prophets in Caesarea: visiting Judean prophet, Agabus (Acts 21:10–11) and Philip's four daughters (Acts 21:9).

Despite Luke's pervasive pairings of male and female characters, his inclusivity need not be taken as unequivocal support for women's equality and opportunity for ministry, certainly not by today's standards. Even in Acts, which hints at gender equality in passing references to "both men and women" (5:14; 8:3; 9:2; 13:50; 17:4, 12; 22:4), men remain the chief preachers, teachers, and authorities. Luke's intention, however, unusually countercultural, is remarkable for his day.

Jesus-Followers Parallels

In Jesus' Sermon on the Plain, he sets forth a guiding principle about teacher-student relations: "A disciple is not above the teacher, but everyone who is fully qualified will be like the teacher" (Luke 6:40). Jesus' disciples, therefore, follow his example in word and deed. And that is what we find in Acts. Jesus' emissaries do not merely witness to him, but perpetuate what he did and taught from the beginning (Acts 1:1).

Even the casual reader notices the parallels between his two volumes:

Gospel of Luke	*Acts of the Apostles*
Preface	Preface
Birth of Jesus	Birth of the church
The Spirit descends on Jesus	The Spirit descends on the apostles
Mission and ministry of Jesus	Mission and ministry of the church

| Journey of Jesus to Jerusalem | Journey of Paul to Jerusalem and Rome |
| Trial of Jesus | Trial of Paul |

This pattern includes healing ministries (Luke 5:17–26 and Acts 3:1–10; 14:8–10). Further, as Jesus raised a widow's son and Jairus's daughter from the dead (Luke 7:10–17; 8:49–56), so Peter resuscitates the widow-aiding Tabitha (Acts 9:36–43) and Paul revives the lifeless youth Eutychus (20:7–12). Like his exalted Lord, the dying Stephen echoes Jesus' final prayers from the cross (Luke 23:34, 46) in Acts 7:59–60. As Jesus escaped the tomb, so Peter is supernaturally freed from prison in Jerusalem (Acts 5:17–21; 12:1–17); likewise, Paul experiences a miraculous jailbreak (Acts 16:25–34) and a resuscitation after being stoned and left for dead (14:19–20). As Jesus exposed and expelled the devil (Luke 4:1–13), likewise Peter (Acts 5:3, 16), Philip (8:7), and Paul (Acts 13:9–11; 16:16–18; 19:11–19; 26:18).

As Luke constructs a network of common experiences between Jesus and his followers, we must not mistake similarity for sameness. The apostles may preach and heal in Jesus' name, but they do not replace or replicate Jesus.

Likewise, within each volume there are double stories. In his Gospel, Luke offers two images of God—a man looking for his lost sheep and a woman looking for her lost coin (Luke 15). In Acts 9, Peter raises a paralyzed man and a dead woman (see also Luke 5 and 8). Acts 3 and 14 contain strikingly similar healing stories. In Acts 16, Luke narrates contrasting stories about two women—a rich businesswoman who became a Christian and a slave girl cleansed of a spirit of divination.

Talbert finds additional correspondences between the Gospel and Acts. For example, Jesus' healing of a lame man in Luke 5:17–26 matches the healing of a lame man in his name in Acts 3:1–10. Similarly, both Jesus and Peter are invited to the house of a Roman centurion (Luke 7:1–10; Acts 10). In their respective trials, both Jesus and Paul are declared to be innocent three times. Further investigation shows that Luke applies a similar scheme on a smaller scale in the organization of sections and sub-sections within the two books. For example, there are remarkable parallels between Luke 9 and Luke 22–23, and between Acts 1–12 and Acts 13–28.

According to James Dunn, intertextual parallels occur not only between Luke and Acts, but also within Acts. The following table from Acts illustrates parallels between Peter and Paul, key figures in the missions to Jews and Gentiles respectively.[4]

---

4. Dunn, *Acts*, xiv.

Peter	Paul
2:22–29	13:26–41
3:1–10	14:8–11
4:8	13:9
5:15	19:12
8:17	19:6
8:18–24	13:6–11
9:36–41	20:9–12
12:6–11	16:25–41

The presence of such correspondences suggest that Luke must have begun his two-volume work with a preliminary plan. While careful architecture is evident in other literary works of the period, the presence of such techniques could well have a liturgical function, leading to the conviction, unique to Luke, that the story of Jesus and of the church are incomplete without the other.

Use of Sources

As any good writer, Luke depends upon many sources. For Luke, they consist of three groupings: (1) preceding documents, (2) eyewitness reports, and (3) his own account, based on careful investigation. When we examine Luke's sources, one looms large, explicit and pervasive throughout: the Jewish scriptures in Greek translation (known as Septuagint and abbreviated as LXX). In his writings Luke ranges far and wide across the Old Testament, confirming Jesus' pronouncement at the end of the Gospel: "These are my words that I spoke to you while I was still with you—that everything written about me in the law of Moses, the prophets, and the psalms must be fulfilled" (Luke 24:44). Likewise Peter launches the early church's mission in Acts with proof-texts from the prophet Joel and Davidic psalms (Acts 2:16–21, 25–28, 31, 34–35) and Paul sums up the mission with an Isaiah citation (Acts 28:25–27).

In addition to Luke's engagement with an array of Old Testament passages, a more extensive and allusive appropriation of scriptural images and patterns follows from Luke's knowledge of Israel's Bible. This phenomenon, labelled "intertextuality," has attracted a great deal of attention in Lukan scholarship. For example, by casting Jesus in the messianic mold of David and Solomon and in the prophetic pattern of Moses and Elijah, Luke demonstrates reliance on biblical portraits of these predecessors.

Outside the transfiguration scene, where Moses and Elijah have a brief but significant role (Luke 9:29–33), two major Acts speeches invoke Moses' active role as Israel's prophet-leader and legal mediator. After recounting Jesus' rejection by Israel and resurrection by God, Peter cites Deuteronomy to announce that Jesus is the long-awaited prophet like Moses, to whom the people must listen (Acts 3:22–23; see Deut. 18:15–20). Stephen recalls the same text in shorter form in Acts 7:37. According to Acts, Jesus fulfills the expectation of a faithful prophet like Moses, repudiated by God's people but vindicated by God's power. This image also informs Jesus' ministry in Luke's Gospel, where Jesus overcomes Satan's three tests by citing Moses' exhortation from Deuteronomy (Luke 4:4, 8, 12; see Deut. 8:3; 6:13, 16). The stage is set for Jesus' vocation as a Moses-style, Deuteronomy-shaped prophet.

Of particular interest is Luke's engagement with the book of Deuteronomy in his Travel Narrative (Luke 9:51—18:14). While the parallels do not suggest Luke's primary dependence on Deuteronomy, as on Mark, his narration's seemingly random order of events may owe a debt to Deuteronomy's sequence of ideas. For example:

- The parable of the Good Samaritan (Luke 10:25–37) and Deuteronomy 6–7. The narrative introducing the parable cites Deuteronomy 6:5, and the character of the merciful Samaritan "foreigner" challenges the ethnic cleansing policy of Deuteronomy 7:2.
- The parable of the Great Banquet (Luke 14:15–24) and Deuteronomy 20:1–9. Luke's excuses for not attending the messianic feast recall exemptions from holy war allowed in Deuteronomy 20:5–8.
- The parables of the Lost Sheep and the Prodigal Son (Luke 15:3–7, 11–32) and Deuteronomy 21:15—22:4. Jesus' story on recovering the lost sheep resembles Deuteronomy's command to return a stray sheep to its rightful owner. Furthermore, concerns over inheritance rights and paternal love link the parable of the Prodigal Son with Deuteronomy 21:15–17. However, the parable's conclusion makes clear its disapproval to the remark about stoning a stubborn son in Deuteronomy 21:18-21.

These cases illustrate Luke's critical engagement with the book of Deuteronomy in both sympathetic and antithetic directions and indicate that Luke wishes his readers to study Jesus' teachings in the central section of his Gospel in light of parallel passages and themes from Deuteronomy.

As Moses seems to be prominent on Luke's radar, so are Elijah/Elisha and the narratives in 1 Kings 17—2 Kings 9. As well as appearing with Moses at Jesus' transfiguration (Luke 9:30, 33), Elijah appears four times in Luke's Gospel, one as a model for John the Baptist (Luke 1:17), twice as a reflection of Jesus' prophetic identity (9:9, 19), and once as the subject of Jesus' proclamation (4:25-26). Like Elijah and Elisha, Jesus cures lepers (5:12-16; 17:11-19), supports widows (7:11-17; see 18:1-8), and nourishes the hungry crowd (9:10-17).[5] Although Elijah partially prefigures Jesus' ascension, Elijah's ascent closely matches Jesus' Spirit-promising farewell to his disciples (Acts 1:4-5, 8-11; 2 Kgs. 2:1-16).

Given Luke's claim that he "carefully investigated" many accounts, which go unnamed, we can imagine that, in addition to biblical sources, he had access to particular items of tradition or information about John the Baptist, Mary the mother of Jesus, Herod Antipas, the Galilean women disciples, and members of the apostolic Twelve. Some of the actual eyewitnesses were no longer alive when Luke wrote, since the Gospel preface seems to derive from a second or third stage of Christianity, following that of pioneering writers/evangelists (second stage) and eyewitnesses to Jesus' mission (first stage). Since Paul's writings and mission stem from the second phase, the author of Luke–Acts appears to be a later Pauline enthusiast and annalist.

For his Gospel, Luke's use of literary sources certainly includes the Gospels of Mark and Matthew (or instead, possibly the hypothetical "Q"), though without naming them. Beyond the addition of a prologue, birth stories (Luke 1-2), and resurrection appearances in Jerusalem (Luke 24), Luke's Gospel follows Mark's outline of Jesus' life. Apart from the occasional transposition of episodes, Luke imposes on Mark only four major modifications: one major omission (eliminating Mark 6:45—8:26 at Luke 9:17), one minor omission (eliminating Mark 9:42—10:12 at Luke 9:50), and various interpolations (such as additions of Luke 4:16-30; 5:1-11; 6:20—8:3 ["little interpolation"], 9:51—18:14 ["big interpolation"], and 19:1-28 to the Markan sequence). The latter, Jesus' journey to Jerusalem, is a Lukan creation (mostly "L" material).

About 40 percent of Luke is not drawn from Mark or Matthew. In the past it was believed that "L" represented the material available to Luke other than Mark or "Q." Lately, scholars are suggesting that Luke was the creative genius who wrote the "L" material. If that is true, by examining this uniquely

---

5. Moses also miraculously feeds God's people, but healing lepers and restoring life to a widow's deceased son better fit Elijah and Elisha (1 Kgs. 17:8-24; 2 Kgs. 4:1-37).

Lukan material, insight might be gained into Luke's purpose, perspective, and theological peculiarities.

Over the past two centuries, an enormous amount of research has been devoted to the study of the four Gospels. The earliest stages of this investigation involve what is called *source criticism* or synoptic criticism, the literary analysis of the written Gospels as sources, focusing on their similarities and differences as well as on their relationships and literary interdependence. This type of investigation led to an obvious conclusion, that three of them—Matthew, Mark, and Luke—have much in common, and that the fourth—John—is quite different. The first three are often called Synoptics (from the Greek word *synopsis*, meaning "seeing together), and John simply called The Fourth Gospel.

Noting that the Synoptics have a great deal in common, often agreeing in style, vocabulary, and phraseology, a theory developed known as the priority of Mark. According to this perspective, Matthew and Luke followed Mark's order, improving its style and language while adding respect for the disciples and reverence for Jesus. Almost as widely held as the priority of Mark is the view that the material common to Matthew and Luke, but not in Mark, was derived from a common source called "Q," after the German word *Quelle*, meaning source. Though no copies of this document survive, some scholars believe that this material circulated only in oral form, though the majority hold that it was reduced to writing before it was utilized by Matthew and Luke. While this basic model, called the two-source theory, continues to have widespread scholarly support, the literary relationship of the Synoptic Gospels has been explained in other ways.

An alternative explanation, known as The Two-Gospel Hypothesis or the Griesbach hypothesis, named after Johannes Griesbach, its eighteenth-century proponent, contends that Luke used Matthew's Gospel as a source and that Mark produced his work last, as an abridgment of Matthew and Luke. An advantage of this theory is that it explains the literary agreements between these Gospels without having to posit the existence of a hypothetical "Q" source. Another group of scholars, led by Michael Goulder, John Drury, and John Spong, have also denied the existence of the "Q" source, but they have built their argument independently of the Two-Gospel Hypothesis. They do not question that Luke used Mark as a source, but they maintain that Luke's parallels with Matthew can be accounted for both by direct dependence on that Gospel as well as by the lectionary needs of the emerging church.

In addition to the schools of thought relying on Markan priority, another view emerged regarding the manner by which Luke composed his Gospel. This view, known as the Proto-Luke Hypothesis, asserts that Luke wrote an original Gospel before he became acquainted with Mark, and that our edition of Luke's Gospel represents a later version, into which blocks of Markan material were incorporated. This view helps explain unusual features in Luke's Gospel, such as the eleven doublets found therein (8:16 and 11:33; 8:17 and 12:2; 8:18 and 19:26; 9:3–5 and 10:3–12; 9:23 and 14:27; 9:24 and 17:33; 9:26 and 12:9; 9:46 and 22:24; 20:46 and 11:43; 21:14–15 and 12:11–12; 14:11 and 18:14), and the seventeen places where Luke, demonstrably using Mark 1:7—14:11, diverges from Mark's order.

Furthermore, Luke's Gospel contains two mission charges, one addressed to the Twelve and drawn from Mark, the other addressed to the seventy and mostly unique to Luke, with some dependence on Matthew. However, when Jesus later reminds the Twelve that they had gone out "without a purse, bag, or sandals" (22:35), he is echoing the charge given to the seventy (10:4). This editorial lapse is understandable if, when Luke first wrote the account of the Last Supper, he had only one mission charge to which he might refer.

Other editorial markers also point to the validity of the Proto-Luke theory, including the likelihood that 3:1–2 originally opened Luke's Gospel (the sixfold date has a ring about it that is reminiscent of the beginning of the prophetic books); the introduction of John the Baptist in 3:2, as though for the first time; and the attachment of the genealogy of Jesus to the story of his baptism instead of to the story of his birth, as in Matthew's Gospel. If the birth stories were not included in the earliest draft of Luke's Gospel, this would be further evidence that the book went through various stages of composition.

As a working hypothesis for our study, then, we shall assume that Luke began his literary undertaking by collecting information about Jesus from eyewitnesses and others, to which he added his own material (this draft would constitute "proto-Luke"). At some later time, when a copy of Mark became available, Luke augmented his draft with Markan insertions. He then combined this draft with material gained from Matthew (and or teaching material from "Q"), adding his version of the infancy stories and the prologue to bring his work into its final form. In every stage of composition he clearly left the imprint of his unique artistry and vision.

At the close of World War I, attention shifted to the preliterary stages of the Gospels, and what is called *form criticism* was applied to the units of tradition about Jesus that had circulated orally before they were incorporated in written Gospels. Reacting against the excesses of form criticism, around 1950 New Testament scholarship shifted attention away from the analysis of individual units in the gospel tradition and concentrated on the Gospels as unified compositions of literary authors. Out of this approach came a method called *redaction criticism*, which viewed the Gospel authors as editors, and *narrative criticism*, which focused on the end product, with the Gospel documents as a whole. Noting that each Gospel possesses a unique literary quality, narrative critics guided readers to discover the leading theological insights and purposes of each author. Viewing the Gospels as literature and the evangelists as theologically creative, redaction and narrative critics raised questions about the purpose, perspective, and peculiarities that make each Gospel unique.

While traditional readers of the Gospels have in mind a composite picture of the life of Jesus, made up of features from the four Gospels, redaction criticism makes an effort to isolate the individual characteristics of each Gospel in order to appreciate the special contribution made by its author to a fourfold task: understanding (a) God's plan for humanity, (b) the church's mission, (c) the uniqueness of Christian life, and (d) the person and work of Jesus Christ. We will return to these topics in chapters 6 and 7 as we focus on Luke's historical and theological purpose for writing Luke–Acts, a task preceded by liturgical considerations.

The use of literary sources in Acts is more difficult to delineate, since we have no similar written Christian sources from this period with which to compare Acts. Since some of the events Luke records in Acts possibly overlap with his own lifetime, the sources for Acts would have been more personal and firsthand than those for his Gospel. As Luke traveled about, staying at Christian residences where apostles, missionaries, and other early Christian leaders often lodged, these venues may well have become places where oral and written Christian traditions were not just passed on but also collected. Luke's interest in hospitality, eating, and lodging in his writings helps us recognize the invaluable role Christian homes played early on in the transmission of the gospel and other early church traditions. Though the preface of Acts (1:1–2) does not acknowledge literary sources (except Luke's "first volume"), the situation is sketchy here, for beyond Old Testament usage, Luke may also have appropriated available apostolic speeches, Pauline traditions, eyewitness diaries, and other oral and written forms of early Christian tradition.

If indeed the "we" passages reflect the author's own experience, Luke would have had personal experience of what Paul and others said and did in places such as Troas and Philippi. Equally important, in his travels with Paul the author is said to have stopped in places such as Judea, including Caesarea and Jerusalem, as well as events during Paul's sea voyage to Rome and Paul's stay in Rome. At Miletus Luke would have heard Paul's farewell speech to the Ephesian church officials (Acts 20:13–38), who could have provided insight into Paul's ministry in that city. At Tyre, where he is said to have stayed seven days, he may have learned about the church up the coast in Antioch, things he may not have learned from Paul.

During a lengthy stay in Judea, lasting about two years and involving visits to both Jerusalem and Caesarea, he could have learned about things recorded in Acts 1-8. For example, we are told that Luke stayed with Philip for several days, during which time the material in Acts 8 could have been gathered. While in Jerusalem, he could have had personal contact with key figures such as James, Mary the mother of John Mark, Mary Magdalene, Joanna (from whom he could have heard stories about the Herods), and possibly Mary the mother of Jesus. Even if Luke was not able to consult such major figures, he could have talked to additional eyewitnesses and others who knew early Christian figures.

It is also possible that during his time in Caesarea, while waiting for Paul's case to be resolved, Luke gathered certain Petrine traditions the Jerusalem church may not have known, including the Cornelius material. He could even have traveled to Damascus and Antioch during this time, though nothing in the "we" passages suggests such a trip. Of course, all this is conjecture, but conjecture based on the text of Acts.

There are signs in the way Luke handles his information that he was not interested in simply making up stories about the early church, but rather was limited to and by his sources. When his knowledge was limited, as with the early Christian mission in Galilee, he says nothing about it (while Galilee is mentioned in the summary statement in 9:31, this is the only mention in Acts of a Christian community in Galilee. Had he not lacked for knowledge, it would have been strange for Luke not to record a mission in the home territory of Jesus and his apostles). Since Luke knew the most about Paul, it is not surprising that Pauline material is briefly introduced at 8:1-4, in preparation for 9:1-31 and for all that follows in Acts after chapter 13. As is his custom, Luke often introduces his subjects in summary passages or by brief reference before treating them more fully (hence Luke introduces Stephen and Philip in Acts 6:5 as a preview to lengthier accounts in 6:8—7:60 and 8:5-40).

While no view is without difficulties, the evidence of Acts seems to point to Luke as an occasional companion of Paul. At the same time, Luke reflects a certain distance from the events he records, suggesting a date sometime in the 80s of the first century as the period of its composition. This helps to explain why Luke doesn't reflect familiarity with Paul's letters or why he leaves out descriptions of major disagreements and tensions in the early church reflected in Paul's early letters (see, for example, Gal. 2:1-21). If Luke had been in his twenties or thirties when he first traveled with Paul in the 50s, he would have been in his 50s or 60s by the year 90.

CHAPTER 5

Luke's Liturgical Task

Summary: Chapter 5 examines the Jewish lectionary pattern of reading appointed scriptures during worship services or other festal occasions, considering whether the liturgical life of the synagogue served as the organizing principle of the three Synoptic Gospels. Noting that Jesus, his original disciples, and early Christians were all Jewish, Michael Goulder proposed that the Gospel of Mark is organized around the liturgical year of the Jews, beginning with the Jewish New Year and culminating in the celebration of Passover. Because Mark only covers six and a half months of the Jewish liturgical year, Matthew and Luke are about 40 percent longer, providing "Jesus material" sufficient to cover the sabbaths and festivals of the remaining five and a half months of the Jewish year.

Matthew's Gospel, written for a primarily Jewish Christian audience, inserts concentrated blocks of "Jesus material" to correlate either with the five books of the Hebrew Torah or with the great festivals of the Jewish liturgical year. Luke's Gospel, written for a primarily Gentile or Hellenized Jewish Christian audience, followed Matthew's pattern while deemphasizing or even deleting exclusively Jewish practices that Luke's community was abandoning. The book of Acts, like Luke's Gospel, may have functioned liturgically as well, though not in the same way as the Synoptics.

Assignment: Read chapter 5 of *Power Revealed*. [If you have not finished reading Luke–Acts in its entirety, do so as soon as possible.] Answer the following questions, writing the answers in your journal. [If you are in a study group, be prepared to share your views with others in the class.] 1. Do you identify with "high" or with "low" church liturgy? Which do you prefer and why? 2. After reading this chapter, do you find Goulder's lectionary theory plausible, convincing, or far-fetched? Explain your answer.

Learning Objectives: After completing this chapter, participants will be able to:

- Describe the difference between "high church" and "low church" tradition and liturgy.
- Explain the concept of a liturgical year.
- Explain the concept of a lectionary.
- Understand how Mark's Gospel aligns with the Jewish liturgical year.
- Identify the five teaching discourses in Matthew's Gospel and explain their correlations with the Hebrew Pentateuch (or Hexateuch) and the five great Jewish festivals.
- Explain Luke's liturgical task, both regarding his Gospel and the book of Acts.
- Describe and assess Goulder's lectionary theory.

Any study of church history or Protestant denominationalism is sure to lead to the terms "high church" or "low church," or "high liturgy" and "low liturgy." Originally, these terms defined movements within the Anglican/Episcopal tradition. According to this terminology, "high churches" are highly ritualistic, using rituals associated with state-related churches or with Roman Catholic elements in worship. By contrast, "low churches" are often associated with dissent, autonomy, and spontaneous worship. Such churches regularly abandon or frown upon elaborate rituals, ornate clerical vestments, hierarchical priestly patterns, worship based on sacraments, and the use of elaborate music, ornamental altarpieces, and pulpit furnishings such as paraments (used to highlight church seasons and festival days). Many of these customs and practices go back to the fourth century, when Christianity was established as the official religion of the Roman Empire.

After Constantine, a distinctively Christian culture progressively developed within the context of the Roman Empire. One of the results of Christendom (the expansion of Christianity as imperial religion) was the organization of space in Christian terms. Worship, no longer confined to small spaces such as houses or burial chambers, now took place in elaborate basilicas. As church architecture and organization expanded, so liturgy expanded to fill the enlarged space allotted to it. Building on pagan rituals such as sacrifices, festivals, and processions, Christian liturgy began to take on the characteristics of such public worship, including open-air processions, pilgrimages, elaborate rituals (such as bowing and genuflecting), rich garments, and the use of musical chants.

In addition to space, Christianity also extended its cultural influence through the sanctification of time. The life of individual Christians was marked at each stage by rituals that came to be called sacraments, numbering seven. For example, baptism and confirmation became marks of growth, associated with birth and entry into the community. The sacrament of repentance (or "penance") and the Eucharist sanctified the turn from sin during the course of adult life. Ordination represented initiation to the priesthood, and the remaining sacraments were matrimony and final anointing (for the terminally ill).

Time itself was sanctified by an elaborate liturgical year that served to bring the biblical past into the present by celebrating moments in the history of salvation and the life of Christ. Sunday, the traditional Christian celebration of the resurrection, was declared a public holiday by Emperor Constantine. Over time, a seasonal liturgical cycle emerged, revolving around Easter. It was preceded by the forty-day period of Lent and followed by an "Easter season" that concluded with the feast of Pentecost. A similar cycle centered on Christmas. It was preceded by the season of Advent and followed by a "Christmas season" that concluded with the feast of Epiphany. The time outside these cycles was designated "ordinary time." During those Sundays, liturgical readings were taken from Gospel stories concerning the words and deeds of Jesus. Eventually another liturgical cycle developed, centered on the celebration of the lives of the saints, beginning with the martyrs, then the "confessors" (those who remained faithful during persecution but did not die as martyrs), and then others who lived meritorious lives.

If you are a Christian and attend a Roman Catholic, Eastern Orthodox, Episcopal, or Lutheran church, you are probably acquainted with a lectionary. This practice, also observed in some Methodist, Presbyterian, African-American, and other Protestant churches, comes from the Jewish pattern of reading appointed scriptures during worship services or other festal occasions. According to the Jewish Talmud, the practice of reading appointed scriptures on given days or occasions dates back to the time of Moses and began with the annual festivals of Passover, Pentecost, and the Feast of Tabernacles.

Typically, a lectionary goes through the scriptures in a logical pattern. The one year Jewish lectionary reads the entirety of the Torah within the space of a year, while the three-year lectionary requires shorter weekly readings. Eventually readings included other sacred writings of the Jews, such as readings from the prophetic writings, known as "latter prophets," and the historical books, known as "former prophets." The early Christians adopted the Jewish custom of reading passages from the Old Testament during worship. They soon included the writings of the apostles and evangelists.

Today many Christians follow the Revised Common Lectionary (RCL), organizing readings from the Old Testament, the Psalms, the New Testament letters, and the Gospels. Both Catholic and RCL versions are organized into three-year cycles of readings, designated A, B, or C. Each yearly cycle begins on the first Sunday of Advent, Year A reading the Gospel of Matthew during Advent, Year B the Gospel of Mark, and Year C the Gospel of Luke.

Another lectionary, known as the Narrative Lectionary, follows a four-year cycle of Bible readings designed for preaching sermons that extend from the Sunday after Labor Day to the Day of Pentecost, with texts highlighting the major story arcs of the Bible. From September to Advent, the readings come from the Old Testament; from Christmas to Easter, one of the four Gospels is read; from Easter to Pentecost, the texts are from Acts and Paul's letters; and from Pentecost to September, preachers are free to create their own sermon series to address other topics or Bible passages.

Aware of this long-standing tradition within Judaism and Christianity, in 1972 Michael Goulder wrote *The Evangelists' Calendar*, proposing that the liturgical life of the synagogue was the organizing principle of the three Synoptic Gospels. Noting that Jesus and his original disciples were all Jewish, together with the fact that early Christians saw in the Hebrew scriptures the anticipation of the person and work of the Messiah, Goulder proposed that the Gospel of Mark is organized around the liturgical year of the Jews. Noting that one of the earliest texts of Mark's Gospel, a text known as Codex Alexandrinus,[1] is divided into forty-nine distinct lections for use in worship, Goulder found in this Gospel an appropriate story about Jesus designed to be read against the background of a one-year synagogue cycle.

Setting Mark into a Jewish Liturgical Framework

The climax of Mark is the story of the passion and crucifixion of Jesus, an event so central to understanding the meaning of Jesus that Mark devotes 40 percent of his Gospel to the last week in the life of Jesus (11:1–15:47). For Goulder, the first and most obvious fact that arises out of the story of

---

1. Codex Alexandrinus, one of the earliest and most complete manuscripts of the Bible, dates to the late fourth or fifth-century. It is considered the best manuscript of the New Testament.

the crucifixion of Jesus is that it is told against the background of the Jewish observance of the Passover celebration (usually celebrated in late March or early April). Accepting this premise, observers can roll Mark's text backward across the synagogue's liturgical year, uncovering a remarkable set of associations:

- Hanukkah (the Jewish celebration of Dedication), comes about three months prior to the Passover, at the start of winter. The story in Mark's Gospel that coincides with that celebration is the account of Jesus' transfiguration (9:2–10).
- Sukkoth (the Jewish feast of Tabernacles), an eight-day celebration of the harvest, comes several months earlier, in late October. The story in Mark's Gospel that coincides with that celebration is the parable of the sower and Jesus' explanation of that parable (4:1–34), which not only displays a clear harvest theme, but also contains sufficient material to cover the eight days of Sukkoth.
- Yom Kippur (the Jewish Day of Atonement), is observed some five days before Sukkoth begins. This coincides with Mark 1:40–2:12, its stories of healing, cleansing, and forgiveness clearly conveying the meaning of Yom Kippur.
- Rosh Hashanah (the Jewish New Year), is observed ten days before Yom Kippur. The Jews observed the day liturgically by blowing the shofar, announcing that the kingdom of God was at hand and urging the people to prepare by repenting. This coincides with the story of John the Baptist, whom Mark casts as a human shofar, announcing that the kingdom of God is dawning in the life of Jesus and urging people to repent (1:1–11).

As this pattern indicates, aligning Mark's story with the Jewish liturgical year means that the start of the first Gospel corresponds to the Jewish New Year. In Mark's case, Gospel readings would cover six and a half months of the liturgical calendar, culminating in the celebration of Passover, with which Mark associates the Christian Easter as its climax and conclusion. This pattern explains why Mark is shorter than Matthew or Luke. Mark needed to cover only six and a half months of the liturgical year. Matthew and Luke are longer—about 40 percent longer—because they needed to stretch Mark by providing Jesus stories sufficient to cover the sabbaths and holy days of the remaining five and a half months of the Jewish year.

The various portions of Mark that tell the Jesus story appear designed to be read during the Jewish observances of New Year, Atonement, Tabernacles, Dedication, and Passover, each coinciding with the narrative story line that Mark had developed. This analysis indicates that the gospel tradition—in addition to being a retelling of the Jesus story based on the Hebrew scriptures—was also organized around the liturgical year of the Jews, under whose influence the Christian story was born. According to Goulder, Mark's Gospel is neither biography nor history so much as it is corporate memory, informed and affected by the Hebrew scriptures and organized according to Jewish worship practices.

Before people thought about organizing the details of Jesus' life in some biographical pattern, he was proclaimed in the synagogues through the tradition of Jewish storytelling. That explains why, as long as the Christian community was made up primarily of Jewish followers of Jesus, early Christians would understand how to read their Gospels, but when the Christian community ceased to be Jewish, that understanding vanished.

Setting Matthew into a Jewish Liturgical Framework

If Mark, the first Gospel to be written, followed a Jewish liturgical framework, what about Matthew and Luke, which made extensive use of Mark? In 1951, British scholar B. W. Bacon identified five teaching discourses in Matthew's Gospel, each of which concluded with a formula statement: "When Jesus had finished these sayings . . ." (see 7:28; 11:1; 13:53; 19:1; 26:1). The five discourses are:

1. Sermon on the Mount (chapters 5–7)
2. Discourse on Missions (chapter 10)
3. Discourse on the Kingdom or Rule of God (chapter 13)
4. Discourse on Church Matters (chapter 18)
5. Discourse on Eschatology (chapters 24–25)

A search of Matthew reveals that the author used the phrase "when Jesus had finished" five times only, in each case bringing one of the five teaching blocks to a conclusion. In no other Gospel are these units so identifiable. Furthermore, by introducing these units, Matthew more than doubled the teachings of Jesus found in Mark. Luke, on the other hand, seemed to have no need for concentrated blocks of teaching material, so he broke up Matthew's long discourses into more manageable segments. Aware of the uniqueness of these units, Professor Bacon suggested that Matthew was depicting Jesus as a new Moses, the five blocks of teaching material functioning as a kind of Christian Torah or Pentateuch, rivaling the first five books of the Hebrew scriptures, attributed to Moses.

While Bacon established recognition of these five teaching units, his correlation of the five with the Pentateuch did not stand the test of time. For example, the first teaching discourse in Matthew, the Sermon on the Mount, bore no discernible relationship to the book of Genesis, which was the first volume of the Torah. It rather had a strong connection with the book of Exodus, giving a new interpretation of the law from a new Mt. Sinai. In 1954, another British scholar, Austin Farrer, suggested that the genealogy chapter of Matthew 1 was actually designed by the author to parallel the book of Genesis, since both dealt with beginnings. This meant, however, that Farrer had six units instead of the five identified by Bacon. Since Farrer needed a sixth book to make things come out evenly, he added the next book in the Hebrew canon, the book of Joshua.

By making the genealogy of Matthew's chapter 1 serve as his Genesis, Farrer could now correlate the Sermon on the Mount with the giving of the law in Exodus. Then he saw a connecting link between the commissioning of the Twelve in Matthew's chapter 10 with the book of Leviticus by suggesting that the twelve disciples were chosen to serve as the priests of the new Israel. The harvest notes of Matthew's third teaching block in chapter 13 Farrer then likened to the gathering of the people into the church and thus parallel to the book of Numbers, which got its name from the order to count the people of Israel. Next, Farrer pointed out that chapter 18 of Matthew contained numerous references to Deuteronomy. Finally, he saw Matthew's last teaching unit as designed to present Jesus as the new Joshua, capping his argument with the note that, just as Joshua crossed the Jordan River to enter the Promised Land of Canaan, so Jesus crossed the barrier of death to enter the Promised Land of the kingdom of God.

While Farrer's proposal intrigued biblical scholars, they did not find it convincing. It fell to Michael Goulder, a student of Farrer, to discover a more convincing association. The five teaching blocks in Matthew were not related to the Torah, said Goulder, but rather to the five great festivals in the Jewish liturgical year. The first three Gospels (the Synoptics), Goulder asserted, were not written as biographies, but rather were designed as lectionary books, intended for reading in public worship on consecutive weeks of the year. Over time, passages from Mark, Matthew, and Luke, initially written as sermons or texts to illustrate or accompany the regular sabbath synagogue readings from the Torah and the other sacred writings of the Jews, were serialized by gifted Jewish Christians to create Gospels. When these Jewish Christians were finally banished from the synagogues around 85–90 CE, they simply took the Gospels with them.

According to Goulder's theory, the task of addressing Mark's incompleteness was handled adeptly by Matthew, a Jewish Christian scribe living in Syria, who was deeply in touch not only with the scriptures of the Hebrew people, but also with the great festivals of the Jewish liturgical year. Once the passion accounts were pegged to Passover-Easter, the correspondences with the festal calendar begin to establish themselves. Taking the sixty-nine numbered divisions of Matthew in Codex Alexandrinus as a guide for the Matthean lections, Goulder then showed how sections of the Gospel correspond with the appropriate Jewish fasts and festivals.

According to Goulder, the five blocks of teaching material in Matthew were designed to fall on or near the five great festivals of the Jewish liturgical year. The following correlations can be made between Matthew's five blocks of teaching material and Jewish festival celebrations:[2]

- The Sermon on the Mount (Matt. 5–7) with Pentecost
- The Discourse on Missions (Matt. 10) with New Year[3]
- The Discourse on the Kingdom or Rule of God (Matt. 13) with Tabernacles
- The Discourse on Church Matters (Matt. 18) with Dedication
- The Discourse on Eschatology (Matt. 24–25) with Passover[4]

Goulder suggests that there is sufficient space for readings for ordinary sabbaths intervening between these festivals and fasts. Chapter 14–16, for example, would provide enough readings for the three months between Tabernacles (Matt. 13) and Dedication (Matt. 17–19).

In chapters 1 through 12, Matthew rearranged Mark's order and material, adding such new material as the genealogy, the birth narrative, an expansion of the temptation narrative, the Sermon on the Mount, and significant blocks of additional teaching material. Thus Matthew accomplished his primary task, the front-end loading of Mark. In Matthew 13 through

---

2. This material is adopted from John Spong's popularization of Goulder's thesis; *Liberating the Gospels*, 101–18.

3. For Goulder, the text from Matthew's Gospel to be read on New Year's was 11:2–15, a passage that reintroduces John the Baptist, Mark's human shofar who announced the New Year theme of the coming of the kingdom of God. The second great block of teaching material in Matthew thus serves to introduce the Baptist story, articulating such New Year's themes as judgment, the need for preparation, and the promise of rest in the coming kingdom (10:5—11:1).

4. In addition to principal Jewish festivals, Goulder's system also provides for minor festivals and fasts such as the 9th of Ab, correlated to the topic of fasting with Matt. 9:9–14, and Purim with the marriage feast in 22:1–14.

28, where he followed Mark more closely, Matthew's approach consisted of inserting new material into Mark's established order.

Setting Luke into a Jewish Framework

If Luke were a Gentile "God-fearer," he would have first embraced liberalized (Hellenized) Judaism before converting to Christianity. Luke's community of Christians, quite different from Matthew's, would have followed a similar pattern. Its Jewish members would have been more Hellenized and therefore less traditionally Jewish than Matthew's. Luke's community would also have included more Gentiles, meaning that exclusively Jewish practices would have been deemphasized or even deleted in that setting.

For Luke's community, Jewish rituals and festivals that originally reflected the Jewish agricultural cycle would have faded, since Hellenized Jews tended to live in cities and no longer maintained Palestinian concerns. However, they had not abandoned all ties with Judaism. Luke's community originally worshiped on the sabbath/Sunday of each week. At this service of worship lectionary readings from the Jewish scriptures were still used, primarily from the Torah, but without ignoring the Former or the Latter Prophets. By the standards of more strictly orthodox Jews, Hellenized synagogue worship services were considerably shorter, for liberalized Jews participated in far more activities on the sabbath than did their orthodox counterparts. For example, Hellenized synagogues regularly shortened the readings from the prophets.

When Mark's Gospel first appeared in Luke's community, it was enormously popular. It ordered Christian worship as never before, but it did not cover the full year. In addition, Luke's congregants were less inclined to value Matthew, primarily because that Gospel emphasized the very ritualistic Jewishness that Luke's community was abandoning. In this respect we note that when comparing Luke with Matthew, whenever Matthew changed Mark to make it more traditionally orthodox, and thus more attractive to his more conservative Jewish-Christian audiences, Luke followed Mark's rendering. Luke appeared to have appreciated Matthew's additions, but often not in the explicit way Matthew presented them. Matthew's lengthy teaching segments, for example, were far less significant to a community that no longer observed so literally the major Jewish festivals for which Matthew had written. Eight-day festivals, vigils, and midweek observances were not part of the Hellenized Jewish experience. Therefore, with the exception of the passion story, which was already shifting from the Passover model to that called Holy Week, Luke's community simply had lesser needs, but also newer ones.

The implications of this approach to Luke are significant, for they indicate that the order for the life of Jesus given by Luke was not driven by chronological accuracy or by the desire to harmonize with existing Gospels, but rather that the order was primarily the liturgical year of the Jews. The order of the Jewish scriptures, primarily of the five books of Torah, then, became the organizing principle by which Luke wrote his Gospel. This understanding also helps us to see how Luke used his sources. He rewrote Matthew 1:1—4:11 as his Genesis (Luke 1:5—4:13). He relied on Mark 1:21—3:19 to formulate his Exodus (Luke 4:14—6:19). He edited Matthew to develop his readings for Leviticus (Luke 6:20—8:25), and he transcribed Mark 4-9 with notable omissions to provide readings appropriate for Numbers (Luke 8:26—9:50). Finally, in his most creative contribution, he wrote the expanded "journey" section of his Gospel (Luke 9:51—18:14) to correspond to the readings from Deuteronomy. Having completed his readings appropriate for Deuteronomy, Luke filled out the balance of chapter 18 with material from Mark. Then he added the story of Zacchaeus (Luke 19:1-10) and a revised version of Matthew's parable of the pounds (Luke 19:11-27) to bring his journey account to a close with the entry into Jerusalem (Luke 19:28-44), where the events of the final week of Jesus' life would unfold.[5]

According to Goulder, the book of Acts, also written by Luke to be used in worship, undoubtedly came to supplement his Gospel as a second Christian reading. A hint of how the Gospels developed can be found in Acts 13, where we learn that on the sabbath after Paul and his companions arrived in Antioch of Pisidia, they entered the synagogue and, after the reading of the law (that is, the Torah), the rulers of the synagogue invited them to speak to the congregation gathered for worship. The book of Acts then records a version of a sermon Paul delivered on that occasion (Acts 13:16-42). His sermon was filled with biblical references, including references to Deuteronomy, the Psalms, the historical writings, the servant figure from Isaiah, and a closing quotation from Habakkuk. This sermon, crafted by Luke, revealed how the Jewish mind worked as it employed the Hebrew scriptures. From this and other speeches in Acts we are introduced not only to early Christian homiletics (how Jews and Christians crafted sermons), but we learn to read the Gospels in a new and more traditional way. Unfortunately, when Jewish Christians began moving in a Gentile direction, the Jewish liturgical connection that first shaped the Gospels was lost.

5. Spong, *Liberating the Gospels*, 127–28.

In Acts 27:9, we learn that Paul observed "the fast," a reference to the Jewish Day of Atonement (Yom Kippur). Earlier, we read that the disciples of Jesus gathered regularly in the temple (2:46), meeting at the time of prayer (3:1). In the circles where Luke lived, certain Jewish worship practices influenced Christians as late as the ninth and tenth decades of the Christian era, though in a Hellenized and less orthodox form.

Reactions to Goulder's Lectionary Theory

While Goulder's basic instinct may be right, biblical scholars have greeted his theory with skepticism. Starting with Mark, some scholars find the argument of a lectionary for half a year highly implausible. For Goulder, however, it explains why Matthew and Luke came into existence, to fill the liturgical void created by Mark. Further, the theory is at times inevitably too rigid, the need to divide the text evenly causing problems. Another difficulty involves the book of Acts. Although Goulder suggested that Acts too is a liturgical book, he was never able to produce a lectionary theory for Acts. The spacing between festivals is a problem, but a greater difficulty occurs when one notes that in 20:16, Pentecost appears a second time, with the festival of Atonement mentioned in 27:9. If one were to take serious note of these markers in the text, it would be hard to make Acts a series of readings for a year.

The book of Acts, like the Gospels, may have functioned liturgically, though not in the same way as the Synoptics. If we are accurate in assessing its date to around 90 CE, it would have been written at a time when the church and synagogue were separating. Acts would thus have filled a growing liturgical need in the newly independent church. Since Jesus, not Moses, was the founder of this new faith tradition, it made sense to substitute a Gospel reading for the Torah reading and a passage concerning the developing church for the second Jewish reading, traditionally taken from the history of the Jewish kingdom.

As evidence for this claim, it is important to note that the book of Acts is approximately the same length as the Gospels of Matthew and Luke. If both Gospels were designed to provide a lection per week, as well as to provide reading for the festivals and fasts of the Jewish liturgical year, we may assume that the length of Acts makes it appropriate as a lectionary book. The fact that it is divided into fifty-two lections in the early manuscripts further strengthens that claim, such number providing a reading per sabbath of the Jewish year.[6]

---

6. Readers should keep in mind that the system of dividing the Bible into chapters

Further confirmation comes from the obvious reference in Acts to the major Jewish festival of Pentecost. To the Jewish people, Pentecost celebrated the giving of Torah by God to Moses at Mt. Sinai, and it was observed fifty days after Passover. Acts modified that interpretation, building its account of the coming of the Holy Spirit into the life of the church as the dominant theme of its observance of Pentecost. For the Lukan community, and henceforth for Gentile Christianity, what Torah was for the Jews, the Holy Spirit was for Christians. Unlike Matthew, who provided the Sermon on the Mount as his Pentecost reading, Luke in his Gospel relocated his Sermon on the Mount material to another place in his drama (see Luke 6:17–49), making his Pentecost story the account of John the Baptist's announcement that one would come after him who would baptize with the Holy Spirit and with fire (Luke 3:16).

Luke was clearly anticipating in his Gospel the Pentecost story in the book of Acts. It is easy to imagine this portion of Luke being read alongside the Pentecost story in Acts in the worship life of Luke's Christian community.[7] With regards to Acts, the lectionary theory solves many problems that Gentile commentators of the past confronted when they viewed Acts solely as a narration of church history. That assumption, myopic and misleading, had the effect of hiding for centuries the essential Jewishness of Luke–Acts and the liturgical role in synagogue worship for which this two-volume set was composed.

Criticism of Goulder's theory also involves the charismatic nature of early Christian worship, which seemingly excludes the likelihood of a lectionary. Paul's picture of Christian worship, such as in 1 Corinthians 14, makes no mention of the reading of set passages and hardly seems consistent with the use of a lectionary. Furthermore, Galatians 4:10, Romans 14:5, and Colossians 2:16 can be used as evidence that the first century church did not observe Jewish fasts and festivals, though in some respects these passages point to the contrary. They show that there was a desire, at least among Jewish Christians and Jewish Christian sympathizers, to keep the festal occasions. Passages such as 1 Timothy 4:13 and evidence from the Gospel of John, set against references to Jewish festivals such as Passover in chapters 2, 6, and 13–20, another festival in chapter five, Tabernacles in

---

and verses is not original to the books of the Bible but of comparatively recent origin. The Hebrew Bible was first divided into verses in 1448 and the New Testament in 1551. The first English translation of the entire Bible to make use of chapter and verse divisions was the Geneva Bible in 1560.

7. For additional liturgical correspondences between Luke's Gospel and Acts, see Spong, *Liberating the Gospels*, 174–78.

chapters 7 and 8, and Dedication in 10:22, add strength to Goulder's claim that festal worship was widespread among Christians in the first century.

According to Christian apologist Justin Martyr (100–165), scripture reading was central to second-century church worship, followed by exhortation and exposition in the liturgy: "The memoirs of the apostles or the writings of the prophets are read as long as time permits; then, when the reader has ceased, the president verbally instructs and exhorts to the imitation of these good things."[8] Evidence for a Paschal vigil is also widespread among Christians, who, at least from the second century, were keeping the Paschal fast on the Saturday night before Easter, and possibly even a two-day fast from Good Friday to Saturday.[9] Furthermore, as late as the fourth century, John Chrysostom (347–407) criticizes a Judaizing tendency in Christianity, saying, as New Year and Tabernacles approach: "Others will join the Jews in keeping their feasts and observing their fasts. I wish to drive this perverse custom from the Church right now."[10]

It is the nature of theories such as Goulder's to be speculative, for it is unlikely that we can ever know with certainty the truth of this matter. To reject the liturgical theory as speculative is to miss the point. Such general criticism of the theory is unconvincing, especially if Goulder is right that breakaway religious movements are often conservative in matters of worship (this principle holds true as late as the Reformation, as evident in dissident movements such as Lutheranism and Anglicanism). Since we lack adequate evidence for Goulder's thesis, our alternatives are limited to speculation or ignorance, which, in this case, is not bliss! Worship has always been central to Christianity, and in on age of high illiteracy, such as the first century, the Jewish pattern of reading appointed scriptures during worship services or other festal occasions would have been indispensable for Jewish Christians as well as for pious Gentile Christians.

---

8. *1 Apol. 67*. Cited in Goodacre, *Goulder and the Gospels*, 320.

9. For many Christians, this vigil is now celebrated as Maundy Thursday, on Good Friday eve.

10. *Discourses Against Judaizing Christians*, I.5. Cited in Goodacre, *Goulder and the Gospels*, 325.

CHAPTER 6

Luke's Historical Task

Summary: Chapter 6 examines Luke's purpose for writing Luke–Acts, linking four broad historical categories: apologetic, sociological, ecclesiastical, and eschatological. Luke's apologetic agenda addresses the scandal of the cross, explaining why early Christians would worship and even follow Jesus of Nazareth, convicted and crucified by Roman officials. Written for believers, Luke–Acts was forged in a context of dispute with non-Christians. Luke's answer to the crucifixion was clear: in Jesus God had brought to completion the great plan of redemption foretold and prefigured in the Hebrew scriptures, a plan enacted at the cross, confirmed by the resurrection of Jesus, and disseminated by God's Holy Spirit. Luke's sociological agenda addresses all humanity, explaining how through Jesus God is restoring men and women of all social classes to their proper dignity as children of God. Luke's ecclesiastical agenda addresses the charge of atheism, one that grew during the 70s and 80s as Jewish Christians began separating from Judaism and as Christianity became an increasingly Gentile phenomenon. Luke's two-volume work, written during this period, functions as the church's first great apologia for the Christian faith. Luke's eschatological agenda addresses the early church's expectation of the imminent establishment of God's reign on earth, associated with Jesus' anticipated return to earth. Uncertain about end-time events, Luke's focus turns to what had already happened in Christ and to what is happening in the present through the coming of the Spirit.

Assignment: Read chapter 6 of *Power Revealed*. [If you have not finished reading Luke–Acts in its entirety, do so as soon as possible.] Answer the following questions, writing the answers in your journal. [If you are in a study group, be prepared to share your views with others in the class.] 1. Explain the meaning of the statement: Luke's entire Gospel is a commentary on the good news about the arrival of the reign or kingdom of God through the ministry of Jesus. 2. Explain the problems early Christians faced with Roman and Jewish authorities, and how Luke addressed these issues.

Learning Objectives: After completing this chapter, participants will be able to:

1. Explain Luke's apologetic agenda.
2. Explain Luke's sociological agenda.
3. Explain Luke's ecclesiastical agenda.
4. Explain Luke's eschatological agenda.

While the identity of Luke and the location of his community cannot be determined with finality, we can be more certain of the issues Luke and his community faced. Chapters 6 and 7 takes an expansive view of those issues and concerns by investigating clues within Luke's writings. The book of Acts is considered a great asset in this regard, for community concerns are more transparent there than in the Gospel, though the two are connected.

The lectionary theory developed by Michael Goulder, discussed at length in chapter 5, proposes a simple solution to the question of Lukan purpose: Luke wrote to meet a liturgical need. The first Christians worshipped in synagogues, and needed Christian liturgical scriptures to augment (or replace) Jewish ones. Since that explanation is based mostly on conjecture and cannot be substantiated through internal evidence, we set it aside, examining here themes and arguments for which we have better textual support.

If the early church was primarily Jewish Christian, consisting mostly of Jewish converts and Gentile "God-fearers," as Acts 1–12 indicate, the need for historical, theological, and ecclesiastical continuity between Judaism and Christianity was imperative. In this regard, an understanding of Jesus and the early church set against a Jewish backdrop would be necessary—and welcome. However, after the destruction of Jerusalem and the temple in 70 CE, and as church membership became increasingly Gentile, new understandings of Jesus and the Christian movement became necessary. Thankfully, Luke's writings address both needs.

While it is impossible to know exactly why Luke wrote, we can be certain that he wrote with intent. With respect to his Gospel, it seems evident that he was conforming to the standard of purpose that Mark and others had set, its fullest expression found in the Fourth Gospel: "so that you may come to believe that Jesus is the Messiah, the Son of God, and that through believing you may have life in his name" (John 20:31). For Acts, however, the purpose is less clear. We wonder, when Luke explained his pastoral intention to Theophilus in his Gospel prologue (that you might "know the truth" about the things in which you have been instructed), whether there were pressing issues involved, and if so, their historical background.

Answers to Luke's purpose are varied, and for good reason. Luke seemed to have more than one purpose when he wrote, and more than one pressing concern. While a number of proposals have been made regarding his purpose for writing Luke–Acts, the following broad categories can be identified: historical issues (which may be grouped into four categories: apologetic, sociological, ecclesiastical, and eschatological) and theological factors (which may be grouped into three categories: missional, pastoral, and christological). These concepts necessarily interrelate, with evident overlap. This chapter examines historical problems confronting the early church, while chapter 7 explores theological features.

Luke's Apologetic Agenda: The Scandal of the Cross

The early church had a problem, one that would not go away. From the start, the followers of Christ were perceived as disreputable. Their founder, Jesus of Nazareth, had died a criminal, tried for sedition and crucified by Roman officials as an insurrectionist. Because this event could not be ignored, or dismissed, it had to be explained.

While Luke–Acts was written for believers, it was forged in a context of disputes with the non-Christian world. Perhaps Luke was concerned about the relationship between Christians and their neighbors, eager to improve relations between church and state. The Christian proclamation of a crucified Messiah was difficult to substantiate in Roman times, as Paul indicates in 1 Corinthians. Writing a mere twenty-five years after the death of Jesus, to a cosmopolitan city proud of its pluralism, multiculturalism, and inclusivism, Paul identifies the scandal thus: "For Jews demand signs and Greeks desire wisdom, but we proclaim Christ crucified, a stumbling block to Jews and foolishness to Gentiles, but to those who are called, both Jews and Greeks, Christ, the power of God and the wisdom of God. For God's foolishness is wiser than human wisdom, and God's weakness is stronger than human strength. . . . But God chose what is foolish in the world to shame the strong; God chose what is low and despised in the world, things that are not, to reduce to nothing things that are" (1 Cor. 1:22–25, 27–28).

Justin Martyr, who composed his *Dialogue with Trypho* in the second century, grappled with Jewish objections to the idea of a crucified Messiah, quoting Trypho as saying that "this so-called Christ of yours was dishonorable and inglorious, so much that the last curse contained in the law of God fell on him, for he was crucified."[1] The Latin author Minucius Felix concluded that only "abandoned wretches" could possibly center their worship on "a man put to death for his crime and on the fatal wood of the cross."[2]

Against such objections, Luke–Acts sought to create a frame of reference that could disclose the transcendent significance of Jesus' death. Luke refers to the crucifixion early in Acts, putting into the mouth of Peter the core of his own theology: "this man, handed over to you according to the definite plan and foreknowledge of God, you crucified and killed by the hands of those outside the law" (Acts 2:23). He sees the ministry of Jesus from baptism to ascension as the working out of a drama of world redemption in which, though human beings are free to act on their own volition, the plot has been determined by God. Humans may reject the purpose of God, as the Pharisees and lawyers did when they ignored John's baptism (Luke 7:30), but the cross is the proof that God can turn even the ultimate rejection into victory.

The divine plan was both foretold and prefigured in the Hebrew scriptures. It was an integral part of the apostolic tradition that the life, death, and resurrection of Jesus had occurred "in accordance with the scriptures" (1 Cor. 15:3–4). This theme, developed in various ways by other New Testament writers, is also of special interest to Luke, who introduces the idea of fulfillment into contexts where it was not present in his source (see Luke 18:31 and Mark 10:33). He also affirms that this method of scriptural interpretation had its origin in Jesus, who found in the Old Testament the pattern for his own ministry (Luke 4:21), and taught his disciples how to use the Old Testament as Christian scripture (Luke 24:27, 44). From these last passages we learn that Jesus fulfilled not just a few isolated promises made by the prophets, but the whole intent and pattern of Old Testament teaching and history, including the exodus and the Passover. In 9:31, when Luke calls Christ's death "his exodus" (Luke's Greek word here for "departure" is "*exodon*"), "which he was about to accomplish in Jerusalem," and later links that death with the fulfilling of the Passover in the kingdom of God (22:16), he is speaking of events through which Israel interpreted its history. These references, unique to his Gospel, are Luke's ways to underscore that in Jesus

---

1. Justin, *Dialogue* 32.1.
2. Minucius Felix, *Octavius* 9.4.

God has brought to completion the great plan of redemption of which the Old Testament story was a prophetic forecast.

Because Luke believed that Jesus fulfilled divine purpose, he constantly portrays him as acting under the authority of divine necessity. In Mark's Gospel, Jesus had once spoken of the necessity of his death (8:31), but Luke uses the same Greek verb *deî* (translated "it is necessary" or "I must") no less than ten times in connection with Jesus' ministry (2:49; 4:43; 9:22; 13:16, 33; 17:25; 22:37; 24:7, 26, 44). We are not meant to think that Jesus was a fatalist, but that at every period in his life he responded willingly to the necessity that was laid upon him by his vocation. Though God is not responsible for the betrayal by Judas or for other events that led to Jesus' crucifixion, not even these happened outside God's determined plan (Luke 22:22).

Luke often describes the ministry of Jesus as God's direct activity in human history (1:68, 78; 7:16; 19:44), an activity also expressed by Luke through his numerous references to the Spirit's presence in Jesus' ministry (4:14, 18), including his birth (1:35), baptism (3:22), and temptation (4:1). In Acts the Spirit leads and guides the disciples, as he did Jesus in the Gospel (Acts 1:2, 16; 2:4, 13; 4:13; 10:44; 16:6–7). Luke more than all other Gospel writers stresses the role of the Spirit. In his Gospel and in Acts, the Holy Spirit is the means, the person who empowers Jesus as well as the disciples for preaching, teaching, and healing. For Luke, the Holy Spirit is the key that makes proclamation, salvation, liberation, and radical discipleship possible.

Unlike Paul the Jew, for whom the cross of Jesus was both a stumbling block, and Paul the Christian, for whom the cross was a ground of hope and glory, in Luke–Acts, the cross and death of Jesus have little evidential value. In the speeches of Acts, the death of Jesus is treated curiously, as an act of ignorant wickedness and rejection on the part of the Jews rather than as a means of salvation (Acts 2:23–24). Even in his Gospel, the death of Jesus is told rather than explained. Luke regularly omits passages in Mark that might suggest a doctrine of atonement. Matthew and Mark's "to give his life a ransom for many" (Matt. 20:28; Mark 10:45) is not in Luke's parallel (22:27), and at least the shorter account of the Last Supper (Luke 22:15–19) found in the "Western text" of Luke (which many scholars prefer as independent of Paul) omits the words "my body, which is given to you" and "this cup that is poured out for you," and thus all reference to vicarious death.[3]

---

3. Because Luke's autographs (his original Greek manuscripts) are not extant, we only have copies produced by later Christians. Examination of these ancient manuscripts reveals two different versions. One set of manuscripts preserves what scholars call the "Alexandrian" text, while a different set preserves what is called the "Western" text. The differences between these traditions is particularly noticeable in the text of Acts, where the Western text is almost ten percent longer than the Alexandrian text.

For Luke, the resurrection is the significant thing about Jesus. His death is but a prelude. The resurrection is the fulfillment of prophecy, the demonstration of messiahship, and the occasion for repentance in view of coming judgment. For Luke the resurrection of Jesus is the distinguishing article of faith for the Christian. No New Testament writer more often refers to the resurrection as predicted in scripture or cites more texts in its support than does Luke.

Luke's Sociological Agenda

Luke believed that only Jesus and those with whom he chose to share his messianic identity really understood God's gracious purpose (Luke 10:21–22; see also Matt. 11:25–27). For believers, that purpose was revealed in every episode of Jesus' ministry. God's purpose is nothing less than the restoration of men and women to their proper dignity as children of God (Luke 19:10).

In Luke, the intention of Jesus' ministry is set forth in the opening scene in the synagogue at Nazareth (4:14–30), when Jesus declares that he has come in the power of the Spirit to proclaim the promised Jubilee, the year of God that is to end all oppression and bondage. Those who took this to mean liberation from Rome were to be disappointed, for Jesus had in mind sociological rather than political reversal, liberation from physical, mental, and moral illness rather than from political persecution. For Luke, the good news of the gospel is about the arrival of the reign or kingdom of God through Jesus' ministry (11:30; 16:16; see also 7:28). The evidence required to support this conviction is that which Jesus offered to John the Baptist: "the blind receive their sight, the lame walk, the lepers are cleansed, the deaf hear, the dead are raised, the poor have good news brought to them" (7:22). This to Luke is no prelude to a future kingdom; it is the kingdom

---

The Western text does not contain stories or episodes lacking in the Alexandrian text, but is simply wordier throughout. In addition to making more use of titles and pious language, the Western text also explains matters that are obscure or confusing in the Alexandrian text. The Western text also exhibits a harsher attitude toward the Jews than is found in the Alexandrian text, portraying the Jews and their leaders as more hostile toward Jesus and the apostles. The Alexandrian text is favored by modern scholars as more accurately representing Luke's original text, though occasionally the reading of the Western text is preferred. Bible translators do not follow either text reading slavishly, but decide each verse on a case by case basis, often relying on recommendations in Bruce Metzger's *A Textual Commentary on the Greek New Testament*, which lists significant options for each verse and then offers the opinion of a committee of translators as to which text seems best and why.

already exerting its power. Indeed, Luke's entire Gospel is a commentary on this theme.

Luke's concern to present the radical inclusiveness of Jesus' ministry is evident in the numerous scenes in his Gospel in which Jesus reaches out to those who are oppressed, excluded, or otherwise at a disadvantage in society. The list of such persons is a long one, and Luke uses all of his rhetorical powers to present to his audience examples of witnesses who can testify to the presence of the kingdom because they have discovered in Jesus the friend and champion of the sick, the poor, the penitent, and the outcast, as well as of women, Samaritans, and Gentiles.

Luke refers to "sinners" more than does any other Gospel (seventeen times). Interestingly, the pattern of the majority of the references to sinners in the Gospel is with tax collectors. The term often emerges in the context of table fellowship and Jesus' practice of eating with those scorned by the religious authorities. While Jesus' disciples are criticized for eating with "tax collectors and sinners" (5:30), Jesus responds that he has not come to call the righteous but sinners to repentance. In the Sermon on the Plain (6:17–49), Jesus challenges his disciples to do more than the sinners who love and who do good to those who can reciprocate (6:32–34). When the Pharisees and scribes see the tax collectors and sinners coming to Jesus, they grumble and complain that Jesus "welcomes sinners and eats with them" (15:1–2). Jesus responds by telling the parables of the lost sheep, the lost coin, and the prodigal son.

It is interesting that Luke was not content to show that the good news of the kingdom only involved the oppressed. Rather, in truly inclusive fashion, he shows how Christ's gospel is likewise for the oppressor, usually the upper echelon of the social ladder. Popular theology held that the rich were blessed of God, but Jesus turned such assumptions on their head, maintaining that they, too, were captives who needed to be set free, whether from money, power, or pious religiosity. Thus we see Jesus eating with tax collectors and Pharisees and redeeming people like Zacchaeus, a tax collector and a rich man, who begins immediately to right his wrongs of overtaxing (19:1–10). Likewise, Luke points out that it is a Roman centurion in whom Jesus finds more faith than in all of God's chosen people Israel (7:1–10). This agenda in the Gospel prepares for similar treatment in Acts of people like the Ethiopian eunuch, Cornelius, and others of social status.

Not surprisingly, Luke refers to the blessings of poverty and the dangers of wealth more than does any other Gospel. Luke's handling of the beatitudes and woes in 6:20–26 is part of the pattern of his characterization of Jesus' response to wealth and poverty throughout the Gospel. Whereas Matthew spiritualizes the beatitudes, "Blessed are the poor in spirit" (Matt.

5:3), Luke faces the economic realities of poverty, "But woe to you who are rich" (Luke 6:24). Significantly, Jesus exhorts guests at a banquet to invite the poor, the crippled, the lame, and the blind when they give a banquet (14:13, 21). The poor man Lazarus, who lay at the rich man's gate, is carried to Abraham's bosom, while the rich man who feasted every day is condemned to perpetual torment (16:19–31). How hard it is, Jesus laments, for those who have wealth to enter the kingdom of God (18:24).

As the Cuban-born theologian Justo González notes, we do not study Luke because he was an inspiring writer, though he was. Nor do we study Luke because he narrates an inspirational account of the early church, which he does. "We study Luke because, through the agency of that same Holy Spirit whose work and power Luke emphasizes, his Gospel becomes God's Word to us, leading and accompanying us as we seek to join Jesus in the great reversal he announces and brings about."[4] Reversal is a central theme of Luke–Acts. In an imperial world where power and guidance came from Rome, and in the context of Judaism, where power was centered in Jerusalem, Luke tells a story that begins in Galilee—a marginal land by both Roman and Jewish standards—and then moves on to bring that message and its power first to Jerusalem, and then to Rome.

Within the context of Luke's geopolitical reversal, the Third Gospel offers numerous instances of reversals no less astonishing. Mary announces this at the beginning of the Gospel: "He has scattered the proud in the thoughts of their hearts. He has brought down the powerful from their thrones, and lifted up the lowly; he has filled the hungry with good things, and sent the rich away empty" (1:51–53). In Luke's Gospel, Jesus shows particular compassion for those whom his society would consider the worst sinners, and has harsh words for good religious people. The first shall be last, and the last, first. Things hidden to the wise have been revealed to babes. The greatest is the one who serves. In the book of Acts, Luke's unfinished history includes a grand reversal—religious, social, and economic—as a sign of the power of God's reign, and invites us to consider the reversals that we encounter in our day as possible signs of that reign.

Luke's Ecclesiastical Agenda: The Scandal of Atheism

Like the crucifixion of Jesus, another scandal early Christians faced was the charge of atheism. Roman law recognized only national religion. Religion, to a Roman, was largely a matter of public ceremony, and loyalty to one's

---

4. González, *Luke*, 11.

country required participation in the worship of that country's gods. Officially, non-conformity was treason or "atheism," and the penalty was death. In practice this law was difficult to enforce, for every country had foreigners, and where there were aliens, there would be other religions. The policy adopted by Rome was that foreign religions, though illegal, might be tolerated, provided they did not disturb the peace or interfere with the official cult. Violations of this privilege were handled, not in criminal courts, but by local authorities with wide discretionary powers.

The first Christians, being Jewish, were officially regarded as a Jewish sect, meaning they benefitted from the exceptional tolerance Rome had granted the Jews since the time of Julius Caesar. However, that policy—and with it security—came to a violent end on the night of July 18, 64 CE, when a fire broke out in Rome that lasted a week and destroyed half the city. Rumor laid the blame on Emperor Nero, and to divert suspicion, he needed a scapegoat. Nero's choice fell on the Christians because, as Tacitus recounts in his version of the fire, they were already "detested for their outrageous practices."[5] Christians had been harassed by Jewish elements, who regarded them with distrust, and by pagan neighbors, who labeled them antisocial. Like unpopular minorities, they were accused of nameless atrocities, but officially they had not been banned. The fire of Rome led not merely to Nero's persecution of Christians in that city, but to a permanent change of legal status for Christians throughout the empire.

Once the initial persecution of the church by Nero came to an end, Christians found themselves in a precarious situation. Their legal security had gone, for their faith was now regarded as a new, and therefore illegal, religion. Their chance of survival lay in avoiding the unfavorable notice of the civil authorities, and this in turn depended on their ability to retain the good will of their neighbors.

While Christianity initially may have functioned as an appendage of Judaism, by the year 64 it was moving out on its own. The move to independence from Judaism was accelerated by Roman destruction of the Jewish temple and the cessation of the sacrifices that had played such a large role in Jewish worship.

Prior to the fateful year 70, Judaism tolerated varieties of opinions within its fold. Between the years 30 and 70, Jewish followers of Jesus continued worshiping in the synagogues. During that period, it was quite clear that Jewish people began incorporating Jesus into their faith story. Within the synagogues, Jewish Christians were at best an enriching new tradition and at worst a minor irritation. However, when the survival of the Jewish

---

5. *Annals*, xv, 44.

faith tradition was at stake, the level of toleration dissipated perceptibly. Acrimony grew between Jews committed to Jesus and traditional Jews who claimed orthodoxy for their convictions, tying their claims to the belief that the God they worshiped could be found only in the unchanging completeness of the Torah. The shift to a survival mentality set the stage for heightened negativity to develop.

After the fall of Jerusalem, many followers of Jesus, both Jewish and Gentile, began to interpret the Roman defeat of the Jews and the loss of the temple as God's punishment of traditional Jews for their rejection of Jesus. Thus the stage was set for hostility. Echoes of this rising hostility can be found overtly in the Gospels, particularly in Matthew (21:43; 23:31–38; 27:25). As rhetoric heightened, the lines around what Jews could tolerate within Judaism tightened considerably so that Jewish Christians, offended by this increasing hostility, began to move more and more into Gentile circles.

From that point on, fewer Christians wished to identify with the rigidly orthodox survival mentality that began to characterize Judaism, while fewer Jews wanted to see any aspect of the Jesus tradition left within their faith traditions. Somewhere in the late 80s a split occurred between the synagogue and the followers of Jesus. We can sense the pain of that split in John 9:22, which states, "the Jews had already agreed that anyone who confessed Jesus to be the Messiah would be put out of the synagogue."

Once that split had occurred, Christianity began to move more and more into the Gentile world. Because the Gospel of Matthew was written during this separation and the Gospel of John shortly thereafter, the Fourth Gospel's blatant negativity toward orthodox Jews (John 8:44) and its descriptions of exclusion from the synagogues reflect that final fracture (John 9:22; 12:42). By the start of the second century, Jewish Christians faded into increasingly Hellenized and Gentile circles, and thereafter Jewish Christians ceased even to think of themselves as Jews, while those who claimed Jewish identity became more firmly entrenched in their tradition. By the middle of the second century there were hardly any Jews left in the Christian movement.

While the church was adapting to these changes, the first great apologia (literary defense) for the Christian faith was written, the two-volume work we call Luke–Acts. The author's purpose was to supply Theophilus and others like him with the truth about this maligned movement. Following the teaching of Paul in Romans 13:1–7, Luke did his best to show that the church does not have a negative attitude toward the state.

Had Christians been condemned as lawless followers of an executed offender? Luke shows that Jesus and his disciples had justly been pronounced innocent by representatives of Roman law. Luke underscores the innocence of Jesus repeatedly throughout the trial and crucifixion scenes. Three times Pilate declares that he finds no crime in Jesus (Luke 23:4, 14, 22). When Pilate sends Jesus to Herod, Herod returns him and Pilate reports that Herod found him innocent (23:6–12, 15). At the cross, the "penitent thief" crucified with Jesus also maintains that Jesus has done nothing wrong (23:41), and the centurion who witnessed Jesus' death proclaims, "Certainly this man was innocent" (23:47).

Paul, like Jesus, is repeatedly said to be guilty of no crime (Acts 16:39; 17:6–9; 18:12–17; 19:37–41; 23:29; 25:25; 26:31–32). The missionary to the Gentiles is not only a Roman citizen, but a loyal and trustworthy citizen, as are Christians in general. Paul makes good use of this privilege (Acts 16:38–39; 21:39; 22:25–29), for as Luke wishes to show, God is using even the Roman state to spread the gospel. Luke speaks of this in Paul's trials, events he records three times (before the Sanhedrin, 22:30—23:10; before Governor Felix, 24:1–27; and before King Herod Agrippa II, his wife Bernice, and newly appointed Governor Porcius Festus, 25:23—26:32). Repeating this narrative three times underscores Luke's concern to show that the Roman Empire was not essentially antagonistic toward, nor should it oppose, the church, just because it had become a separate entity from synagogue-based Judaism.

Is Christianity an eccentric, foreign superstition? Luke proves that it is the true Israel, the fulfillment of the religious aspirations of the Old Testament, deserving all the tolerance that Rome has shown to the Jews, and that, unlike the nationalistic creed of the Jews, Christianity is a world religion, adequate to meet the spiritual needs of the empire. Luke shows that the Christian movement (known as "the Way"; see Acts 9:2; 18:25–26; 19:9, 23; 22:4; 24:14, 22) is no innovation, but was intended by God all along.

Have Christians been denounced as revolutionaries who are threatening the Roman world? Luke's story tells how Christ turned his back on political revolution in order to accomplish a profounder revolution in the realm of ideas and values.

Are Christians suspected of antisocial behavior? Luke portrays the founder of their faith as a figure of nobility, grace, and charm, able to reproduce these same qualities in the lives of his followers and to raise to decency and dignity even the outcasts of society.

While Luke's motives may have been varied, and are now not easy to trace throughout his work, nevertheless some apologetic aims can be determined from such passages as:

- "I truly understand that God shows no partiality, but in every nation anyone who fears him and does what is right is acceptable to him. You know the message [God] sent to the people of Israel, preaching peace by Jesus Christ—he is Lord of all" (Acts 10: 34–36).
- "Simeon (Peter) has related how God first looked favorably on the Gentiles, to take from among them a people for his name" (Acts 15:14).
- "Paul said in his defense, 'I have in no way committed an offense against the law of the Jews, or against the temple, or against the emperor'" (Acts 25:8).

Luke's Eschatological Agenda

From Paul's epistles and the Gospel of Mark, it is apparent that early Christians lived in the imminent expectation of Jesus' return (an event the New Testament calls the *parousia* or second coming of Christ). Jesus first coming, followed by his post-resurrection appearances, was widely regarded by early Christians as signaling an imminent and permanent reappearance at the end of the age, when, as Paul states, Christ "hands over the kingdom to God the Father, after he has destroyed every ruler and every authority and power" (1 Cor. 15:23–24). Indeed, like that first generation, for whom "the appointed time has grown short" (1 Cor. 7:29), many Christians today continue to anticipate Jesus' imminent return to earth.

For early Christians, the church's "blessed hope" (Titus 2:13) involved more than Christ's return, for it also included the community's resurrection hope and the promised season of universal restoration. The ascension scene in Acts 1:6–11 notes the apostles' preoccupation with Jesus' immediate establishment of God's reign by their urgent question, "Lord, is this the time when you will restore the kingdom to Israel?" Acts contains additional mention of "the last days" (see 2:17–21; 3:19–26; 17:31), a theological conception also present in Luke's Gospel, particularly in the apocalyptic teaching of Jesus in Luke 21:8–36, shared with the other Synoptic Gospels, Matthew and Mark. However, due to the limited futuristic references in the Gospel and in Acts, some scholars find the delay of the *parousia* to be the purpose for Luke–Acts.

Of the major modern commentators on Luke, one of the first to study Luke as theologian, is the German scholar Hans Conzelmann, a pioneer in redaction criticism. His 1957 book *Die Mitte der Zeit*, available in an English translation as *The Theology of St. Luke*, identified the main occasion for Luke's writings with this eschatological crisis in the life of the early church.

While many early Christians believed the *parousia*, or second coming of Christ, was an event that was going to occur very soon, this did not happen, and the prospect of a future return of Jesus diminished over time (2 Pet. 3:8). By the end of the first century, when Luke wrote, the church was coming to terms with the fact that it needed to settle down for the long haul. As time passed and Jesus still did not return, Christians were forced to reassess their beliefs about both the present and the future.

Conzelmann believes Luke wrote to address this situation. He viewed Luke as a capable and original theologian who reworked Judeo-Christian tradition according to a specific theological agenda. The overriding theological concept that emerges from Conzelmann's study is Luke's understanding of "salvation history." According to Conzelmann, Luke's conception of human history, from creation to the end of the world, is arranged into three epochs: (1) the period of Israel, (2) the period of Jesus' earthly ministry, and (3) the period of the church. The period of Jesus' life on earth represented the "middle of time." As such, it was central to all history, but, just as it was preceded by a long "period of Israel," so it was to be followed by a lengthy "period of the church." The break between the first two periods is indicated in Luke 16:16, when Jesus says, "The law and the prophets were in effect until John came; since then, the good news of the kingdom of God is proclaimed." The break between the second and third periods is indicated by the division between the Gospel and Acts, where the church is described as a community that must persevere for an extended period of time in the absence of its Lord. Viewed thus, Luke wrote Acts to explain how this period of the church was inaugurated and to delineate what life and faith during such a time must be like.

As simple as this arrangement seems, it has far-reaching theological implications. For one thing, it assumes a significant interim between the time of Jesus' earthly ministry and the end of the world. According to Conzelmann, that mindset led Luke to write not only a third Gospel but also the first history of the Christian movement. After all, why write another account of Jesus and a book about history if you are expecting the end of the world to come any day? Recognizing that the *parousia* was losing its significance as a key factor in Christian hope and therefore as a decisive motive for Christian living, Luke is said to have written for a new generation of believers, his purpose being to strengthen their faith and to offer them pastoral guidance to meet challenges that might cause them to doubt. If the church is to endure, it must make peace with the world and learn to coexist with society.

Impressive as it is, Conzelmann's proposal has not fared well in recent years. A better understanding of Luke's historical paradigm is that, like Paul and other New Testament authors, he divides history not into three parts, as Conzelmann claims, but rather into two epochs, namely, the "former age" (the time of prophetic promise), and the "new age" (the time of eschatological fulfillment in the church). Within the eschatological time of the church, there are also two great periods, the mission to the Jews (Acts 1–12), and the mission to the Gentiles (Acts 12–28), divided by the conversion of Cornelius in Acts 10–11.

By emphasizing the idea of promise and fulfillment, Luke establishes Jesus' relationship to the time of Israel before him. Similarly, the themes of apostolic tradition and the gift of the Holy Spirit assure continuity between the past time of Jesus and the current era of the church. Because the church proclaims the message concerning Jesus, based on apostolic tradition, it becomes the guardian of tradition and the channel of salvation in the present age. The gift of the Holy Spirit is reinterpreted by Luke to become a provisional substitute for the *parousia* that makes it possible to live in the interim.

As to his eschatological perspective, some scholars think Conzelmann has gotten it precisely backwards. A. J. Matill argues in his book *Luke and the Last Things* that the evangelist writes with fervency because he believes the *parousia* is imminent. In Luke's Gospel, Jesus instructs his followers to proclaim the nearness of the kingdom of God (10:9, 11) and promises to return as a sign to "this generation" (11:30; 21:32). In Acts, the final judgment is referred to as something that will happen "soon" (17:31; 24:15, 25). Mattill finds Luke's works to be replete with apocalyptic imagery and thus concludes that the evangelist writes to give the church new impetus for its task now that the end is in sight.

While both perspectives have merit, perhaps a better understanding of Luke's intention is to regard the *parousia* as delayed without abandoning the thought that it is still imminent. German theologian Hans Bartsch makes such a proposal, suggesting an approach similar to that found in the final chapter of the book of Revelation, where the concluding verses reiterate four times that the eschatological return of Christ will happen "soon" (22:6, 7, 12, 20). Given the undeniable delay in Christ's return, contemporary Christians can interpret such language in two ways: (1) as a reference not to time, but to the nature of Christ's *parousia* (not when but how Christ comes, namely, suddenly, as opposed to soon), and (2) as a reference to God's mysterious ongoing presence, namely, that the God whom we worship is the one who came in Jesus and is forever present in the Spirit. This God is the one whose coming is always "soon," for God is the beginning and the end, the one in whom "we live and move and have our being" (Acts 17:28). Thus, those who await Christ's coming are forever heralding the coming age, the age of the Spirit believers now inhabit.

Whatever we make of Conzelmann's thesis, the book of Acts can be read as evidence that Christians in Luke's day were beginning to think differently about the future. The emphasis in Luke–Acts lies not on delay, but on what has already and is now happening, what has already been fulfilled and is now being fulfilled. As Fitzmyer suggests, the shift is from focusing primarily on what will happen to emphasizing what has happened and is happening "today" (see Luke 4:21; 5:26; 19:5, 9; 23:43) or "daily" (see Luke 11:3; 16:19; 19:47).

Despite Conzelmann's arguments, Luke does not radically distinguish between the time of Jesus and the time of the church. In fact, he does not radically distinguish the time of Israel from the time of Jesus or the church because in his view the community of Jesus' disciples is the logical development of Israel according to God's plan. Jew and Gentile united in Christ are the beginning of Israel's restoration.

For Luke, the coming of Christ and equally importantly his death and resurrection have modified the conception of eschatology. Jesus' resurrection is an eschatological event that triggers other eschatological events such as the sending of the Spirit, but it will take a further coming of Jesus to trigger the final eschatological events, such as the general resurrection (Luke 20:27-40; Acts 24:15) and the final judgment of the world by Jesus (Acts 17:31). In short, Christ's first coming divided the eschatological events into already and not yet, which suggests that Luke views the present as some sort of eschatological age in which some "final" things have already happened and others are anticipated. The present, we learn, is an age of decision, when ignorance can no longer be overlooked. If we accept this conclusion, then it is improper to speak about Luke believing in a "delay" of the *parousia*, for the concept of delay implies that the event is late, that it did not occur at the expected and predicted time. The unpredictability of the *parousia* means one cannot know the timing of the End. For Luke, ignorance of the "when" is countered by certainty of the "that."

While scholars take issue with practically every point that Conzelmann made, his treatment of Luke's theology has been the starting point for many discussions in recent years. There is, however, consensus on one matter. Even if scholars disagree on the particulars of Luke's theology, they recognize Luke as a theologian of prominence who consciously planned and deliberately executed his work.

CHAPTER 7

Luke's Theological Task

Summary: Chapter 7 continues the discussion regarding Luke's purpose in writing Luke–Acts, addressing three broad theological categories—missional, pastoral, and christological. Luke's missional agenda, clearly central in the book of Acts, demonstrates how Christianity spread into the Gentile world, faithfully fulfilling its twofold task in society—to evangelize others and to live by the ethics of love and mercy that Jesus had taught. To accomplish this task, the various factions in the church needed to work together, a theme Luke pursues in Acts. Luke's pastoral agenda addresses the challenge of proclaiming the whole gospel to the whole person in the whole world, a task early Christians embraced wholeheartedly, using the life of Jesus and the corporate life of his disciples as models. In this regard, important examples for congregational life include table fellowship, worship and prayer, sharing possessions, devotion to apostolic teaching, and practicing servanthood. Luke's christological agenda answers the following question regarding Jesus: "Who is this who speaks and acts thus"? By way of response, Luke heightens the reverence for Jesus portrayed in his sources, primarily in Mark's Gospel. Likewise, in comparison with Mark, Luke increases respect for the apostles, who by the late first century had come to be regarded as the pillars of the church.

Assignment: Read chapter 7 of *Power Revealed*. [If you have not finished reading Luke–Acts in its entirety, do so as soon as possible.] Answer the following questions, writing the answers in your journal. [If you are in a study group, be prepared to share your views with others in the class.] 1.

In your estimation, what is the role of the church in society? In particular, how does the church fulfil its servant role? 2. As part of their evangelistic task, should Christians evangelize non-Christian Jews, or are they under an older and different covenant with God than Gentiles? (If possible, support your conclusion with both Lukan and Pauline passages.) 3. Explain your understanding of the relationship between christology, discipleship, and Christian mission.

Learning Objectives: After completing this chapter, participants will be able to:

1. Explain Luke's missional agenda.
2. Explain Luke's pastoral agenda.
3. Explain Luke's christological agenda.

When readers consider the topics of chapter 6 and 7, Luke's "historical" and "theological" tasks, they might think themselves distinguishing strictly historical considerations from specifically theological ones. Such compartmentalization, however, is inaccurate, for in biblical perspectives all things cohere. Therefore, when believers think biblically, they are thinking both historically and theologically. Modern Christians have been taught to distinguish between secular or spiritual categories, and that has led to dualistic thinking, an essentially unbiblical way of conceptualizing reality. If God is Lord of reality, all things are under God's sovereignty, whether religious, scientific, historical, political, economic, or sociological.

When scholars speak of theology, they often have one of three definitions in mind:

- God and divinity
- religion and religious topics
- reality as a whole, but from a nuanced point of view

Because of this overlap in terminology, when speaking theologically, it is important for individuals to clarify which definition they have in mind. Recognizing the limitation behind dichotomous labeling, we continue exploring Luke's purpose for writing, encouraging readers to determine how chapters 6 and 7 interrelate. Having examined Luke's historical background, specifically apologetic, sociological, ecclesiastical, and eschatological issues facing the early church, this chapter explores Luke's purpose for writing by examining missional, pastoral, and christological issues.

Luke's Missional Agenda

While we may never be certain about Luke's eschatological expectation, there is little doubt that Luke wished to demonstrate how the gospel spread into the Gentile world. Every verse of the New Testament presupposes the new people of God, a new community called the church. From the beginning, Christians were described as "the body of Christ," followers of Jesus who showed by their lifestyle that they were a part of the new order that Jesus had announced and that they believed had now arrived.

Theologically, the church was a microcosm of the transformation that God's new order would bring for the whole world. To be in the church was to have a foretaste of life as God's new people. Socially, the church in the Roman Empire was an alternative society, based not on selfishness and greed and exploitation, but on the new freedom and fellowship that Jesus had announced: freedom to love God and to love and serve others (Mark 12:29-31). As the church expanded across the Mediterranean world, it was indeed a new society—a context in which people of diverse social, racial, and religious backgrounds were united in a new and radical friendship. Because they had been reconciled to God, they found themselves reconciled to each other.

Jesus conceived his mission to be that of calling the remnant of Israel—twelve disciples, corresponding to the twelve-tribe structure of Israel—to covenant faithfulness. And when the meaning of Jesus' life, death, and resurrection came upon these disciples with overwhelming power at the festival of Pentecost (Acts 2), a powerful movement emerged, rightly termed the Age of the Spirit. This small community became a dynamic and militant church, with a message that "turned the world upside down" (Acts 17:6) and a gospel they carried enthusiastically to the ends of the earth. The Acts of the Apostles gives the story of the emerging church. The expansion was amazingly rapid. Within ten years of the death of Jesus, there were Christian communities throughout Palestine and Syria; in twenty years, across Asia Minor and into Greece; and in twenty-five years, in Rome.

Christian expansion, as narrated in the book of Acts, resulted in a twofold shift: geographically, the center of the church gravitated from Jerusalem to Rome; ethnically, the church's identity shifted from Jewish Christians to predominantly Gentile Christians. According to Acts, the church expanded because it fulfilled faithfully its two tasks in society: to evangelize, that is, to serve as Christ's witnesses "to the ends of the earth" (Acts 1:8; see also Matthew's Great Commission in 28:19-20), and to live by the ethics of love and mercy that Jesus had taught.

While stressing the newness of the church, we must also keep in mind the relation of this community to the entire Old Testament heritage. In a sense, the church regarded itself as the "New Israel," for like ancient Israel, congregants had a special role in history. The Old Testament narrates how a people was formed to be the bearer of God's purpose in history and the instrument of God's saving work. Israel was not primarily a race or a nation but a covenant community created by God's action. Having delivered Israel from slavery in Egypt, God made them a covenant people. Through many tumultuous years, God educated and disciplined them in order that they might understand more deeply the meaning of their special role.

It was Second Isaiah who understood most profoundly Israel's place in God's worldwide purpose. According to this prophet, Israel was called to be a "light to the nations" (Isa. 49:6) and a servant whose sufferings would benefit all humanity (Isa. 49:3; 53:4-6, 11-12). However, in the intervening years, this expansive vision was obscured. The last two centuries before Jesus witnessed a resurgence of Jewish nationalism that led in time to wars with Rome. In 70 CE the Romans destroyed the temple, leveled Jerusalem, and removed the last vestiges of Jewish statehood.

Thus, in the fullness of time, God acted once again to reconstitute the community of Israel—no longer bound by ethnic or nationalistic limitations but open to all people, Jew and Gentile alike, on the basis of faith. Acts was written as a tool of the church's evangelistic mission. Clearly, the literary theme that follows the triumph of the gospel from Jerusalem to Rome testifies to the power and necessity of evangelism. The prophetic boldness and effectiveness of the church's mission, led and empowered by the Holy Spirit, expresses this same theme. If the missionary episodes are read as indicating normative patterns of outreach for subsequent generations of Christians, then Acts may have been written to invigorate the missionary consciousness of Lukan congregations, in continuity with the missionaries of the earliest church. However, to be effective in mission requires ecclesiastical unity.

In the nineteenth century, the influential German Protestant theologian Ferdinand Christian Baur (1792-1860) put forward a theory about Acts that would become a hallmark of the famous "Tübingen school" of theology. Baur believed that Acts was written to repair a divisive breach in early Christianity, a division that was rooted in the various traditions and congregations established by Peter and Paul. It is clear from New Testament documents that Peter was recognized as a leader among Jewish Christians, whereas Paul was known as the apostle to Gentile Christians (an interesting though one-sided passage highlighting some of these differences is found in the second chapter of Paul's letter to the Galatians; see especially 2:7). By the time Acts was written, Baur theorized, the Petrine and Pauline parties in the church had become warring factions that threatened to split the new religion into two separate faiths. According to this scenario, the book of Acts was written to reconcile these factions and to restore unity to the church. Luke presents both Peter and Paul as heroes of the faith and, from the descriptions he provides, their approaches to ministry and theology appear to be quite compatible.

While noting that the situation of first-century Christianity was more complex than Baur envisioned, the idea that Luke wrote Acts to help unify a fragmented church remains persuasive. While Luke's idealistic portrait of a unified church goes beyond reality, it represents an ideal that continues to exist in the hearts and minds of Christians today. While Luke's picture may not reflect social and historical reality, it presents a picture of how Christianity should be. According to Baur, Luke's representation of the early church makes a theological statement about the church that transcends contemporary concerns for accurate historical reporting.

As we learn from the Gospels, from the start the followers of Jesus struggled to comprehend the meaning of their experience, disagreeing with one another over the identity of Jesus and his mission. According to scholars, the first converts to Christianity were no different, reflecting more diversity in belief and practice than exists in today's multidenominational and multicultural church. It would take several centuries and numerous councils for Christian authorities to sort out church dogma, and even then disagreements continued, culminating in the sixteenth century Protestant Reformation, which, in returning to the seemingly singular authority of scripture, unleased a new and endless flurry of sectarianism.

Like contemporary churches, the New Testament church was not a perfect body. As we discover in biblical writings such as 1 Corinthians, Paul addressed numerous flaws, among them sectarianism, divisiveness, perfectionism, superiority, insincerity, arrogance, immorality, liturgical improprieties, and eucharistic malpractice. Paul rebukes some members, while condemning sinful behavior. Further dissension appeared later in the apostolic churches, mainly over "false teaching."

The first Christians, themselves Jews or proselytes to Judaism, struggled to comprehend the meaning of their experience. When Gentiles joined the church, concerned to evangelize their world, a natural question they might have asked is, "If the Christian church is the true Israel, why is it rejected by the majority of Jews?" The answer to this question, while important, needs clarification. For example, in his important book, *Luke and the People of God*, Jacob Jervell finds this question unhelpful, its premise faulty. According to Jervell, Luke presents the mission to the Jews as having been completed, not due to failure, but rather due to success. Despite accounts of rejection by small groups of Jews, Acts depicts large numbers of Jews accepting the gospel: three thousand in 2:41, five thousand in 4:4, and many more in 6:7 (see also 21:20, where all are "zealous for the law").

According to Jervell, Luke presents the mission to Israel as coming to an end in Acts 28:17–31 because this phase of the mission is now complete. Israel has been successfully reached with the gospel, and the time has come to take the gospel to the nations. Of course, not all Jews have accepted God's word of salvation, but that, Jervell contends, is precisely what the Hebrew scriptures predict (see the references to Isaiah 6:9–10 in Acts 28:26–27). The Jews who do believe represent the repentant remnant of Israel. For Luke, the influx of Gentiles does not contradict this but confirms it, for he reads the scriptures as declaring that when Israel is restored, (meaning, when the full number of Jews are converted), something that has already occurred, then the Gentiles will repent (Acts 15:12–18).

While Jervell's view that "Israel" refers only to converted Jews and not to a church made up of Jews and Gentiles remains unpersuasive, he has caused scholars to rethink basic presuppositions about Luke–Acts.[1] While there is no clear evidence in Luke's writings that he considers Gentiles part of reconstituted Israel, viewing "Israel" as an exclusively Jewish phenomenon would have put him in serious disagreement with Paul and would have introduced the very kind of dispute Luke faithfully avoided. As Paul puts it in his discussion in Romans 11:17–24, Gentile Christians are a "wild olive shoot" grafted onto the olive tree (Israel). The tree, including root and branches, is Israel. The branches broken off are the unbelieving Jews, and the branches grafted in are Gentiles who believe in Christ. Luke would certainly have agreed with Paul that this relationship is the presupposition for the Gentiles' sharing in the promises. As Peter, Paul, and the apostolic leaders maintained, the church is not an entity separated from Israel, and rather than having its own covenant with God, is rather encompassed under God's "new covenant" with Israel (see Heb. 8:6–13 and Jer. 31:31–34). Because unrepentant Jews have forfeited their membership in the people of God, God has extended salvation to the Gentiles. This was God's plan all along, and continues to be the church's understanding of mission.

For Paul and Luke, salvation history begins with missionary work to unbelieving, unrepentant Jews. Hence, the ongoing mission to the Jews in Acts, despite rejection by some. The portion of Jews who believe in the Messiah and are willing to repent appear as the true, restored Israel. To this

---

1. According to Jervell, "In Luke's writings 'Israel' always refers to the Jewish people. At no time does it serve to characterize the church . . . The early understanding of the church . . . as the *new* Israel that is made up of Gentiles and Jews is not present in Acts." *People of God*, 49.

group is added the influx of repentant, believing Gentiles, which, together, constitute the church, the true Israel of God (see Gal. 6:16). Thus, the mission to Jews is a necessary stage through which the history of salvation must pass in order that salvation might proceed from the restored Israel to the Gentiles. From its inception, the mission to the Gentiles is in accordance with scripture. That mission fulfills scripture in the sense that the promises are first fulfilled to repentant Jews (Jewish Christians), then to Gentiles.

We should note that Luke's emphasis in Acts is different from Paul's because Paul wrote a generation earlier, when this internal threat was not so keenly felt. While both contend that only a remnant within Israel repented of sin and turned to God in faith, Paul is clearly dissatisfied with a divided Israel as a permanent solution. He, therefore, posits the full restoration of historic Israel at the return of Jesus following the Gentile mission (see Rom. 11:25–36). Acts does not register so sharp a dichotomy between the Jewish rejection of the gospel and the Gentile embrace of it as found in Romans.

This same difference is reflected by the principal opponents of Paul's Gentile mission within the church. In the Pauline letters, Paul is opposed by "Judaizers"—Jewish Christians who stipulated that all Gentile converts must also be catechized and circumcised according to the traditions of ancient Judaism. As a working symbol of this Judaizing movement within the church, Paul refuses to circumcise Titus, a Greek convert (see Acts 15:1–2; Gal. 2:1–10). However, when Luke wrote Acts, the principal internal threat to the church's faith were "Gentilizers" who threatened to erase anything Jewish from the church's core identity. To mark this different context, Luke tells the story of Paul's circumcision of Timothy, who symbolizes the mission's resistance to the Gentilizing of the church's Jewish legacy (see 16:1–5; also 15:19–21, 28–29; 21:25). Surely Luke was right to worry. The dilution of the church's Jewish legacy led to Marcionism in the next generation and has contributed to the anti-Semitism that continues to this day.

An interesting question arises at this point concerning the origins of the Christian mission to the Gentiles. While much of the impetus belongs to Paul, the "apostle to the Gentiles," there is little question that he built on the presuppositions of the primitive church, based, no doubt, on the teaching of Jesus. In Mark's Gospel we are told great multitudes came to Jesus, not only from Galilee and Judea but also from Gentile regions such as "Idumea, beyond the Jordan, and the region around Tyre and Sidon" (Mark 3:8). Although Jesus remains in Galilee until chapter 4, Jesus for the first time enters Gentile territory (5:1–20), a step that leads to the spreading of the news of Jesus' ministry in the Decapolis (5:20). After conflict with Jewish authorities (7:1–13), Jesus again goes into Gentile territory, eventually traveling through the region of Tyre and Sidon (7:24), returning to Galilee through the Decapolis (7:31). In chapter 8, after another dispute with the Pharisees, Jesus again crosses the lake to the north shore, from where he continues to Caesarea Philippi (8:13, 22, 27). For Mark, then, the essence of the Galilean part of Jesus' ministry is Jesus' rejection by the official representatives of Judaism, hence his turning to the Gentiles. This view is summarized in 7:24–30, where a Gentile woman comes to Jesus and asks for help. Jesus answers that the children (the Jews) are to be fed first, but it is obvious by his response that "to the Jews first" already includes the subsequent turning to the Gentiles.

The middle part of Mark's Gospel (8:27—10:45) focuses on the disciples, and significantly, localizes Peter's confession of Jesus as the Messiah on Gentile soil. As Mark turns to the passion of Jesus in Jerusalem and to the concluding part of his Gospel (10:46—16:8), the purpose of Jesus' suffering is "to give his life a ransom for many" (10:45). Mark's emphasis throughout this final segment of Jesus' life, whether in his account of the cleansing of the temple (see " a house of prayer for all the nations," 11:17), the eschatological discourse (see "the good news must first be preached to all nations," 13:10), or the account of the passion (see the climax of the account in 15:39, the confession of the Gentile centurion, "Truly this man was God's Son"), is on the mission to the Gentiles.

What is clear in Mark's understanding is that the missionary purpose is directed nearly exclusively to the Gentiles. As Jesus already in his lifetime went beyond Israel, so in his closing teachings he makes clear that the gospel is to be preached to all the nations in the world, with no need of any further missionary command to do so. It is possible, from a reading of Mark's Gospel, to infer that the author believed that by his time the period during which salvation was being offered to the Jews had already passed. Thus, for Mark, the way has become free for the salvation of the Gentiles. Thus Mark seems to have developed in his Gospel what Paul radically expressed earlier in 1 Thessalonians 2:15–16, namely, the forfeiture of Israel's right of priority (see 7:27) by the eschatological "first" of 13:10.

In Luke's Gospel and in Acts, the situation is different. According to Luke, the entirety of Jesus' ministry takes place geographically within Jewish territory.[2] There is no direct parallel to Mark 13:10. In the eschatological discourse of Luke 21:5–36, the missionary task is not mentioned. For Mark's reference to the global preaching of the gospel Luke substitutes the enigmatic

---

2. The sole exception being his cure of the Gerasene demoniac in Luke 8:26–39, but even here, there is no mention of the Decapolis in 8:39, as in the Markan parallel at 5:20. To the Jews the pig was an unclean animal, and the eating of pork expressly forbidden (Lev. 11:7–8). The presence of pigs is a reminder that Jesus was here in predominantly Gentile territory.

remark about the times of the Gentiles being fulfilled (21:24). On the other hand, in 24:47 Luke has a saying that is closely allied to Mark 13:10, but it comes from the risen Lord. In 23:47, the christological confession of Mark's Gentile centurion, "Truly this man was God's Son" (Mark 15:39), becomes a bland proclamation, "Certainly this man was innocent" (23:47).

Why does Luke make such changes? In part, because Luke has a second book in mind, but equally so, because of his geographical framework. Why Jerusalem? Because it is the place of salvation, the center from which Jews looked for salvation (Luke 9:51; 13:22, 33, 35; 17:11; 18:31; 19:11, 28). Jesus must accomplish or finish his earthly work there so that salvation and its message may go forth from Jerusalem to the world, as the Hebrew scriptures had proclaimed.

The belief that salvation comes from the Jews engenders the "to Jerusalem" orientation of Luke's Gospel, which in turn explains why Luke relates the story of Jesus going up to the temple as an infant (2:22–24), why the prophecies of Simeon and Anna about Jesus as the world's savior come from the temple (2:25–38), why Luke wishes to show that Jesus is in the line of the Old Testament prophets (13:33), and why Jesus' life and teachings are presented as fulfillment of the prophecies of the Old Testament (4:18–21; 16:31; 18:31; 24:27, 45). The disciples must remain in Jerusalem until they receive power from on high, for not only is Jerusalem the place from which salvation comes, but also the place from which empowerment to preach comes as well (Luke 24:47, 53; Acts 1:4). Thus Luke 24:47 foreshadows the fact that Acts will deal with the horizontal spread of the gospel "beginning from Jerusalem" unto all the nations.

In the Gospel, all things point to Jerusalem; hence Luke's lengthy travel narrative (9:51—19:27). From Jerusalem, as Acts 1:8 indicates, salvation extends geographically, unfolding through three stages: Jerusalem, Judea and Samaria, "to the ends of the earth." As the structure of Luke's second work makes clear, changes in the Gospel allow Luke to pave the way for the missionary command at the beginning of Acts, thereby dismissing from Jesus' earthly life any direct reference to missionary work among the Gentiles.

This does not mean that Luke's Gospel does not contain allusions to the salvation that the Gentiles are to receive. Already at the end of his birth narrative, in the *Nunc Dimittis* (Luke 2:29–32), Simeon speaks of the salvation of God prepared "for revelation to the Gentiles." Then follows the account of John the Baptist in 3:3–22, with the quotation from Isaiah, which Luke enlarges to incorporate the sentence from Isaiah 40:5 that speaks of "all flesh" seeing the salvation of God (Luke 3:6). This sheds light not only on "the salvation of God" in Acts 28:28 but also on "all flesh" in Acts 2:17.

The risen Lord's instructions to the disciples at the close of the Gospel about preaching the gospel among the Gentiles (Luke 24:27, 44–49) refer to the fulfillment of the scriptures and open his followers to a new understanding of the Old Testament. As it was written, Christ had to suffer and rise again, and must also be preached among the Gentiles on the ground of Old Testament prophecy. This emphasis enables Luke to adopt a new line of thought in connection with the words about mission, changing Mark's gospel tradition to underscore that the early Christian mission is founded, not only on Jesus' command, but also on Old Testament prophecy.

According to Luke's account, the turning point of the Christian mission comes with the conversion of Cornelius in Acts 10. However, in chapters 2–9 the mission to the Gentiles is already prepared in a threefold way. First, the study of Pentecost, with its list of Jews and proselytes coming from all nations (2:9–11), and the quotation from Joel about "all flesh" (2:17), shows a worldwide horizon already opening up. Those who are being gained through the gospel gather first in Jerusalem. According to Luke, thousands join the apostolic fellowship and receive baptism.

The occasion of the next step is the action against Stephen, and the persecution connected with it (8:1). This forced the early Christians to disperse, but it only empowered their witness. According to Acts 8:1, they scatter throughout Judea and Samaria. Acts 9:32–42 speaks of visits by Peter to Lydda, Sharon, and Joppa, all in Judea. Acts 8 tells of the work of Philip in Samaria, the conversion of Simon Magus, and the visit of Peter and John. For Luke, their presence in Samaria means the official legitimation of Samaria's conversion to Christianity (9:31).

As early as Acts 9, we learn that some of the fleeing Christians were scattered as far as Damascus, well beyond the borders of Judea. Here begins the third stage in the preparation for the mission to the Gentiles, the conversion of Paul, about whom we are told that he has been chosen to be an apostle to the Gentiles (9:15). The transition to the Gentile mission is carried out through Peter as the apostles' representative. The importance for Luke's outlook of the conversion of Cornelius is told in Acts 10:1—11:18. Even the Jerusalem Council, which the Judaizers made necessary (15:1–21), merely readopts and strengthens the decision made in Caesarea, and thus Peter's task, as presented in Acts, is fulfilled. Acts 11:18 expresses the new awareness: "Then God has given even to the Gentiles the repentance that leads to life."

Only then are we told that those who were scattered because of the persecution traveled as far as Phoenicia, Cyprus, and Antioch (11:19), though Acts explains that they continued speaking the word to "no one except Jews." Missionary work became legitimized through Barnabas, the emissary of the Jerusalem church, and it was he who brought Paul from Tarsus to Antioch to the missionary work begun by that church, its members for the first time called "Christians" (11:26). With the sending out of Barnabas and Paul (Acts 13:1–3), there begins a new period in the history of early Christianity. Not only is the door now opened to a universal mission, but the mission is placed in the hands of the next generation.

In principle, the early church's period is concluded, and a transitional period begins, in which the author of Acts stands, and which will last until the events of the last days. For Luke, Paul becomes the prototype for the church's missionary activity. But even Paul is not free to go to the Gentiles until he has preached to the Jews of the Diaspora and they have rejected the message. This is expressed first in Acts 13:46–47, with the quotation from Isaiah 49:6, partly reproduced in Luke 2:32 and Acts 1:8, and then repeated in 18:6 and 28:25–28. However, the ongoing work of the Gentile mission continues under the direct guidance of the risen Lord, through the activity of the Holy Spirit, but always as the fulfillment of scripture.

Thus the large structure of Luke's conception stretches from Luke 2:30 and 3:6, across 24:47, to Acts 28:28. It can be seen from this trajectory the degree to which Luke finds in the mission to the Gentiles a dominating theme. Because of his view of salvation history, he does, indeed, assume a gradual development, so that the universal preaching of the gospel predicted in the Old Testament is only indirectly indicated during Jesus' lifetime, and is not carried out, even in the early church, until after a transitional period.

Luke's Pastoral Agenda

Within the New Testament, the book of Acts sets out to tell the story of the infant church. Written around 85 CE, Luke described the early church in ideal terms. Jesus had appointed apostles, and these became their leaders. Luke pictured the Jerusalem church as a charismatic fellowship so loving that believers shared what they possessed. For example, Barnabas gave all he owned to the church's funds, Peter and John perform miracles of healing, Peter raised the dead, and all are filled with the Spirit. United in practice and belief, they preached that the Messiah had come, had been crucified, had risen from the dead, and was coming again. Good Jews, they worshipped regularly in the temple.

The typical church established by Paul was, Luke tells us, an outgrowth of the synagogue. Jews were scattered over the Roman world, which in first-century Judaism became, briefly, in some sense a missionary religion (Matt. 28:15). Many Gentiles were attracted by the monotheism and the high moral standards of the Jews. Some even underwent circumcision and became Jewish proselytes; others, called "devout" or "God-Fearers," attended the synagogue but were not actually enrolled. It was among these Gentiles that Paul had his greatest success. This was likely true of other traveling evangelists. Paul welcomed all races without requiring the circumcision that was essential in the Jewish law.

Inevitably, this easing of the law produced friction. Synagogues split. Many Jewish Christians were distressed that Paul seemed to be abandoning the true Mosaic faith. Not only non-Christian Jews but also Jewish converts to Christianity attacked Paul verbally and sometimes physically. He was at times forced to flee, leaving behind a young church to face the opposition. According to Acts, after considerable dispute the church agreed to accept uncircumcised Gentiles. A formal assembly of apostles and elders considered the matter at Jerusalem around 49 CE, and at this council James, the brother of Jesus and a leader of the Jerusalem church, announced the consensus that all races, circumcised and uncircumcised, were to be welcomed.

However, despite the agreement of the Jerusalem Council, which accepted Gentiles into full church membership with limited restrictions (see Acts 15:28–29), the ecclesiastical controversy continued, for Paul's epistles are full of evidence that there were for a time Jewish Christians who insisted on greater adherence to Jewish laws and practices. What, then, does it mean to be a follower of the Way, a Christian disciple?

For Luke, the universalization of the gospel embraces not only all ethnic diversity but also people up and down the social scale, including both the oppressed and the oppressor. Furthermore, Luke and Acts also demonstrate a concern for the physical as well as the spiritual welfare of humankind, so that the gospel's liberation is not merely to come to all people but is to affect every aspect of their lives. Such a total salvation requires a total response of discipleship.[3] In Luke's Gospel, Jesus' disciples must be prepared to leave everything and follow (Luke 5:11), renounce all (14:33; 18:18–30), take up their cross daily (9:23), and put their hand to the plow and not look back (9:62)—agendas reiterated in Acts. The whole gospel must be proclaimed to the whole person in the whole world—that is Luke's pastoral agenda. Why? Because there is only one, all-sufficient Savior, and all must acquiesce to that Lordship.

For Luke, discipleship consists in being molded by God's Spirit, but more specifically, by the tradition about Jesus. Thus, remarkable correspondences can be discerned between what Jesus says and does in Luke's Gospel and what the disciples say and do in Acts. Indeed, as Jesus tells his followers,

---

3. The topic of soteriology (salvation) is discussed in appendix B.

"A disciple is not above the teacher, but everyone who is fully qualified will be like the teacher" (Luke 6:40). Thus, in his writings, Luke intends to illustrate graphically how Christians living after Easter should take the earthly Jesus as their model.

There is more to being a Christian, however, than simply patterning one's life after that of Jesus. In Luke's view, disciples must follow Jesus by experiencing his call (5:11, 27–28; see Acts 9:1–31). Furthermore, disciples are not solitary individuals but participants in community. This dimension of the Christian life is emphasized throughout Acts, but it is also foreshadowed in the Gospel through the corporate life of Jesus' disciples, a community consisting of females as well as males (8:1–3).

Luke's concept of discipleship applies not only to the way Christians are to live but also to the mission they are to fulfill (Luke 5:1–11; 24:46–49). Luke records two stories in which Jesus sends the disciples out as missionaries (9:1–6; 10:1–24), emphasizing that the disciples are sent by Jesus but also that they are to undertake this mission in partnership with others. In both cases, discipleship consists of being molded by a tradition, being empowered by an experience, and participating in a community.

In addition to what has already been said about individual discipleship, Luke understands the basis of Christian community to be the tradition about Jesus. This affects all aspects of congregational life, including fellowship, worship and prayer, teaching, and mission. In Acts, Luke states that believers live communally, sharing possessions (Acts 2:44; 4:32). While such idealism might seem foreign or far-fetched to modern Americans living in relative prosperity, this image seems to build on patterns in Luke's Gospels, taken from the corporate life of Jesus' disciples. There we find unusual attention given to meals, banquets, and table fellowship. Banquets and food feature prominently in Jesus' parables and teaching. In all, Luke mentions nineteen such meals, thirteen of which are peculiar to his Gospel. As if to call attention to the prominence of this motif, Luke reports that Jesus' opponents call him a "glutton and a drunkard" (7:34) and criticize him for eating with tax collectors and sinners (5:30; 15:1–2).

Modern readers may have difficulty appreciating this theme, unless they realize that in the biblical world, food is life and the sharing of food is the sharing of life. Thus, examples of Jesus' participation in table fellowship become "acted parables" about life, and Jesus' instructions about eating together show how people should live together. Besides generosity, hospitality, and humility, another possible interpretation is to view meals in Luke's Gospel as inclusive events, so when Jesus is depicted as eating with tax collectors and sinners, this also points metaphorically to eating and living inclusively, with people of other faiths, cultures, races, and social classes. Furthermore, meals also represent occasions for conversation, reconciliation, and role reversal, by which the lowly are raised up and the proud are put down (7:36–52). In other words, where Jesus gives instructions concerning matters of table etiquette, readers can look beyond the surface to deeper issues of fear, prejudice, bias, and inequity.

Worship and prayer are also important themes for Luke. Only in the Third Gospel do Jesus' disciples ask him to teach them to pray (11:1). This he does, not only by teaching them a model prayer (11:2–4), but also by his own example throughout the Gospel. Luke's Gospel portrays Jesus at prayer far more often than the other Gospels. In Luke's Gospel, Jesus offers three parables on prayer not found elsewhere (11:5–8; 18:1–8, 9–14). Likewise, Jesus is frequently represented as encouraging his disciples to pray (18:1; 21:36; 22:40). Underlying prayer is communion with God, an important feature of individual and corporate life.

Another important element in prayer is petition and intercession, that is, prayer for spiritual ends. The goals of prayer are to receive the Holy Spirit (11:13; see Matt. 7:11), to not lose heart (18:1), to escape temptation (22:40, 46), and to be ready for the Lord's return (21:36). Yet other essential elements of prayer are worship, praise, and thanksgiving. Luke's Gospel begins and ends with references to people worshiping (1:8–9; 24:52–53), and it contains more liturgical material than any other New Testament book. These themes recur in Acts as well, where prayer is said to mark every significant stage in the unfolding of God's plan. Likewise, worship, adoration, and praise typify the life of God's people. Luke conceives of Christians as people who worship and pray together.

In his description of an ideal Christian community in Acts 2:42, Luke mentions all of the aspects of life together that we have examined so far, adding yet another characteristic of early Christians, that they "devoted themselves to the apostles' teaching," by which is meant that they gathered to hear the teaching of one or another of the church's leaders. This element, while an important aspect of Christian worship, is evident in Luke's Gospel as well. For example, in his passage on Mary and Martha (Luke 10:38–42), Jesus commends Mary for listening to his teaching, unlike Martha, who is distracted with serving and hosting. In short, those who want to grow must first be taught.

Likewise, Christian growth is important to Luke, and he associates such growth with the ministry of teaching. Jesus' own disciples are good examples of this, for the growth they exhibit between Luke's first and second volumes may in large part be attributed to the teaching Jesus provides at the end of the Gospel (24:27, 45). Their minds are opened (24:45), and they are now able to understand what was previously concealed (9:45). As to the content of the teaching Jesus provides, Luke is quite specific: "he interpreted to them the things about himself in all the scriptures" (24:27). In Acts, the figure of Apollos is an excellent example of Luke's thinking in this regard. Having received limited instruction in the way of the Lord, he is able to teach accurately about Jesus, but only after receiving additional instruction is he able to show from the scriptures that Jesus is the Christ (Acts 18:24–28).

Luke-Acts not only contains the content of Christian proclamation, but also presents a theological basis for the church's mission in the world. That basis lies in the concept of servanthood, presented so clearly throughout Luke's Gospel (see Luke 22:27, where Jesus establishes the pattern of servanthood when he declares, "I am among you as one who serves"). Underlying the church's mission to evangelism, which leads to growth and expansion, the calling of every believer is to servanthood. This is the Bible's stress on election, that when God calls a people, they are called not to privilege but to service. The Bible makes it clear that just as ancient Israel's call was for the healing of the nations (Gen. 12:3)[4] that, too, continues to be God's call for the church. Christians are called to be servants and are expected to perform acts of love and mercy for others, in imitation of Christ. Luke's writings, of course, offer the church an exemplary portrait of Jesus as the Servant of God.

Luke's Christological Agenda[5]

To understand Christian mission and discipleship, we need to understand Luke's characterization of the person and work of Christ, for these matters are intimately connected. For example, Luke's Gospel regularly depicts Jesus as a prophet like Moses, who is filled with the Holy Spirit, speaks God's word, and works signs and wonders among the people. Significantly, not only Jesus but also his followers are depicted thus. In Acts, every protagonist is presented in prophetic terms. Like Jesus, all are filled with the Holy Spirit, all speak God's word, and all work signs and wonders among the people. For Luke, christology shapes discipleship, and discipleship shapes mission. Likewise, God's plan shapes mission, and mission shapes discipleship.

In the early church there was an increase of respect for the apostles, who came to be regarded as the pillars of the church. As a result, Luke often softens the hard edge of Mark's portrayal of the disciples, omitting

---

4. The biblical word for healing, health, wholeness, and goodness is "salvation," similar in meaning to the Hebrew word *shalom*. In the Bible, the election of a people becomes the basis for good news, what the New Testament calls "gospel."

5. Luke's christology is discussed more fully in appendix A.

the statement that the disciples' hearts were hardened (Mark 6:52), Jesus' rebuke of the disciples for their failure to understand about the loaves (Mark 8:17–21), Jesus' rebuke to Peter, "Get behind me, Satan" (Mark 8:32–33), and the disciples' final abandonment of Jesus (Mark 14:50–52).

Likewise, Luke heightens the reverence for Jesus portrayed by Mark. Whereas Mark uses "the Lord" only once to refer to Jesus, Luke does so sixteen times. Luke also suppresses or weakens references in Mark to such human emotions of Jesus as grief and anger (Luke 14:10; see Mark 3:5), and he eliminates Jesus expression of amazement in Mark 6:6. Luke also omits unflattering statements about Jesus such as found in Mark 3:21, or questions Jesus asks in Mark 6:38, 9:16, 21, and 33, which might be taken to imply his ignorance. Luke also omits Mark's story of the cursing of the fig tree, an episode unbecoming to the gracious and noble character of Jesus Luke wishes to portray.

Luke's Gospel centers around the person of Jesus, connecting the question of his identity to the plot of the Gospel during the Galilean ministry. Regularly we hear the question, "Who is this who speaks or acts thus?" The scribes and Pharisees question (5:21), John the Baptist questions (7:20), even his disciples wonder (8:25). In 9:18 Jesus asks his disciples the question of his identity: "Who do the crowds say that I am?" The repeated question sustains the issue, even as the identity of Jesus, revealed from the annunciation of his birth, is confirmed and amplified for the reader. The Galilean ministry concludes with Peter's confession, "[You are] the Messiah of God" (9:20). Shortly thereafter, at his transfiguration, the voice from heaven declares, "This is my Son, my Chosen" (9:35).

It should come as no surprise that Luke's two-volume narrative, filled with numerous themes, also evinces multiple possible purposes for its composition. I have suggested seven practical and theological issues, but these are only representative of the struggles that Luke and other first-century disciples of Jesus experienced in living out their faith in a violent and uncertain world.

In addressing a variety of issues and questions, Luke's aims cohere around a central theological question, how first-century events involving Jesus and his followers fulfill God's purposes in the world. They also lead to the central issue of our lives, how current events and issues in our lives fulfill God's plan for history and human society.

As we make our way through Luke and Acts, we will discover few clear answers to these questions and concerns, no fill-in-the-blanks, no set of dogmatic propositions, no systematic theology. However, we will encounter a rich tapestry of stories, offering an imaginative resource for reflection.

Luke's narratives, written in the swirl of confusion and conflict, aim to supply God's people much needed "assurance" (*asphaleia*) that God faithfully works all things for good according to God's eternal purposes (see Rom. 8:28–30).

UNIT III

Exegetical Topics

CHAPTER 8

The Infancy Narrative (Luke 1:1—2:52)

Assignment: Read chapter 8 of *Power Revealed* and chapters 1–2 of Luke's Gospel. Answer the following questions, writing the answers in your journal. [If you are in a study group, be prepared to share your views with others in the class.] (1) After reading Luke 1–2, determine which aspect(s) of Luke's infancy narratives you find that most clearly reveal the theological agenda of Luke–Acts. Explain your answer. (2) Read the infancy narrative in Matthew 1–2 and make a list of the major similarities and another list of the major differences between Matthew and Luke's accounts. How do you account for these similarities and dissimilarities?

Outline of Luke 1:1—2:52

I. Annunciation of John the Baptist's Birth 1:5–25
II. Annunciation of Jesus' Birth 1:26–38
III. Mary's visit to Elizabeth 1:39–56
IV. Birth, Circumcision, and Naming of John the Baptist 1:57–80
V. Birth, Circumcision, and Naming of Jesus 2:1–21
VI. Presentation of Jesus in the Temple 2:22–40
VII. Jesus at Age Twelve in the Temple 2:41–52

The Priority of Easter over Christmas

For modern Christians, Christmas has long surpassed Easter as the favorite holiday. Christmas is the season of romance, pageantry, candlelight, and midnight services. In the celebration of Christmas the promise of peace, the exchange of gifts, the yearning for togetherness, and the family feast all find expression. It celebrates the innocence of childhood by portraying the God who draws near to humanity in the humility of a powerless infant. All these images are enhanced in the birth narratives of Luke's Gospel. These narratives, celebrated in poetry and art, have become a treasured part of the folklore of Western civilization, revered by all who look to the past for guidance and inspiration.

Paradoxically, we may speak of the Gospels as developing backwards, for the oldest Christian preaching about Jesus concerned his death and resurrection. We see this clearly in the formulas of Acts 2:23, 32; 3:14–15; 4:10; Acts 10:39–40; 1 Corinthians 15:3–4. For early Christians, Easter, not Christmas, was the entry point for their faith. For the cross—and the empty tomb—presented a new image of God. This image defied conventional wisdom, for it called into question the monarchical model as the primary analogy by which God could be understood. The image of a weak man, beaten, broken, and crucified, became the symbol through which the triumphant God was perceived. The first witnesses to what we now call Easter were invited to open their minds to new possibilities, such as embracing the scandal of the cross. Over time, additional possibilities emerged, such as God being incarnated in a child, born in a manger, heralded by magi but also by lowly shepherds.

The birth narratives we now possess, found in the Gospels of Matthew and Luke, both achieved their final written form late in the first century. Despite agreement on certain features, the two accounts represent quite distinct, even divergent, traditions. Though traditional Christians tend to blend them into a single narrative, this can only be accomplished at the price of ignoring discrepancies and distorting irreconcilable data. For example, Matthew tells of the visit of the wise men, the flight into Egypt, and Herod's command to kill the infants in Bethlehem. None of these appears in Luke, who reports the conception and birth of John the Baptist as well as of Jesus. Interspersed in his narrative Luke includes half a dozen poetic passages, three of which are widely used in the church as liturgical hymns. These canticles, known by the first words of their Latin translation, are the Magnificat (1:46–55), attributed to Mary; the Benedictus (1:68–79) of Zechariah, the father of John; and the Nunc Dimittis (2:29–32) of Simeon, a devout Jew of Jerusalem. Unlike Matthew, Luke also tells of shepherds, the

CHAPTER 8—THE INFANCY NARRATIVE (LUKE 1:1—2:52)

manger, the presentation of Jesus in the temple, and an account of Jesus as a twelve-year-old.

As we examine the birth narratives, two principles should be kept in mind. (1) These accounts are not historical, certainly not in the modern sense, for they combine history and theology. Symbolic language is obviously present in the story of Jesus' birth. Do virgins conceive? Do angels sing to shepherds? Do stars wander through the sky so slowly that magi can follow them? Would wise men travel with symbolic interpretive gifts for a newborn child, including myrrh as a sign of what that baby's eventual death would accomplish? Even in the first century these things would be recognized as the stuff of fairy tales, not unlike narratives of those who seek a pot of gold at the end of the rainbow. Modern people, concerned with objectivity and literalness, ask, "What happened?" The biblical writers, deeply involved with faith and tradition, asked a quite different question, "What does it mean?" The Gospels, like the rest of scripture, were written to inspire faith.

How far the reports of Jesus' birth and infancy in Matthew and Luke are historical and how far they are poetic and theological interpretations has been debated at length. Some light can be thrown on this approach to historical narrative by the Jewish distinction between two types of scriptural exposition: *halakah* (from the verb "to walk") was the commentary on scripture that adduced from it rules for daily life, and *haggadah* (from the verb "to tell") was the recital of scriptural stories to bring out their religious significance. Whereas Jewish orthodoxy consisted more in rightness of practice that in rightness of belief, halakhic traditions were preserved with scrupulous precision, whereas haggadic traditions were regarded as a legitimate field for creative imagination.

(2) The birth narratives in the Gospels should also be read as resurrection accounts, for they are told from that perspective.[1] The birth of Christianity was an Easter event, not a Christmas event. This is the perspective

---

1. See, in this regard, the presence of the phrase "after three days" in Luke 2:46 and "on the third day" in John 2:1. The expression "the third day" is employed six times by Luke in reference to the resurrection (Luke 9:22; 18:33; 24:7, 21, 46; Acts 10:40), and the expression "after three days" twice more (Acts 25:1; 28:17) simply as a time demarcation with no reference to the resurrection. In Hebrew thought, the phrase "three days" did not generally constitute a reference to calendar time, but carried symbolic significance (see Gen. 42:17–18; Exod. 3:18; 10:22; 19:11; 2 Kgs. 20:5, 8; Hos. 6:2; Jonah 1:17). Reference to "three days" was in many instances either the critical Day of Judgment or the day when a new reality dawned. The third day also had eschatological overtones, evoking images that Jews associated with the climax of history (Isa. 25:6–8), the Day of the Lord. As in Jewish history, so Jewish Christians began to assert that on the third day God had raised Christ and exalted him to God's right hand. For Christians, the third day became the day of resurrection. To literalize its meaning in the New Testament would be to miss its meaning.

from which the nativity tradition, the life and teachings of Jesus, and the crucifixion are told. It is also the perspective from which the New Testament books were written, including all of Luke–Acts.

During Jesus' lifetime, there was no talk of his divinity, of incarnational concepts, or of Trinitarian formulas. However, after his death, everything changed. The earliest phase in biblical christology, labelled *adoptionism* or "exaltationism," is indicated in the opening of Acts, especially in the speeches by Peter and others. The clearest example is Acts 2, Peter's speech on the Day of Pentecost, where the crucified "man" Jesus, by virtue of being "exalted at the right hand of God" (2:33), has been "*made* both Lord and Messiah" (2:36). In another sermon attributed to Peter, recorded in Acts 5:29–32, the resurrection is also described as the "exaltation" of Jesus to God's right hand (5:31).

It seems clear that the exaltation of Jesus was the original meaning of Easter, rather than the later explanation that came to be called resurrection. Also supporting this idea are the words found in Paul's letter to the Philippians about the self-emptying of Christ in the incarnation, where the only concept of resurrection it mentions is exaltation (Phil. 2:9). As these passages suggest, the raising of Jesus was a demonstration of God's power, not of Jesus' power.

As the exaltation story was told and retold, the action of God raising Jesus began to be expressed in terms of Jesus himself rising from the grave. With this change, exaltation became divided into two events: resurrection (Jesus rising from the dead in an active sense) and ascension (God exalting Jesus into heaven in a passive sense). What was once a single proclamation became over time two distinct narratives. Christians now found themselves two steps removed from the primary Christian experience. Over time, as emphasis on the resurrection increased, it came to mean Jesus' return to life rather than Jesus' exaltation into heaven. It is at that stage of development that the focus turns to the empty tomb and the appearances of the resurrected Jesus. In addition, only at this point does the claim of physical, bodily resurrection enter the Christian conception. Christians now found themselves three steps removed from the primary experience.

The manner of relating that narrative happened in two ways. In Mark, Matthew, and John, Easter is primarily both resurrection and exaltation. Mark has no post-resurrection appearances, though the implication is that the exalted Lord will appear to the disciples in Galilee (Mark 16:7). The only account of an appearance of the risen Lord to the disciples in Matthew takes place on a Galilean mountain, where the exalted Lord came to them out of heaven with a divine commission (Matt. 28:16–20). In the Fourth Gospel the first appearance of the risen Lord was to Mary Magdalene, and Jesus forbade her to touch him, because he had not yet ascended to the Father. Rather, she is commanded to tell the disciples that he is ascending "to my Father and your Father, to my God and your God" (John 20:17). Then, later that day, the ascended Lord appeared to the disciples and they received the Holy Spirit (John 20:19–23).

Luke follows a different pattern. He separates the resurrection from the ascension by a period of forty days (Luke 24; Acts 1). He also uses the ascension narrative both to close the resurrection appearances and to prepare the church for the coming of God's Holy Spirit at Pentecost. It seems apparent that Luke makes linear and narrative what had originally been instantaneous and a matter of proclamation.

In addition to the resurrection, a parallel line of development occurs within christology. To trace the expanding claims made for Jesus in the New Testament, we begin with Paul, the first author of any part of the New Testament. In the epistle to the Romans, written about AD 58 (some twenty-eight years after the death of Jesus), Paul begins to develop explanations for his experience of Christ. God, he says to the Christians in Rome, had "declared" Jesus to be "Son of God with power according to the spirit of holiness by his resurrection from the dead" (Romans 1:4). This is an important passage, not only because it represents an early (pre-Gospel) tradition, but because it defines three key ideas. First, according to this Pauline statement, God declares or designates Jesus to be "Son of God." There is no sense here of divine equality or of what later came to be called incarnation. Next, Paul states that God made this declaration according to the "spirit of holiness." The Holy Spirit was not yet viewed as a separate and distinct aspect of God. Third, this designation of Jesus as God's divine son is said to have taken place by his "resurrection from the dead."

For Paul it was the Easter experience, not the incarnation or Jesus' birth, which constituted the basis for the claim he was making about Jesus. Paul seemed not to know of a divinely initiated virgin birth, for this belief is not mentioned in any of his letters. In this early strata of theological thinking we find a point of view that later came to be called "adoptionism." This means that late in his career it was Paul's understanding that God had adopted Jesus into the being of God. In Paul's mind, this adoptive status was not conferred upon Jesus prior to the resurrection.

Some ten years after Paul had written his epistle to the Romans and some forty years after Jesus' death, the Gospel of Mark came into existence. Here, for the first time in Christian history, the biographical details of Jesus' life were chronicled in written form. Mark's account, however, starts with the encounter of Jesus and John the Baptist at the Jordan; Mark tells us nothing about Jesus' birth or youth, not even the name of his father. An outline similar to Mark's appears in the sermon in Acts 10:37–41. There we find no mention of Jesus' birth, but rather a sequence beginning with the baptism and ending with the resurrection.

In his first verse, Mark informed his readers of his purpose for composing this book: "The beginning of the good news of Jesus Christ, the Son of God." He took Paul's earlier words and adapted them to his purpose in an interesting way. He accepted two parts of Paul's earlier declaration, but gave to them narrative form. Later in chapter 1, Mark took Paul's words (that God had declared Jesus to be God's son) and described just how it was that this declaration occurred. The voice of God spoke from heaven, Mark declared, and said of Jesus, "You are my Son, the Beloved; with you I am well pleased" (Mark 1:11).

Next, Mark took Paul's idea that this declaration came by way of the "spirit of holiness" and created a specific setting. He wrote that the heavens tore apart, enabling the "Spirit" to descend on Jesus "like a dove," that is, in a physical way (Mark 1:10). Up to this point, Mark seemed to be following the Pauline script closely, but he made a profound alteration, changing the moment when this declaration took place. Whereas Paul had made the declaration occur at the time of the resurrection, Mark inserted it into his story of the baptism, which inaugurated Jesus' ministry (Mark 1:11). He did so in order to demonstrate that the power of God was at work throughout the life of Jesus. That could not have been the case if Jesus had become the Son of God at the time of the resurrection.

By the time Matthew wrote, some ten to twenty years after Mark, Matthew began his story of Jesus' life with the narrative of his birth, thereby moving Paul's account of Jesus' divine designation back to his nativity. For Matthew, God still declared Jesus to be the Son of God, only this declaration is now placed into the mouth of the angel who appeared to Joseph in a dream (Matt. 1:20). Matthew goes on to say that this divine nature was preordained by the prophet Isaiah, but the status is still accomplished, even for Matthew, by the Pauline "spirit of holiness," though by Matthew's time that concept had become the more explicit "Holy Spirit." This Spirit is not yet fully distinct as a separate part of the triune God, for in Matthew's birth narrative the Spirit appears to function as the male agent in conception. When Matthew wrote his Gospel, the Holy Spirit as a distinct person was inconceivable. As yet, no account of the coming of the Holy Spirit as a separate power, either at Pentecost (Luke) or at Easter (John), had yet been written, and the doctrine of the Trinity would not be formulated until the fourth century.

Luke, writing five to ten years after Matthew, changed some of Matthew's details, but essentially left the story line intact. Luke's annunciating angel, for example, was far more specific than Matthew's. Luke's angel now has a name, Gabriel (Luke 1:26). This divine creature appears, according to Luke, in person, not in a dream, and it is Mary, not Joseph, who is the recipient of this angelic revelation. Mary's baby is designated by this angel as both "the Son of God" (Luke 1:35) and "Son of the Most High" (Luke 1:32). In the third Gospel, Jesus is clearly God's son from conception, and Paul's "spirit of holiness" is becoming a specific divine agent.

The Fourth Gospel, written during the last decade of the first century, bypasses the narrative about Jesus' birth and declares that Jesus is said to have shared in God's identity prior even to his conception and birth. Preexistence now becomes a category by which Christians could talk about Jesus. For John, there never was a time when Jesus was not God's son. By the start of the second century, Jesus' identity with God was complete, providing a biblical basis for the concept of the incarnation.

What we have described is a grand theological story, designed to capture the imagination. Paul's early affirmation has reached its biblical limit. At the resurrection God had declared Jesus the divine son, adopted into who or what God is. That designation had been accomplished by the spirit of holiness, a character that morphed over time, first into the Holy Spirit and then into the very essence of God. Finally, the origin of the Son's designation was moved backward in time, from the resurrection, to the baptism, to the conception, and in John's Gospel, to the origin of the creation itself.[2]

Proto-Luke

There are various reasons to believe that an early version of Luke existed, and that it did not include the birth narratives of Luke 1 and 2. The following reasons are given in support of this argument.

1. According to this theory, Luke 3:1–3 was the original opening of the Gospel. The elaborate dating process that begins this unit has about it a ring reminiscent of the beginning of the prophetic books in the Old Testament.

2. Chapter 3 introduces John as though for the first time. In addition, the analogy between John the Baptist and Jesus, emphasized in the early chapters, is avoided in the rest of the Gospel.

---

2. The discussion on the development of claims about Jesus is adapted from Spong, *Christianity Must Change*, 73–82.

3. The reference to Jesus' baptism as "beginning" in Acts 1:22 suggests that the infancy narrative may have been prefixed to the Gospel after the book of Acts was completed.
4. The attachment of a genealogy of Jesus to the story of his baptism instead of to his birth, as in Matthew's Gospel.
5. The fact that characteristic features such as the part played by Mary, the virgin conception, and the Davidic descent of Jesus, do not appear again either in the Gospel or in Acts.
6. Language and stylistic differences between the birth story and the rest of the Gospel, including the frequency of Semitisms in the first two chapters of Luke.

While these considerations do not constitute proof of the Proto-Luke theory, they enable us to assume that Luke composed his work in stages. As a working hypothesis, we presume that Luke began his literary undertaking by collecting information about Jesus from eyewitnesses and others. Subsequently, when a copy of Mark became available, he augmented his original document with Markan insertions.[3] He then appears to have had access to either Matthew or the Q material, that is, to material common to Matthew and Luke but not to Mark. He then added the infancy stories and the prologue to bring his work into its final form.

At various stages he added material classified as "L," identified by scholars as Luke's special source. It includes everything that cannot be assigned to the Gospels of Mark and Matthew or to the "Q" document. Once that generalization is made, it becomes obvious that the "L" source is more than a single source. The canticles of Zechariah, Mary, and Simeon in the birth narrative, the genealogy, many of the unique parables, and major parts of the birth narratives—each might represent a different source that Luke collected at various stages of composition. Some of this material might have been written, some of it was surely oral, and some Luke may well have created. He would certainly have been the first person to put this particular part of the oral tradition into written form. But the fact remains that Luke wove all of these sources into his own narrative, making each part serve the needs of the whole and revealing in a consistent way his unique themes.

This brings us to an important question: Why were infancy narratives composed? Of course, curiosity might have been involved. Christians

---

3. According to this hypothesis, Proto-Luke could have been written by Luke in Caesarea during the time of Paul's imprisonment there (Acts 23:33—26:32). After Luke had accompanied Paul to Rome, he would have expanded his text with material from Mark's Gospel, which he would have encountered there for the first time.

wanted to know more about their master, about his family, his ancestors, and his birthplace. However, apologetics is a more significant reason. Some aspects in Luke's account help to explain the superiority of Jesus over John the Baptist. In the first century, as we know from Luke's Gospel (see 3:16) and also from Acts 19: 1–7, John the Baptist had a significant following among non-Christians, and was probably viewed by some as a rival to Jesus. (To help offset this potential rivalry, see John 1:15 and also 3:30, where John the Baptist declares concerning Jesus, "He must increase, but I must decrease.")

Some scholars find in the birth stories of Jesus an anti-docetic aspect.[4] More plausible is the suggestion that the story of Jesus' birth offered an explanation against the charge that Jesus was illegitimate (see John 8:41). Luke's account offers an explanation that allowed for an irregularity in the birth of Jesus, while at the same time defending the purity of the mother and the sanctity of the child.

Ultimately, partly apologetic and partly theological factors may have been involved in the development of Matthew and Luke's infancy accounts. Matthew's account draws a parallel between Joseph the legal father of Jesus and Joseph the patriarch who dreamed dreams and went to Egypt. In midrashic fashion[5] Matthew has Jesus delivered from the hands of wicked King Herod, who slaughtered male children like the wicked Pharaoh during Israelite slavery in Egypt. Such parallels and reminiscences with Old Testament accounts would have helped develop a Christian understanding that Jesus the Messiah relived the history of his own people.

Both Matthew and Luke constructed their infancy narratives into a story that allowed the covenant relationship between God and God's people to enter a new phase, one that moved the covenant from Israel to the followers of Jesus. Matthew and Luke also saw christological implications in stories that were circulating about Jesus' birth. More importantly, they saw the possibility of weaving such stories into a narrative of their own composition that could be made the vehicle of the message that Jesus was the Son of God acting for the salvation of humanity. As we shall see, Luke also used his account as a vehicle through which to introduce major themes of his Gospel.

Writing for Jews and God-fearers familiar with Old Testament stories, Luke's infancy narrative serves as a transition from the Hebrew scriptures to

---

4. In this respect see also Colossians 2:9 and 1 John 4:2–3. In later Christianity the creedal slogans "born of the Virgin Mary" and "suffered under Pontius Pilate" were employed to refute docetic claims that Jesus was not really human. However, anti-docetic apologetics seem unlikely in the infancy narratives.

5. For a definition of midrash and further examples of midrashic technique, see the explanation under "Thematic Considerations" below.

the Gospels. Hence, Luke's first two chapters utilize the full imagery of Israel as a historical and theological bridge. Almost every verse in this segment is adapted from lines in the Hebrew Bible.

One of the prominent themes in Luke is that events in the life of Jesus and the early church had happened "according to the scriptures," and that by his coming Jesus had fulfilled the promises and aspirations of the Old Testament. This theme is emphatically stated at the end of Luke's Gospel, where we find the risen Christ interpreting to his disciples "the things about himself in all the scriptures" (24:27; see 24:44). This is also a dominant theme of the first two chapters. These chapters are prophetic not merely because they contain predictions of the births of John and Jesus and of the divine act of deliverance that John heralded and Jesus mediated, but also because they epitomize the spirit of expectancy that pervades the Old Testament.

At the opening of his Gospel, in a few memorable episodes, Luke reminds us of the prophet's faith in the divine control of history, the priest's yearning for the presence of God, the Nazarite's dedication to purity, the hopes for a kingdom of justice and peace associated with King David, and the piety of humble folk who awaited the redemption of Israel. By his allusive use of Old Testament language, Luke makes us aware that behind Zechariah and Elizabeth, Joseph and Mary, and Simeon and Anna lie a host of Old Testament figures who lived by faith in God's promises and died without seeking their fulfillment.

How much of the Jewish character of these stories is due to Luke's sources, how much to his own intimate knowledge of the Greek Old Testament, and how much to his creative artistry is hard to estimate. However, one way or another, he has exquisitely recaptured the atmosphere of Jewish religion at its best. The messianic hope, so beautifully expressed in the Magnificat and the Benedictus, remains the hope of Israel, not yet transformed by the light of the gospel. It involves a confusion of Israel's political hopes with her religious vocation, and a national self-concern from which Jesus had to dissociate himself before he could accept the role of Messiah.

The Internal Structure of Luke 1–2

There is general agreement that Luke arranged these chapters with careful artistry. His infancy narrative includes seven episodes: (1) annunciation of John the Baptist's birth (1:5–25); (2) annunciation of Jesus' birth (1:26–38); (3) Mary's visit to Elizabeth (1:39–56); (4) birth, circumcision, and naming of John the Baptist (1:57–80); (5) birth, circumcision, and naming of Jesus (2:1–21); (6) presentation of Jesus in the temple (2:22–40), and Jesus at age twelve in the temple (2:41–52). Some degree of parallelism is evident in these scenes, particularly between John the Baptist and Jesus. The closest parallelism is between episodes 1 and 2 (the two annunciations), but there is also parallelism between episodes 4 and 5. Episode 3 serves as a further connective between John and Jesus. Episodes 6 and 7, however, appear to be additions, for no narrative parallels can be found with preceding scenes. The canticles also fit awkwardly into the structure; the second canticle or Benedictus(1:68–79) refers to John, while the first and third, the Magnificat (1:46–55) and Nunc Dimittis (2:29–32), refer to Jesus. In terms of parallelism, the Magnificat and Benedictus are close to each other in length, tone, and speakers (respective parents), yet the episodes in which they are placed (3 and 4) are not parallel. The Benedictus and Nunc Dimittis are closely related in that each is a prophetic canticle uttered after the birth, naming, and circumcision of the child, and each refers to the child's destiny, especially in relation to Israel.

As is true of Matthew's Gospel, Luke's infancy narrative had little or no influence on the rest of the Gospel, so that, if the first two chapters had been lost, we would never have suspected their existence. However, a strong connection can be made between Luke 1–2 and Acts 1–2. In Luke we find Zechariah and Elizabeth, Simeon and Anna, characters taken almost from the pages of the Old Testament, who appear as representatives of the piety of Israel, while Mary recites a hymn that evokes the aspirations of Israel's righteous remnant, God's servant Israel (1:54; see Isa. 49:3). As the first two chapters of Luke supply a transition from the story of Israel to the story of Jesus, so the first two chapters of Acts supply a transition from the story of Jesus to the story of the church. There, the apostles are the principal connecting element, for they were with Jesus throughout his ministry and will be the chief human agents in the early days of the church.

If Luke intended parallelism between the two transitional sections of his books, it is not surprising that in many ways his infancy narrative is closer in spirit to the stories in Acts than to the Gospel material that Luke borrowed from his sources. The outpouring of the prophetic spirit that moves people to act and speak (Luke 1:15, 41, 67, 80; 2:25–27) may have little parallel in the ministry of Jesus, but close parallels in Acts (5:19; 8:26; 10:3; 12:7; 27:23). The parallelism that Luke manifests between John and Jesus in the infancy narrative is also at work in the parallelism in Acts between the careers of Peter and Paul. Also, the unusual title "Messiah Lord" (*Christos Kyrios*) given by the angels to the infant Jesus in Luke 2:11 echoes the christology of the speeches in Acts, particularly 2:36: "Therefore let the entire house of Israel know with certainty that God has made [Jesus] both Lord [*Kyrios*] and Messiah [*Christos*], this Jesus whom you crucified."

Because of their content and significance in Luke's Gospel, the canticles have been the object of special attention by scholars, who wonder whether they were composed by Luke or taken from a common source. The style of these canticles is more poetic and Semitized than that of their context; in some respects, the Magnificat and Benedictus hardly seem Christian. It has been suggested that these were originally Jewish or Jewish Christian hymns (possibly from the Jerusalem community, which is so prominent in Acts 2–6). In fact, chapter 2 seems completely separable from chapter 1; it has its own introduction, and is capable of standing on its own. Although prominent in chapter 1, John the Baptist disappears in chapter 2. One even wonders when the story in 2:41–51 was added, for it seems to have a second and duplicate conclusion in 2:52. The story of Jesus at the temple in 2:41–51 is also separable from the rest, and one could argue that 2:40 was the original conclusion of chapter 2.

Some scholars posit a Baptist source for John the Baptist's material in chapter 1. If that were the case, it helps to explain variants in the textual tradition, such as at 1:46, where some manuscripts substitute the name of Elizabeth in the place of Mary. Some scholars argue that the Magnificat would sound more natural on the lips of Elizabeth, since she is the one who has been raised from the humiliation of childlessness. This reading is particularly popular among those who maintain that the entire nativity cycle originated among the followers of John the Baptist and was later adapted to Christian purposes. If that were the case, however, significant editing and rearranging had to have occurred, including moving the Magnificat from its more proper place in the story after 1:25. In addition, the annunciation in 1:26–38 would have been originally addressed to Elizabeth, as a parallel to the annunciation to Zechariah.

When examining the literary emphasis Luke places on parallelism in the infancy narrative, we also note the intense relationship Luke places between John and Jesus. Both were charismatic figures proclaiming the imminence of God's kingdom. Each had a loyal band of followers, held wide admiration among the common people, and died the death of a martyr. Were they related, and if so, were they cousins? Luke is the only Gospel writer to suggest a blood kinship between them (1:36), calling their mothers "relatives" or "kin." This idea is certainly challenged by the Fourth Gospel, which goes so far as to have John say of Jesus, "I myself did not know him" (1:31). The tradition that they were cousins is not biblical but rather seems to have begun with John Wycliffe in the fourteenth century.

Thematic Considerations in Luke 1–2

Midrash

If the Bible is to be read today with intelligence, our knowledge of how it came to be written needs to be expanded. Many people today, unaware of the style of writing that was in vogue in the Jewish world when the Gospels were written, miss the symbolism in the first pages of Luke, tending to read Luke's words as historical fact, as if things actually happened that way. However, to do so is to miss the point, for Luke did not write to record historical facts. When Jesus lived, people did not keep records of ordinary individuals; there was no electronic or print media, as today, no television documentaries or researched biographies. Early Christians were convinced they were living during the final days of history. In such a climate, record-keeping seemed irrelevant.

The way the Jewish tradition viewed and treated scripture is well known. It produced a method called midrash, a type of commentary or scripture that "represented efforts on the part of the rabbis to probe, tease, and dissect the sacred story looking for hidden meanings, filling in blanks, and seeking clues to yet-to-be-revealed truth. It was the assumption of the rabbis developing the midrash that the sacred text was timeless, that it was true in the past, true in the present, and true in the future."[6] This is how Jesus "opened the scriptures" to Cleopas and his companion in the Emmaus road story (Luke 24:27; see 24:44–45), and how early Christians became convinced that Jesus was the key to the Jewish scriptures. The God who had spoken in times past through the prophets was now speaking through his Son (Heb. 1:1–2), and so people like Luke searched the ancient record for hints, clues, and foreshadowings of current events. Retelling stories out of the Jewish past to illumine new experiences was not considered false or misleading, but rather a way to see correspondences and better understand the present. This is what we find generally in Luke's writings and specifically in his birth narrative.

As Raymond Brown notes in his exhaustive study of the infancy narratives, the term "midrash" can refer either to a literary genre or to a technique or style of writing.[7] When applied to the infancy narratives, the first definition means that such narratives should be viewed as a reflective or meditative exercise on a preexistent document, making them an entirely creative (or re-creative) literary endeavor. In this case, Matthew's story of

---

6. Spong, *Born of a Woman*, 18.
7. Brown, *Birth of the Messiah*, 557–63.

the birth of Jesus would have drawn its inspiration from Jewish midrashim[8] interpreting the birth of Moses found in Exodus 1–2. The existence of such midrashim is attested in the *Antiquities* of Josephus and in the *Life of Moses* by Philo, works contemporary with the New Testament. More speculative is the existence of a midrash about the birth of the Messiah at Bethlehem based on Micah 4–5 and Genesis 35:19-21, said to underlie Matthew and Luke's infancy narratives.

The second definition means that the infancy narratives reflect a midrashic style, meaning that certain passages, such as the canticles, reflect a style of exegesis exemplified in midrash. In this case, Luke would have used Old Testament models (Abraham, Sarah, the parents of Samuel, Eli), scenes, and citations to portray his characters and enhance his setting. According to Brown, "the same kind of mind that would compose a midrash in order to make scripture understandable composed birth stories to make christological insight understandable. Sometimes the composition of a midrash . . . involved adding what the author thought were historical details; sometimes it was an exercise of creative imagination."[9] This type of composition, drawing images from the Old Testament or Jewish tradition, and weaving them together to dramatize the conception and birth of a Messiah who was God's Son, constitutes a theology in itself. Such composition, used to produce new christological insight, received legitimation when set against the background of the births of the patriarchs, Moses, and Samuel, and against the hopes of Isaiah, Micah, and Daniel.

Understanding Luke's midrashic style enables us to see how passages like the Magnificat, the Benedictus, and the Nunc Dimittis were created, the Magnificat based largely on the Song of Hannah in 1 Samuel 2:1-10, but all a mosaic of Old Testament texts. For Luke, the presence of characters in his Gospel shaped on Old Testament models showed the continuity between the old and the new. Because Jesus' birth was not part of the earliest known Christian proclamation, called the kerygma, Luke was uniquely free in his depiction of this material. In composing his infancy narrative, then, Luke had no newspaper accounts to follow, only stories handed down, Jewish scripture, and the Jewish interpretive technique called midrash.

---

8. The earliest extant Jewish works known as midrashim date from the second century CE. These rabbinic documents represent detailed and in many cases highly imaginative commentaries on Old Testament texts. Earlier examples, called pesharim, appear among the Dead Sea Scrolls and are attributed to Essene scribes working at Qumran.

9. Brown, *Birth of the Messiah*, 561.

Virginal Conception

From the outset, we need to clarify that when Christians speak of the Virgin Birth, they are not referring to the doctrine of the Immaculate Conception (a Roman Catholic dogma promulgated in 1854, which teaches that Mary, not Jesus, was born in a miraculous fashion, meaning that she was conceived without "original sin"). In addition, we must note that the doctrine of the Virgin Birth refers not to the birth of Jesus but rather to his conception. Hence, it is more accurate to use the phrase "virginal conception" rather than "virgin birth." What is at stake is not the manner of Jesus' birth or how he came forth from the womb, but the manner of his conception. In early Christianity there did develop a belief in virginal birth alongside virginal conception—a miraculous and painless birth in which the hymen was not ruptured—but that is not our concern here, nor is it Luke's concern. When the ancient Christian creeds refer to birth from the Virgin Mary, they couple this with his death under Pontius Pilate, both a way to counter the heresy that questioned the reality of Jesus' humanity. "Born of the Virgin Mary," then, underlies the historicity of Jesus, a much different question than the historicity of his conception without a human father.

It is clear that both Matthew and Luke refer to the virginal conception when they narrate the birth of Jesus, though we can confidently state that it was as peripheral to their account as to the New Testament in general. There are only two passages in Luke's Gospel that imply a virginal conception (1:34–35; 3:23), and in both places the belief is hinted at rather than stated. Apart from these verses, the story reads like an account of a normal human birth, miraculous only because through it God had chosen to act for the deliverance of humanity. Luke consistently refers to Joseph as Jesus' father, and it is through Joseph that Jesus is descended from David (1:27, 32; the earliest reference attributing Davidic ancestry to Jesus is Rom. 1:3).[10] While it is clear that Jesus' family was not of direct royal lineage or of ancestral nobility, it is possible that Joseph belonged to one of the non-aristocratic branches of the house of David.[11]

As we have seen, the infancy narratives in these Gospels belong to a rather late stage of composition, something confirmed by the rest of the New Testament, for the virginal conception was not part of the kerygma (the earliest apostolic tradition), nor is there any explicit reference to such teaching in the New Testament outside the infancy narrative. For Paul, who

---

10. Matthew's Gospel shows a particular interest in the title "son of David" for Jesus. John never uses it, and Mark and Luke use it only four times (Mark 10:47–48/Luke 18:38–39 and Mark 12:35–37/Luke 20:41–44).

11. Brown, *Birth of the Messiah*, 511.

undoubtedly believed in the divinity of Christ, the important fact was that, in entering life normally (Gal. 4:4), Jesus then acquired manhood with all it entailed (Rom. 8:3; Phil. 2:7).

While aspects of the birth of Jesus remain controversial literarily, historically, and scientifically, the stress in the birth narrative is less on the absence of a physical father and more on the power and activity of the Holy Spirit. As is well known, both Matthew and Luke make use of the prophecy of Isaiah 7:14, Matthew by direct quotation (1:23) and Luke by allusion (1:35). In its original Hebrew form this prophecy said nothing of a virgin birth, but in the Septuagint version, the Greek word *parthenos* (virgin) was used, incorrectly translating the Hebrew word *almah* (a young woman). Furthermore, it would never have occurred to a first-century Jew to consider Luke's reference to the overshadowing of Mary by the Holy Spirit (Luke 1:35) as a substitute for normal parenthood. According to Rabbinic Judaism, "There are three partners in the production of man: the Holy One, blessed be He, the father, and the mother."[12]

Our focus, like that of the entire New Testament, should be upon the incarnation—that God became human, that the Word became flesh, and that Christ humbled himself and took on the form of a human—rather than upon the issue of whether Jesus was born of a virgin. It is not human seed that brings Jesus into this world, but rather God becoming human; that is the important aspect.

The question at stake is, "Who is Jesus?" It is only when we see Jesus as God incarnate that we can understand why he came—to restore human beings back into right relationship with God. That is why the infancy accounts indicate that Jesus Christ came into the world in a manner different from that of other humans, because his death and resurrection would have an outcome different from all others. As seminarians learn in graduate school, who Christ is precedes what Christ accomplishes (christology precedes soteriology).

The Temple in Luke 1–2

As Israelites believed that God was eternally King and yet still prayed for the coming of his kingdom, so they believed in his presence and yet looked forward to his coming. For the first Christians, as for Jews in general, the temple was the symbol both of the presence of God and of the fuller presence they expected. One of the final prophecies to be added to the Hebrew scriptures promised that "the Lord whom you seek will suddenly come to

---

12. Niddah, 31a; cited in Caird, *Gospel of St. Luke*, 31.

his temple" (Mal. 3:1), and that before his coming Elijah would return to inaugurate a great repentance (Mal. 4:5–6). It was appropriate, then, that the temple should provide the setting for the opening of Luke's Gospel (1:9–23; 2:22–38, 46–50), as it does for its close: "And they were continually in the temple blessing God" (Luke 24:53). This fits in with Luke's picture of early Jewish Christians who worshipped in the temple daily (Acts 2:46; 3:1; 5:12).

Luke's infancy narrative contains numerous references to the temple. The annunciation of John, for example, including his birth, circumcision, and naming, are told against the backdrop of the temple, as are the circumcision, naming, and the presentation of Jesus. Luke can hardly have had a personal interest in the details of Jewish ceremonials, and it is therefore remarkable that he should mention no less than five times that the observances he mentions are carried out according to Jewish law. Jesus, we are to understand, was brought up in the strictest traditions of Jewish devotion. In the temple we meet Simeon and Anna; both were looking for the "consolation of Israel" (2:25; see 2:38), a standard rabbinic description of the messianic age, which has its origin in the opening words of Second Isaiah (Isaiah 40–55), and it is from these prophecies that a large part of Simeon's song, the Nunc Dimittis, is drawn.

The Mosaic Law provided three ceremonies to follow on the birth of a male child (Lev. 12; Exod. 13:12; Num. 18:16). The first was circumcision, which took place on the eighth day from birth, and was usually the occasion for the giving of the child's name. Then, in the case of the firstborn, there was the rite of redemption by the payment of a five-shekel offering; this could be done any time after the first month. Finally, after forty days, there was the purification of the mother, who until then was regarded as unclean and therefore disqualified from any form of public worship. The purification involved the sacrifice of a lamb and a turtledove or young pigeon, but the poor were allowed to substitute a second dove or pigeon for the lamb; Joseph and Mary made the poor family's offering. Luke appears to have confused the second and third ceremonies.

To the Jews a name was more than a label; it was closely related to the character and nature of the bearer. So pious parents would choose a name expressive of their own faith or of their hopes for their child. John is a shortened form of Jehohanan, which means "God's gracious gift," and the choice of this name could be understood as a grateful acknowledgment of the unexpected goodness of God in the gift of a son to aging parent. Jesus is the Greek equivalent of the Hebrew Joshua, which means "the Lord is salvation."

To illustrate the thirty years of growth that led to the baptism of Jesus, Luke records one incident. At the age of twelve a Jewish boy became bar mitzvah, a son of the Law, able to accept the responsibilities and obligations of an adult.[13] For Jesus this occasion was celebrated by a family visit to Jerusalem for the Passover. When the seven-day festival was over, his parents started for home along with other Galilean pilgrims, not realizing that Jesus was left behind. His parents returned to find him in the temple, described by Jesus as "my Father's house" (Luke 2:49). This reference indicates that the doctrine of divine fatherhood, long a tenet of Israel's faith, had become for him an intimate personal experience.

Luke's Gospel is more than the story of what Jesus did and taught; it is also the story of what Jesus experienced. He was, as the epistle to the Hebrews indicates, the "pioneer of our faith" (Heb. 12:2), blazing a trail for others to follow. It was his calling to explore to the fullest what it means to call God "Father."

Further clarity on this story comes from Luke's model for this unit, 1 Samuel 2. The boy Samuel was given to God by his mother Hannah, and in time he was taken to live in the tabernacle. It was in the place of worship that Samuel came to an awareness of his special mission. And of the boy Samuel, like the boy Jesus, it could be said that he "continued to grow both in stature and in favor with the Lord and with the people" (1 Sam. 2:26; see Luke 2:52).

As a historian, one of Luke's interests is to establish that Jesus was a true Israelite, from birth brought up in the moral and ritual life of Judaism. At every significant period of his life, he was in continuity with Judaism. Those periods for a male child included circumcision at eight days, dedication or presentation to God (in this case at six weeks, when his mother was purified), bar mitzvah at age twelve, and public life at age thirty (see 3:23). These are the moments Luke marks in Jesus' life.

---

13. The general Talmudic principle is that a child reaches manhood at the thirteenth birthday, though the age of twelve is another possibility, so we cannot be certain that Luke's story is about a bar mitzvah ceremony. Nothing in the story indicates that Luke thought of this experience as an obligation on Jesus' part. In the first century, Jewish teachers might have received youngsters in the temple during feasts to prepare them for their religious rite of passage to adulthood. Another, perhaps more plausible possibility for Luke's choice of this event is that he uses it to anticipate Jesus' future action as a teacher, not only in Galilee (see 4:15), but also in the temple, where he will teach every day when he is in Jerusalem (19:47; 21:37).

CHAPTER 9

Jesus' Galilean Ministry (Luke 3:1—9:50)

Assignment: Read chapter 9 of *Power Revealed* and chapters 3:1—9:50 of Luke's Gospel. Answer the following questions, writing the answers in your journal. [If you are in a study group, be prepared to share your views with others in the class.] (1) Which episode in Jesus' Galilean ministry (from his baptism to his transfiguration) do you consider to have influenced most profoundly Jesus' self-understanding and task? Explain your answer. (2) Is there a corresponding event in your life that you consider to have influenced most profoundly (a) your own identity and self-understanding and (b) your current understanding of the person and work of Jesus? Explain your answer.

Outline to Luke 3:1—9:50

   I. Preparation for Jesus' Public Ministry 3:1—4:13
       A. Historical Setting 3:1–2
       B. John the Baptist's Ministry 3:3–20
       C. The Baptism of Jesus 3:21–22
       D. The Genealogy of Jesus 3:23–38
       E. The Temptation of Jesus 4:1–13
   II. The Ministry in Galilee 4:14—9:50

A. Introduction to the Ministry in Galilee 4:14–15
B. Preaching in Nazareth 4:16–30
C. Teaching and Healing in Capernaum 4:31–44
D. Calling and Training Disciples 5:1—6:16
E. Instructing Disciples 6:17–49
F. The Identity of Jesus Disclosed 7:1—9:50
   1. Greater Than a Prophet 7:1–50
   2. Good News of the Kingdom 8:1–21
   3. Powerful Deeds of the Kingdom 8:22–56
   4. The Messiah and the Nature of Discipleship 9:1–50

Chapters 9–14 of *Power Revealed* follow a common format. Previous chapters exposed readers to technical language and issues of current scholarship. There is a good reason for this exposure, for those who assimilate contemporary biblical scholarship are less likely to reach spiritual dead ends, often caused by legalistic and literalistic approaches. Many destructive effects result when legalistic preachers and dogmatic teachers insist on one way to think and live. Even worse, much positive spiritual imagination is lost when we jump to the dogmatic level or freeze the text with literalism.

As you will discover, the material that follows is more homiletical and less technical in nature than that of chapters 1–8. Concentrating on the text of Luke–Acts, our focus will be on the flow of the narrative and on Luke's spiritual intent.

Preparation for Jesus' Public Ministry (Luke 3:1—4:13)

The Gospel of Luke is a gospel of world salvation. Writing in the Roman Empire, Luke is well aware how hard it is to believe that the truth about human destiny is to found in a member of a despised race, executed on a criminal charge at the order of a Roman governor in an outlying province of the empire. He finds a means to overcome this initial handicap by claiming that the events he is about to relate are part of world history. Like Paul before Festus, he wishes to tell his readers that these events did not occur "in a corner" but rather against a global backdrop.

By beginning with the ministry of John the Baptist, Luke is in line with the early preaching of the apostles (Acts 10:37) and with the other canonical Gospels.[1] John occupies this position partly because we need to know about him to understand the baptism of Jesus, but more particularly because the Gospel is not a biography of Jesus but the ongoing story of God's plan for humanity, in which John has his part to play. Following the parallel accounts of the annunciation and births of John and Jesus, Luke describes John's preaching and baptizing ministry. All the evangelists identify John's preparatory role for Jesus' ministry. While John's vision is one of imminent judgment, Luke sees John's role as the first scene in the divine drama of redemption, for only Luke completes the quotation from Isaiah with words that to him were a forecast of the world mission of the church: "all flesh shall see the salvation of God" (3:6).

Baptism was already in use among the Jews as part of a ceremony by which proselytes were incorporated into Israel, a rite that symbolized the cleansing of Gentile defilement. However, John gave baptism a new meaning and a new urgency. He required even Jews to submit to his baptism as an admission that through disbelief and unrighteousness they had forfeited their right be called Israel, the people of God. For John, the coming crisis would involve the overthrow of ancient wrongs, settling accounts on the basis of strict justice. Facing such a prospect, no one could claim preferential treatment on the basis of ancestry. As trees were judged not by their root, but by their fruit, so Jews would be held accountable for unjust behavior.

To each class John spelled out in simple terms the meaning of repentance. To ordinary, selfish folk, blind to the needs of others because of their preoccupation with security, to tax collectors who used unfair laws as a form of licensed extortion, to soldiers accustomed to line their pockets by intimidation and blackmail, John gave the same verdict. All had to recognize and renounce their besetting sin. John's task was to create a tide of messianic expectation, and then to make way for the Messiah. His baptism with water was but a prelude to another baptism, one "with the Holy Spirit and fire" (3:16). This dual baptism, a gracious gift for the penitent and the fire of judgment for the obstinate, prepares Luke's audience for the experience at Pentecost, when the Spirit would descend in tongues of flame (Acts 2:2).

---

1. John's Gospel inserts an early Judean ministry of Jesus, involving conflict with Pharisees, calling select disciples, attending a wedding at Cana in Galilee, return to Jerusalem to cleanse the temple, encounter with Nicodemus, and an encounter with a Samaritan woman. Only in John 4:43 does Jesus begin his Galilean ministry. The early church's kerygma (preaching) contained a succinct outline of Jesus' life, as witnessed in Peter's sermon to Cornelius and his household in Acts 10:34–43. That outline begins with the baptism by John, a ministry in Galilee and then in Jerusalem, culminating in Jesus' death and resurrection and in post-resurrection appearances to the apostles, whom he commissioned as witnesses to the good news.

Altering Mark's order of events, Luke then tells the story of John's imprisonment (3:19-20), not because it happened at this time (see Mark 6:14-29), but because he follows his customary pattern of rounding off one story before going on to the next (see, for example, Acts 11:29-30, where having mentioned Agabus's prophecy of famine, Luke goes on to tell how, some years later, in the reign of Claudius, the prophecy was fulfilled).

The topics of the baptism, genealogy, and testing of Jesus bring into focus the identity and vocation of Jesus as Messiah, Son of God. The baptism of Jesus raises an interesting question. If baptism is for forgiveness of sin, why was Jesus baptized, if, as the witness of the New Testament attests, Jesus was without sin (see John 8:46; Acts 3:14; 2 Cor. 5:21, Heb. 7:26, 1 Peter 1:19)? The story of his baptism, brief as it is, provides an answer. The voice Jesus hears from heaven contains a composite quotation from scripture (Ps. 2:7; Isa 42:1), the first from a royal or messianic psalm, and the second a reference to the servant of God, taken from the first of four servant songs that culminate in Isaiah 53, where the Servant is seen to suffer vicariously on behalf of others. At his baptism, then, Jesus receives direct confirmation of his status as Son of God, and the Spirit anoints him for the way of suffering that lies ahead. Then a genealogy ascribes honor to Jesus as "son of Adam, son of God." Finally, Jesus demonstrates, against demonic opposition, his resolve to accept his vocation as Messiah.

When Jesus goes to be baptized, it is not for private reasons, but as a means to fully identify with human beings in their movement toward God. If Jesus is to lead others into God's kingdom, he must enter by the only door open to them. He must be their representative before he can be their king. As God's Servant, he must be "numbered with the transgressors" (Isa. 53:12). The words from heaven are more than divine appointment; they are the divine approval of the course to which Jesus became committed in accepting baptism.

While Jesus receives baptism—presumably by John, though this is only implicit—what matters is not John's role but the tangible descent of God's Spirit upon Jesus. The setting—Jesus is praying; the heavens are opened; the voice—is part of a religious experience that characterizes Jesus' life with God. However, by adding that the Spirit descended in bodily form, Luke is informing us that though this is a private event, it was nonetheless objective. While Luke rarely mentions the role of the Spirit during the ministry of Jesus, a cluster of references at the outset (see 4:1, 14, 18) supplies the divine signature on Jesus' activity.

Following his baptism, Jesus, "full of the Holy Spirit" (4:1), is led by that Spirit into the wilderness, where for forty days he is tempted by the devil. For many modern readers the mention of the devil invests the story with an air of unreality. Granted that we might be in the realm of myth here, we should not confuse myth with legend or fairy tales. Myth is a literary way of expressing truths that cannot otherwise be expressed. Take the term "devil," or its adjectival form, "diabolical." These terms come from the Greek *dia balein*, meaning "to throw apart." Their Hebrew equivalent, "satan" or "satanic," meaning "antagonist" or "accuser, personalizes all false gods, all idolatrous allegiances, powers, and distortions that create a gap or distance between God and creation. There are at least five truths that are safeguarded by belief in a devil.

1. Evil is real and potent
2. Evil is personal
3. Evil is distorted good
4. Evil masquerades as good
5. Evil is an enemy

Having admitted the reality of evil, we wonder whether someone like Jesus, "full of the Holy Spirit," could experience testing like the rest of us. Was Jesus really tempted to sin? Was he capable of succumbing to evil? As with all profound theological questions, the answer is complicated. One thing is certain; if Jesus were able to sin, his testing would have been significantly greater than that of the weaker person who succumbs to its first onset. It seems unlikely that Jesus ever felt any temptation to do the things that are commonly regarded as immoral or antisocial. If so, how, then, was he tested?

If the nature and strength of one's temptation are in proportion to the goal of one's life, that would certainly hold true of Jesus. A person of dedicated spirit, called to liberate the oppressed and to establish God's reign of justice and peace, would be open to three types of temptation: to allow the good to replace the best; to seek God's ends by means alien to God's character; and to force God's hand by taking short cuts to success. And those are the three temptations of Jesus: to focus on his personal needs first; to put God to the test, rather than trusting God by faith; and to allow the ends to justify the means. Having discovered his messianic task in life, three factors would have been involved: what kind of messiah would he be (would he avoid personal suffering at all costs)? What strategy would he follow to accomplish his task (would he awe crowds with mighty works, using miracles to gain a following)? Would his warfare against evil involve compromise?

In his baptism and temptation, Jesus grappled with his identity, something that continued throughout his ministry. Acknowledging that Jesus was human, meaning that he was limited in knowledge and ability, is the only way to make sense of his temptation. According to Hebrews 4:15, Jesus was tested in every respect as we are, yet without sin. As Jesus was tested—economically (the need to be successful), politically (the need to be powerful), and spiritually (the need to be right)—so too are we, though certainly not in the same way and to the same extent. When used selfishly or for personal gain, success, power, and ideology can weaken and corrupt. However, when applied humbly and compassionately, they can be useful, even transformative.

The last verse of Luke 2, "Jesus increased in wisdom and in years, and in divine and human favor," is a good place to discuss the human consciousness of Jesus. Helping Jesus come to know his identity became the role of the Spirit in his life. For Jesus, his baptism was a breakthrough moment. However, it did not end his search or experience with identity. Throughout his life and ministry, it seems, Jesus' self-knowledge continued to grow.

When we approach the Gospels this way—with Jesus growing and developing in self-understanding—they become more real and alive. The stories become more identifiable and transferable to our own situation. Jesus becomes a real model and mentor of the process of faith itself instead of simply the object of our faith. We like to think that Jesus did not doubt, did not flinch, and did not ever question his identity. However, the greater message is that in his humanity Jesus did have doubts, did flinch, did ask questions—and yet remained faithful. That is what we discover in the temptation scenes. His faith was tested, and he responded, not by hurling divine thunderbolts but by quoting scripture (passages from Deuteronomy, finding a parallel to his own experience in the trials of Israel in the wilderness; Deut. 8:3; 6:13; 6:16), relating his own forty-day sojourn with the forty-year wilderness experiences of the Israelites. By placing himself under the authority of scripture, he placed himself under the authority of God. That was his role, to worship and to serve; to be, in fact, the Servant of the Lord.

When, in my classes on the New Testament, I cover the temptation narrative, I share with students the following quotation from biblical scholar N. T. Wright:

> Jesus did not . . . know that he was God in the same way that one knows one is male or female, hungry or thirsty, or that one ate an orange an hour ago. His "knowledge" was of a more risky, but perhaps more significant, sort: like knowing one is loved. One cannot "prove" it except by living by it. . . . As part of his human vocation, grasped in faith, sustained in prayer, tested in confrontation, agonized over in further prayer and doubt, and implemented in action, Jesus believed he had to do and be, for

Israel and the world, that which according to scripture only YHWH himself could do and be. He was Israel's Messiah; but there would, in the end, be "no king but God."[2]

As a comparison of Luke and Matthew's temptation narratives reveals, the order of the three temptations differs between the two accounts. Since Mark does not contain the actual temptations and because Matthew's order is deemed original, it seems likely that Luke changed the order found in his source. The commentaries vary greatly on Luke's motivation in placing last the temptation to jump from the temple wall, assuming the rationale to be spiritual or theological. That, however, is unlikely. The solution seems obvious when one ponders Luke's perspective. The focus of his historical paradigm was Jerusalem, as we have noted, and that is likely why he placed the temple setting last. For him, Jerusalem was the place of suffering and the goal of Jesus' ministry. It seems right to place this temptation last.

The Ministry in Galilee (Luke 4:14—9:50)

In this segment, Luke follows the structure of the Gospel of Mark, though he abbreviates the period of Jesus' ministry, knowing that he will expand the period of Jesus' journey to Jerusalem (9:51—19:27). Various passages are omitted, including Mark 6:1-6, the so-called "longer omission" at Luke 9:17, where Mark 6:45—8:26 is omitted, and the "shorter omission" at Luke 9:50, omitting Mark 9:41—10:21. The most notable addition to the Galilean ministry in Luke is the section 6:20—8:3, which includes the Sermon on the Plain.

Luke prepares the reader and creates anticipation by providing a summary statement at the outset (4:14-15). Luke is fond of summaries (see also 8:1-3; 11:53-54; 19:47-48; and 21:37-38), using them as transitions to what follows. The ministry in Galilee is introduced by Jesus' "inaugural address" in the synagogue at Nazareth (4:16-30). There he selects a reading from Isaiah 61:1-2, a passage about freedom and liberation, heralding the Jubilee Year, when all financial debts were to be forgiven (the Jubilee legislation, given in Leviticus 25, announces a program whereby every fiftieth year was to be a time when "you shall proclaim liberty throughout the land to all its inhabitants"; Lev. 25:10). This scene, functioning as a keynote of his entire ministry, sets forth the perspective from which Jesus' ministry is to be understood. "This," according to Jesus, "is what I stand for. This is my party platform!"

---

2. Wright, *Jesus and the Victory of God*, 653.

According to Luke, he is unwelcome by the citizens of Nazareth, the town of his birth, so he goes to Capernaum, another town in Galilee, using it as his home base.[3] The rest of chapter 4 amplifies the nature of Jesus' ministry: it is to be a healing and teaching ministry. His healing includes exorcisms and other encounters with mental, physical, emotional, and spiritual bondage. The interpreter must decide at what level to engage these accounts: literarily, scientifically, historically, or spiritually. When Jesus cures a leper (5:12–16), his reputation grows, and large crowds gather to hear him and be healed. Jesus preaching is constantly mixed with healing. Followers of Jesus need to be free, not only in mind and spirit but in body, memory, and emotion. That's the fullness of Jesus' gospel, the good news in his preaching, that God has come to free human beings at every level of their being.

To this point, Jesus has acted alone, unaccompanied by disciples. In 5:1—6:16 Jesus begins to call others to leave everything and join him in the work of God's kingdom. This section is framed by two scenes that feature the disciples: the call of Simon Peter and James and John, sons of Zebedee (5:1–11), and the appointment of the Twelve (6:12–16). Between these scenes Jesus heals a leper and a paralytic, calls Levi to follow him, and eats with tax collectors. Table fellowship seems to be the central symbolic action of Jesus. He is invariably eating with the wrong people. In Luke's Gospel there are ten such examples.

Jesus teaches by his life and not just by his words. He teaches, as the Hebrew prophets did, in what are called symbolic prophetic actions. Jesus is aware that symbols, actions, and images speak more powerfully than words. For him to sit at table with tax collectors is a powerful symbolic action that confronts the hypocritical religious system of his day. This is the meaning of the two two episodes concerning the sabbath: allowing his disciples to pluck grain on the sabbath and healing a man on the sabbath. Here we find Jesus' striking remark: "The Son of Man is lord of the sabbath" (6:5). Both Matthew and Luke omit Mark's pronouncement that the sabbath was made for humans and not humans for the sabbath (Mark 2:27).

Of all the Jewish institutions, the sabbath was the most important for the survival of Judaism in a predominantly Gentile world. Other requirements of the law could be performed—or omitted—in private, but the sabbath commandment obliged Jews to make a public profession of faith by abstaining from work. The rabbis had enumerated thirty-nine activities that were considered "work" within the intention of the sabbath law. Any threat

---

3. The reference to the synagogues of "Judea" in 4:44 should read "Galilee," a correction found in the manuscript tradition. However, as elsewhere in Luke, "Judea" is sometimes used as a synonym for the entire country, as in 1:15, where Herod is called king of Judea, though his rule included Galilee and Perea (see also Acts 10:37).

CHAPTER 9—JESUS' GALILEAN MINISTRY (LUKE 3:1—9:50)

to the sabbath was bound to evoke strenuous opposition, yet Jesus not only broke these regulations but often seems to have gone out of his way to break them. For Jesus, there was a higher principle underlying such regulations, the purpose for which this law was instituted, and thus he seized the initiative with his question in 6:9: "is it lawful to do good or to do harm on the sabbath, to save life or to destroy it?" The question needs no answer; it is always right to do good, and what better day than the sabbath could there be for doing the works of God?

What Jesus learned about sonship at his baptism (that whatever the Father is, the Son becomes), he proclaimed at his keynote address in Nazareth. In Luke 5–6 we learn that the core of Jesus' message is tied up with discipleship, another word for sonship and daughterhood. Disciples first must become as children, learning how to be taught, how to receive love, how to be loved, how to be taken care of, how to be believed in. Often disciples want to be parents, that is, they want power, they want to be in charge. What Jesus discovered in his baptism and temptation was how to step into his ministry as son, not as a father. Rather he lets the Father teach him. This means that Jesus says nothing that he hasn't first heard. What he teaches in his keynote address, he learned from the Father. He is, first, a faithful son; and out of that sonship experience comes the power to be the leader of his spiritual family on earth, the church.

Though Jesus took time out for meditation and prayer, he did not live apart. He lived with disciples, and those included women. Luke is quite clear about that (see 8:1–3). In Jesus' entourage, Luke lists the Twelve (6:12–16), but he also includes a large number of women who joined the apostolic band. Jesus lived a real-world lifestyle; that gave him authority to speak with understanding.

In chapter 5, Luke defines discipleship in the story of Peter. Discipleship is defined in terms of risk and trust. Peter is a veteran fisherman, so Jesus meets him by the sea, in his own environment, and helps him find in that familiar realm a sign of the transcendent. In effect, Peter says to Jesus, "This is my world; if you can turn my fishing world upside down, you are for real." And because Jesus was able to do that, Peter and his companions "left everything and followed him" (5:11). The miraculous catch of fish that precedes the call of Peter seems close to the account in John 21:1–23, which is a resurrection appearance narrative.

If "the Spirit of the Lord is upon me" in chapter 4 was Jesus' keynote address, the last half of chapter 6, often called the Sermon on the Plain, was his "State of the Union" address.[4] In this address, Jesus is not presenting

---

4. Rohr, *Luke*, 110–113.

more legalistic dos and don'ts; this is not a list of actions one must enact to enter God's kingdom. Rather, Jesus is describing for his disciples what it means to be a disciple. The sermon consists of five parts: (1) blessings and woes (6:20–26); (2) on love of enemies (6:27–36); (3) on judging (6:37–42); (4) on integrity (6:43–45); and (5) on hearing and doing (6:46–49). Whereas Matthew's setting is before a huge crowd, for Luke it is given primarily to the disciples, precisely because this is a description of discipleship (but see Luke 7:1, where the larger audience is included, perhaps as potential disciples).

It should be noted that at this point Luke departs from Mark's Gospel and inserts material not found in Mark. Hence Luke 6:20—8:3 has been called the "little interpolation." Luke's truncated version, drawn from Matthew's Sermon on the Mount and possibly other sources, eliminates material in Matthew concerning the relationship between Jesus and the Jewish law, matters that would have been of more interest to Jewish Christians than to Gentile Christians. Luke also sharpens the edge of Jesus' teachings on wealth and poverty by refusing to spiritualize Jesus' words and by adding the four woes (6:24-26). While the Sermon on the Mount extends over three chapters (109 verses), the Sermon on the Plain is packed into part of one chapter (30 verses). Despite the disparity in context, Luke's sequence agrees with that of Matthew, though some of the material omitted from Matthew's sermon is found elsewhere in Luke, but even there the material is often abbreviated. While respecting Matthew's sermon, Luke is free to shape the tradition of Jesus' teachings for his own purposes.

The theme of the next three chapters (7:1—9:50) is the identity of Jesus. Luke shows that Jesus continues the works of the prophets and fulfills their words. Yet, he is greater than the prophets. The theme is carried along by the interplay between recurring questions about Jesus' identity and repeated testimonies to him until finally Peter confesses Jesus to be the Messiah (9:18–20), which elicits further teaching on the meaning of discipleship (9:23–27). This section concludes with the voice from heaven declaring at the transfiguration, "This is my Son" (9:35).

The incidents in chapter 7 set forth themes that will be developed in the coming chapters. For example, the account of the centurion in 7:1–10, a Gentile who loves the Jewish nation and built a synagogue, foreshadows Cornelius, the first Gentile to be converted in Acts 10. After the pattern of Elisha (already previewed in 4:27), Jesus restores health in response to the request of a Gentile military officer. The point of the story is not the healing of the centurion's slave, but rather the extraordinary faith of this Gentile: "Not even in Israel," Jesus exclaims, "have I found such faith" (7:9). God's gracious favor comes to outsiders, even Gentiles, just as Jesus had said it would (4:25–27)—the first enactment of the prophecies voiced by Simeon (2:32) and John the Baptist (3:6). Although Jesus will direct his ensuing ministry to Jewish communities (with the exception of 8:26–39), the encounter with this remarkable Gentile soldier gives a preview of the direction the story will take in Acts.

After the pattern of Elijah (as previewed in 4:25–26), Jesus restores life to a widow's son (see 1 Kgs. 17:17–24; also Elisha in 2 Kgs. 4:32–37). In 7:18–23, John, the imprisoned prophet who was to "prepare the way" for Jesus, sends his own disciples with a question for Jesus: "Are you the one who is to come?" For confirmation of his identity and calling, Jesus points to his acts of healing, echoing Isaiah 35:4–6 with its images of the future restoration of the land. After the departure of John's messengers, Jesus evaluates the people's response to John and himself. They were right to esteem John as a prophet, yet he belongs to the time of preparation (7:28).

Two prominent themes—divergent responses to Jesus' ministry and role reversals—are spliced together in the next scene, a dinner set at a Pharisee's home. This is the first of three such occasions, each producing conflict between host and guest (see also 11:37–54 and 14:1–24). A woman of disreputable character enters the house uninvited and in a gesture of shocking intimacy bathes, kisses, and anoints Jesus' feet. The impropriety of the scene prompts the Pharisee (Simon) to doubt Jesus' status as prophet. Jesus reads Simon's mind and answers with a parable and a rebuke, defending the woman and honoring her at the host's expense. Other dinner guests are left with the question, "Who is this who even forgives sins?" (7:49).[5] Each unit in this chapter portrays Jesus as one greater than a prophet, either by comparison with the Old Testament prophets or with John the Baptist. The story of the Pharisee and a harlot is the culmination of this narrative sequence and is clearly related to what precedes.

At this point, the character of Jesus' ministry changes. On this Mark and Luke agree, though they disagree about the precise nature and cause of the change. According to Mark, it was the growing enmity of the leaders and the enthusiasm of the crowds that prompt Jesus to abandon the more settled ministry of the synagogue and to make the seashore his arena. Luke, even where he is following Mark, eliminates from his version much of the Markan atmosphere of mounting tension; instead, he implies that it was the inner necessity of his own missionary program that drove Jesus to visit smaller towns and villages (8:1).

---

5. There is no reason to confuse this nameless woman either with Mary Magdalene or with Mary of Bethany (see Mark 14:3–9/Matt. 26:6–13; John 12:1–8).

Chapter 8 employs the teaching device of the parable, a brief fictional narrative that illuminates some aspect of life or God's kingdom. Jesus has previously used this device (5:36–38; 7:41–42; see 6:39, 48–49), but beginning with 8:4–15, parables become increasingly prominent, including several in the travel narrative unique to Luke. Parables are not intended as information; they don't call for discussion, debate, or question. Rather, they challenge and call people to decision. Like koans or jokes, they lead to a punch line, one you either get or don't.

This need not mean, however, that all parables have only one meaning, or that the main point of a parable has only one interpretation. Viewing parables as literary art forms means that what a parable says is to a large degree determined by the listener or reader, just as a work of art means different things to different viewers. Of course there are boundaries to what a parable may mean, based on the immediate context of the parable within the Gospel, within Jesus' overall message, and within the community of faith to which the listener belongs. At times the interpretation is given by the biblical text itself.

The first parable in this unit, that of the sower and the seed (8:4–8), is allegorized, that is, its literary form is changed from a punch line to where every statement symbolizes something specif. The interpretation is given in 8:11–15. Most scholars take this interpretation to represent not so much an explanation by Jesus but rather the situation of the early church in its missionary preaching to a variety of conditions and audiences. In that setting, the parable informs early preachers and teachers that their work will not always be productive.

The parable of the sower is followed by the parable of the lamp. Both parables develop the theme of hearing and doing God's Word. The section opens and closes with references to groups who followed Jesus: the Twelve, a group of women, and his mother and brothers.[6] In the context of the foregoing, Jesus' pronouncement in 8:21 opens the way for all who hear and act on God's Word to be included in Jesus' family. Luke is telling us that Jesus has created a new definition of family that transcends bloodlines and marriage. As Hosea said, those who are no people, by receiving God's Word may become God's people (Hos. 2:23; see 1 Pet. 2:10).

The remainder of the chapter provides four miracle accounts, stories that show Jesus setting things free. First comes the calming of the storm

---

6. Mark tells us that Jesus had four brothers and an unspecified number of sisters (6:3). Those who believe in the perpetual virginity of Mary, about which nothing is said in the Bible, argue that they were children of Joseph by a previous marriage or cousins, though there is no justification for evading the plain meaning of the text, that they were younger children of Joseph and Mary. The present passage would lose its point if this were not so.

(8:22–25). The Jesus who can set hearts free to live in the truth can free nature to live in peace, because he controls even the winds and the sea. Rather than viewing this event as a demonstration of Jesus' power over nature, the calming of the storm is, like the story that immediately follows, an exorcism of evil from nature. The language used in 8:24, "he . . . rebuked the wind and the raging waves" is the customary language of an exorcism. From ancient times, and even in some cultures today, large bodies of water are believed to be the abode of evil spirits, said to stir up storms against sailors. Jesus' word of rebuke here is a direct command to evil itself.[7] In the story of the Gerasene demoniac (8:26–39), Jesus also demonstrates power over evil. In the cure of the woman with the hemorrhage (8:43–48), Jesus cures what medicine cannot; in the raising of the daughter of Jairus (8:40–42, 49–56), Jesus displays power over death and sets the child free to live again.

In 9:1–6, Jesus gives these powers to the Twelve, sending them forth to overcome evil, heal, and preach the gospel of the kingdom. This is the first of four scenes in which the disciples are commissioned in Luke: (1) sending the Twelve to preach and heal (9:1–6); (2) sending the seventy in pairs (10:1–11); (3) Jesus' preparation of the apostles for their post-Easter mission (22:35–38); and (4) the commissioning of the eleven and the others at the end of the Gospel (24:48–49). A further commissioning follows in Acts 1:6–8.

In Luke 9 the themes and issues developed in the previous two chapters reach a climax. When reports of Jesus' work reach Herod, he asks, "Who is this about whom I hear such things?" (9:9). This section of Luke provides an answer to Herod's question. Jesus is "the Messiah of God" (9:20), but he is also the Son of Man who will be rejected and killed by the religious authorities. As we learn from Jesus' life, discipleship requires a total commitment of one's life. Jesus identity and role as the Messiah are confirmed and clarified by the events that follow Peter's confession. Here Luke mentions the first passion prediction (9:22), though he omits Jesus' rebuke to Peter following that prediction (see Mark 8:32–33). The five sayings on discipleship (9:23–27) that follow the first passion prediction also serve as an answer to Herod's question regarding Jesus' identity. Lordship and discipleship are always related. Surprisingly, the five discipleship sayings are addressed to "all"—both the disciples and the crowd (see Mark 8:34)—thereby extending the invitation to discipleship to all people.

The feeding of the five thousand in 9:10–17 (a variant of this miracle is told in each canonical Gospel, making it the only miracle shared by all four evangelists) is reminiscent of the great Banquet, the coronation feast of

---

7. Craddock, *Luke*, 115.

God symbolic of the messianic age (see Isa. 25:6-8). In his preaching Jesus made frequent use of this symbol, to denote either the presence of the kingdom with its rich invitation (5:34; 6:21; 14:16-24) or its ultimate, heavenly fulfillment (13:29-30; 22:15-18). The Last Supper was, as we shall see, a dramatic anticipation of the heavenly feast. As the story stands, the feeding of the five thousand it is a miracle story, but it is noteworthy that in none of the six versions found in the four Gospels is it said that Jesus multiplied the loaves; the miracle enters the story only with the twelve baskets of broken pieces. We must allow for the possibility that oral tradition has turned into miracle what might originally have been an act of prophetic symbolism to the church and to the world. The feeding highlights Jesus' compassion and especially his concern for the poor and hungry. In addition, the church find in this event a model for ministry: Jesus working through his disciples. Echoing the feeding of the Israelites in the wilderness during the Mosaic period (see Exod. 16; "a deserted place" in Luke 9:12 is literally "a wilderness place"), the account also reflects the works of Elisha, particularly the feeding of the multitude as narrated in 2 Kings 4:42-44.

At the transfiguration, the voice from heaven declares, "This is my Son, my Chosen; listen to him!" (9:35). Luke provides a clue to the nature of the episode when he tells us that Moses and Elijah appeared to prophecy of Jesus' "departure," which he was to accomplish at Jerusalem. In typical fashion, the insertion of the word "Jerusalem" in 9:31 is uniquely Lukan. The fact that Jesus took with him three disciples, the same three who would later accompany him into Gethsemane, affirms that "departure" means death by crucifixion. The following day, after casting the demon out of the epileptic boy, Jesus foretells his own death a second time (9:44).

The episode of the transfiguration, coming after Jesus' announcement of the passion and immediately after Jesus' sayings on discipleship, serves as a correction about his identity. Because Luke is writing with hindsight, he wishes to give his readers a glimpse of Jesus' "glory" (9:32); the mention of "glory" is found in no other account of the transfiguration. Given the connotation of "glory" in the New Testament as the status of the risen Christ, it is not hard to imagine that Luke did not intend some connection between this episode and the risen status of Jesus (see also Luke's use of "glory" in 24:26; also 2 Peter 1:16-18).

The disciples do not understand, however, that discipleship, like messiahship, entails suffering, because they debate among themselves as to which of them is the greatest. Jesus answers insightfully from the depth of self understanding he received, beginning at his baptism: "the least among all of you is the greatest" (9:48).

CHAPTER 10

Luke's Travel Narrative (Luke 9:51—19:27)

Assignment: Read chapter 10 of *Power Revealed* and chapters 9:51—18:30 of Luke's Gospel. Answer the following questions, writing the answers in your journal. [If you are in a study group, be prepared to share your views with others in the class.] (1) Of the many teachings given by Jesus during his "journey to Jerusalem," which speak most relevantly to your current situation? Explain your answer. (2) Of these teachings, which do you consider most relevant to everyone's life, regardless of circumstances? Explain your answer.

Outline to Luke 9:51—19:27

I. Jesus' Journey to Jerusalem 9:51—19:27
    A. Discipleship: Hearing and Doing the Word 9:51—10:24
    B. The Love of God and Neighbor 10:25-42
    C. Instruction on Prayer 11:1-13
    D. Jesus Answers Critics 11:14-54
    E. Readiness for the Coming Judgment 12:1—13:9
    F. Lessons on the Kingdom 13:10—17:10
        1. Reversals Brought by the Kingdom 13:10-35

2. Kingdom Etiquette 14:1-24

   3. Conditions for Discipleship 14:25-35

   4. Parables of Recovery and Return 15:1-32

   5. Lovers of Money 16:1-31

   6. Forgiveness and Faith 17:1-10

  A. Responding to the Kingdom 17:11—19:27

   1. Ten Lepers Healed 17:11-19

   2. The Coming of the Kingdom 17:20-37

   3. Jesus' Gospel to the Rich and Poor 18:1—19:27

Luke 9:51—18:14 is often called Luke's travel narrative, for in 18:15 Luke rejoins Mark and Matthew's pattern. While a small portion of the travel narrative is also in Mark, much has a common source with Matthew, with a substantial amount peculiar to Luke. The material is arranged as a journey, with Luke on occasion reminding readers of that perspective (5:51; 13:22; 17:11), since the stories in themselves do not usually imply a journey. Some scholars hold that Luke follows the narrative of Deuteronomy, and much does fit that pattern, though not all. For example, some Elijah and Elisha echoes from 1 and 2 Kings are also apparent. Geographical references do not really help one reconstruct the journey, since Luke's travel narrative is more theological than geographical. Jesus moves now toward suffering; to follow him is to face the same.

That Luke found the travel motif helpful for telling the story of Jesus parallels his telling of the story of the church in Acts, which is occupied not only with the expansion of the gospel to Rome, but also with the missionary journeys of Paul, culminating in his lengthy travels to Jerusalem and to Rome. Just as Jesus viewed his going to Jerusalem as the will of God (Luke 9:22, 31), so Paul felt compelled to visit Rome (Acts 19:21), and as for Jerusalem, "I am ready not only to be bound but even to die in Jerusalem for the name of the Lord Jesus" (Acts 21:13).

In Luke's Gospel, Jesus is said to be focused on Jerusalem. This is an issue we raised earlier, but it is an important one, with at least two answers. In the first place, it is the city of Jesus' destiny. However, it is also the symbolic center of God's global action, a microcosm of what God is doing on earth. Ironically, Jerusalem remains a microcosm of the world today, both as home and object of hope to the three great monotheistic religions of the world, but also as a symbol of rivalry, bigotry, and hatred between cultures, races, and religious denominations. Pilgrims and visitors still travel to Jerusalem, as I

CHAPTER 10—LUKE'S TRAVEL NARRATIVE (LUKE 9:51—19:27)   151

have done on several occasions, but it continues to be an unpleasant place to visit and live, a place of paradox and contradiction. As Franciscan scholar Richard Rohr notes, the ancient stones "seem to hold a kind of negative energy in the very place we call the Holy Land."[1]

These ten chapters of Luke consist chiefly of teaching material, but Luke attempts to create a narrative framework by casting the whole section in the form of a journey toward Jerusalem. The result is artificial and full of topographical inconsistences. For example, Jesus starts out from Galilee by the short route through Samaria, but arrives by the longer route through Jericho; and in between he is first in Bethany, a few miles from Jerusalem, and later on at the borders of Samaria and Galilee (10:38; 17:11). In addition, the teaching material, while wide-ranging, frequently seems to lack focus. Readers seeking explanation on every saying or episode are encouraged to consult one or more of the commentaries on Luke listed in the bibliography. While commenting on numerous passages, our focus in this chapter will be twofold: discipleship and the nature of God's kingdom—or what it means to be "kingdom people," the people of God (divine royalty) doing God's work on earth.

In 9:51—19:27 we discover anew the close connection between christology and discipleship. If the first part of Luke (chapters 1–2) introduces Jesus as a royal messiah from the house of David, and the second part (chapters 3–9) narrates Jesus' journey from baptism to transfiguration,[2] focusing on his self-understanding as the Son of God,[3] the third part (chapters 10–19) focuses on the identity and task of disciples as "kingdom people." The fourth and final unit of Luke provides Jesus' final teachings to his disciples, preparing them through word and deed for his death and the path beyond. The death, resurrection, and ascension of Jesus function as an interlude to the next episode in Luke's story, the birth and expansion of the church, when the disciples, led by God's Spirit, become leaders in their own right.

Two personal stories illustrate my perspective. Upon graduating from the Stony Brook School, a college preparatory school on Long Island, New York, I received a gift from one of my favorite teachers. The gift was a book titled *A Leader Led*, a study guide on 1 Timothy. I have always treasured that book, not only because I received it from Thomas Little, the religion professor with whom five students and I traveled across the United States the summer after my Junior year, but because the title suggests my identity

---

1. Rohr, *Luke*, 133.

2. In both episodes, a voice from heaven declares Jesus to be "my Son" (3:22; 9:35).

3. Note how Luke's temptation narrative is book-ended by the question, "If you are the Son of God"; see 4:3, 9.

as leader and my vocation as disciple of Jesus. That's what I see going on in Luke's travel narrative: the training of "kingdom people" as future leaders.

The second story is about Robert Cook, president of The King's College, my alma mater. Dr. Cook, a Christian author, radio broadcaster, and pastor, was associated with Youth for Christ before coming to King's. He often invited me to travel with him on speaking engagements, where I was encouraged to share my testimony. When we traveled, we often prayed, and I peeked on occasion to make sure Dr. Cook's eyes were open as he drove. Like Jesus with his disciples, he taught me through word and deed. Though he died in 1991, his broadcasts are still available on YouTube. The title of his books and programs, "Walk with the King Today," was striking and practical, its premise being that as children of God, you and I are nobility in training, raised at the feet of Jesus and walking daily with the King, the Lord of lords. As we read Luke's travel narrative, let us accompany Jesus as disciples, siblings, and friends—as leaders led.

In its entirety, the story narrated in Luke–Acts is the account of how humans become children of God. The Gospel of Luke focuses on sonship and daughterhood, affirming how men and women, equally yet distinctly, become children of God, beginning with Jesus. If Luke's travel narrative chronicles the adolescence of Jesus' disciples—their coming-of-age—the book of Acts speaks of their emerging adulthood.

Walking with the King in the Heavenly Kingdom (Luke 9:51—13:9)

When Jesus set his face toward Jerusalem, he sent messengers ahead of him, to prepare the way in Samaria. The long-standing feud between Jews and Samaritans flares up again in this section, as does the Elijah theme. In 9:53–54 we find the disciples James and John trying to emulate Elijah, who felt the best way to deal with the enemies of Israel was to call down God's curse upon them. James and John had a lot to learn about discipleship. Intoxicated with limited authority and influence, they saw only one way to solve problems—by force. This is why Elijah's methodology gives way to that of Jesus, with his new way of loving enemies and dying for them.

As Jesus heads toward Jerusalem, he encounters three people with excuses that keep them from the spiritual path (9:57–62). Their reasons are all valid: (1) the necessity of home; (2) duties to aged parents; and (3) relationships with family. The three candidates for discipleship are warned to count the cost. Jesus makes some hard remarks here, but the fact that Luke brings up this issue shows that he is telling his community that the call of God's kingdom (God's rule) is absolute. It is the only thing that matters because it is the only thing that lasts. Jesus obviously isn't telling people to avoid family duties or family funerals, but instead is encouraging them to find ways to be responsible through a transformed consciousness. Family life is divinely appointed, but under certain conditions Jesus' followers must be prepared to sacrifice security, duty, and affection if they are to respond to the call of God's kingdom, a call that makes other loyalties pale by comparison (see Luke 14:26/Mt. 10:37; also Luke 11:23). The point is not to be stymied by life's problems and dilemmas but to keep moving forward, making a difference through one's presence. That's how one grows spiritually, by being attuned to God's Spirit, hearing and obeying God's marching orders. The most difficult choices in life are not between the good and the evil, but between the good and the best.

In addition to the mission of the Twelve (Luke 9:1–6), Luke also presents a mission of the seventy (or seventy-two). This number is believed to come from the list of nations in Genesis 10 (seventy in the Hebrew text, seventy-two in the Greek text). The sending of the seventy is recorded by Luke alone, and it raises some difficult questions, because the same material is placed by Matthew in his charge to the Twelve (Matt. 9:37–38; 10:7–16, 40). Whether the mission is fact or fiction, the number is certainly symbolic. By invoking the number seventy, Luke may be alluding to Moses, who shared the burden of his work with his seventy assistants (see Exod. 24:1, 9; also 18:21–23). Even though their commission, like that of the Twelve, was to the house of Israel, Luke is clearly anticipating the mission to the Gentiles begun at Pentecost (see Acts 2:5).

The missionaries are sent forth in pairs, and for good reason. Gospel work—kingdom work, church work—is not solo activity. The gospel of love cannot be communicated by one person because, in the end, love is something that happens between two. If only one disciple is sent, that ministry would likely be verbal. In the Bible, the gospel spreads between two or more people. That's why group Bible study is so important. God places us in corporate contexts because unless one is in right relationship with at least one other person on this earth, expansion is not possible. Eastern Orthodox know that intuitively, as do Mormon missionaries, who always travel in pairs. In Orthodoxy, no one is saved individually; rather Christians are saved together.

Other aspects of this mission deserve attention. For instance, when Jesus instructs the missionaries in 10:4 not to greet people on the road, he is not saying they should be unfriendly; Rather he is telling them to have a focused purpose, to be intentional about their activity. Their mission is an urgent one because they are harvesters: Israel is ripe for the harvest and must be gathered into the kingdom while the brief season lasts. The focus of their mission is the immanence and nearness of the kingdom (10:9, 11). This does not mean that the arrival of the kingdom is in the future, about which people must be warned during the interval that remains. For Luke the kingdom is present, and that presence is to be proclaimed by word of mouth but also actively demonstrated through deeds of love, compassion, and power. Whether we like it or not, whether we believe it or not, God's kingdom is inexorably present, a reign of peace to those who accept it and a sentence of doom to those who do not. The time is short because the opposition is gathering its forces, so that even now the disciples go out "like lambs into the midst of wolves" (10:3).

The pronouncement of Jesus is against entire towns and cities (10:13-15), which implies that he is looking for corporate rather than individual response to the gospel message. He has come to recall Israel to her true vocation as the holy people of God, and the cities of Israel must choose between self-denying service and defiant nationalism. Repeatedly in the succeeding chapters we shall find Jesus warning Israel that to reject him is to choose disaster on that day when God's transcendent judgment takes historical form.

The passage concerning the return of the seventy (10:17-22) contains a succinct summary of much of Jesus' teaching. It provides the occasion for an inspired statement by Jesus: "Blessed are the eyes that see what you see! For I tell you that many prophets and kings desired to see what you see, but did not see it, and to hear what you hear, but did not hear it" (10:23-24).

The following passage (10:25-37), occasioned by the lawyer's question in 10:29, "And who is my neighbor?" contains the well-known parable of the Good Samaritan. Providing further clarification of the meaning of discipleship, the conversation between Jesus and the lawyer illustrates the difference between the ethics of law and the ethics of love. To the lawyer eternal life is a prize to be won by meticulous observance of religious rules, whereas for Jesus, love of God and love of neighbor is in itself the life of the heavenly kingdom, already begun on earth. Whereas the rabbis believed keeping the law of Moses in its entirety, with its 613 commandments, was the way of showing love to God, Jesus was convinced that loving God meant devotion to God's purpose of compassion and grace. The story of the Good Samaritan tells us that the question, "Who is my neighbor?" is the wrong question. The proper question is, "To whom can I be a neighbor"; and the answer is, "To anyone who needs my help." Importantly, Jesus chose an outsider, a Samaritan outside the Jewish system, to be the true neighbor. In this amazingly anticlerical story, Jesus focuses on the basics—pity, care, compassion—and does not get sidetracked by divisive peripheral issues such as religious membership or religious orthodoxy.

Scholars are now labelling the parable of the Good Samaritan an "example story" rather than a parable, since it appears only in Luke, and only Luke contains example stories (10:30–37; 12:16–21; 16:19–31; 18:10–14). Despite Luke's editorializing, this story likely goes back to Jesus, who intended it not as an example of "proper" behavior but as a portrayal of how the inbreaking of the kingdom transforms people and reorders their thinking. The focal point of the story cannot be the Samaritan's good deed of kindness or compassion, since the Samaritan exceeds all bounds, "not merely ethnic bounds, but even the suggested bounds in the Old Testament of what compassion would look like."[4] What we have here is an ethnic reversal, used to challenge current attitudes regarding ritual standards. The notion of a "good Samaritan" was a contradiction in terms for a traditional Jew, but such reversal is typical of Jesus the sage, "who seems to specialize in oxymorons like good leaven, light burdens, and here a good Samaritan."[5]

The Martha and Mary story (10:38–42), a uniquely Lukan passage, often leads to misunderstanding because we focus on the wrong person, in this case on Mary. As the opening line makes clear, this is Martha's story, not Mary's. As hostess, Martha is the central figure, the stronger character. She is full of good works and entirely free from selfishness. However, she earns a gentle reproof from Jesus because good works and even sacrifice can be spoiled by self-concern and self-pity. Jesus is not contrasting prayer and activism and putting primacy on a life of contemplation. Rather he is saying that the one prerequisite for being a follower of Jesus is listening to God's word. Listening is the better part. Martha is trying to get Jesus to reinforce her cultural understanding of women's roles, and Jesus refuses to do so while still affirming Martha warmly. Both virtues combined—good works and contemplation—represent the ideal. Good works alone can become misery to the doer and tyranny to others.

A comparison of Luke's version of the Lord's Prayer with Matthew's shows the former to be shorter but in some points more original than the latter. Luke's version, however, contains the essentials concerning the nature of discipleship and of the kingdom. Any Jew could have prayed, "Our Father," using the formal and exclusively religious term *Abinu*, but when Jesus prayed, he used the word *Abba*, the word a child used when addressing a human father. Jesus' term for God turned a theological doctrine into an intense and personal experience; he taught his disciples to pray directly,

---

4. Witherington, *Jesus the Sage*, 195.
5. Ibid, 194.

with intimacy. Such a way of addressing God was revolutionary, a uniquely new contribution of Jesus.

The second petition of the prayer calls for the coming of the kingdom. Jesus was telling his followers that God's kingdom comes into this world by our invitation. Only as we say, "Your kingdom come," does God's power invade this world. Some manuscripts contain the Matthean phrase, "Your will be done, on earth as in heaven." This concept is significant, for the prayer recognizes that the characteristics of the heavenly kingdom—communion, unity, family—represent God's nature and will. God's will is not centered on crafting new legalistic requirements but on creating unity. That's why Jesus' basic rules for the kingdom are about forgiveness, reconciliation, healing, and communication. Those capable of union and communion are open to God, those incapable of communion are not open to God because they cannot share life, they cannot give and receive life or love.

A paraphrase for the next phrase might be, "Give us each day our manna from heaven, as you fed our ancestors in the desert." In 11:3 Luke is connecting his Christian audience with the Jewish heritage, and teaching trust. Earlier, during their wilderness sojourn, the Hebrew people gathered manna each day, and were supposed to gather only enough for that day. If they tried to horde or store it for the future, it rotted (Exod. 16:11–35). That's the significance of "daily" bread. We are to live one day at a time, trusting God in the moment.

The next phrase provides a good definition of the word "Christian," namely, "those who forgive sinners." As Jesus indicates, forgiveness and being forgiven are two sides of one coin. The final petition, "do not bring us into temptation," is an admission of weakness before God. Therefore Luke continues Jesus' teaching on prayer with passages that encourage patience, perseverance, and asking for the Holy Spirit (11:13), who not only teaches us how to pray but actually is the one praying when we pray (see Rom. 8:26–27). Discipleship, for Luke, is about being in union with God, listening to God, spending time with God, and letting go of the need to control. If the world defines us on the level of doing and having, God defines us on the level of being. Prayer, too, happens on the level of "being," not on a "having" or "doing" level.

Later in chapter 11 Jesus indicates that there are two spiritual kingdoms in this world, the kingdom of God and the kingdom of Satan. As goodness is personified and personalized, so is evil. This is an undeniable teaching of scripture. The two kingdoms confront one another in a war that knows neither truce nor neutrality; he who does not side with Jesus sides with Satan, and the only power capable of breaking the grip of Satan is the "finger of God" (11:20; see Exod. 8:19).

In 11:29–32, Jesus brilliantly illustrates his message of the kingdom by what appears to be a central metaphor of his teaching, the "sign" of Jonah. The explanation followed in Luke's version is quite different from the one in Matthew 12:40. Those who asked for a sign wanted some spectacular proof that Jesus was the representative of God he claimed to be. He replied that the only proof of his credentials he was prepared to give was that which Jonah offered to the Ninevites; the call to repentance (11:32), through which they recognized the authentic demand of God. However, in light of the full gospel message, Matthew's explanation seems more adequate. The sign of Jonah, the only sign that Jesus ultimately gives, is that revealed in the Eucharistic meal: "Christ has died, Christ is risen, Christ will come again." Without the sign of Jonah—the pattern of new life only through death—Christianity remains largely impotent, another way to "win" and avoid the pain of faith. Alternatively, it becomes a language of ascent instead of the treacherous journey of descent that characterizes Jonah, Jeremiah, Job, John the Baptist, and Jesus. Jesus' way, as he himself characterized the journey of discipleship, is "the way of the cross" (see 9:23–27). Those who miss the sign of Jonah miss the Christian message.

The Jonah-Job-Jesus pattern of spirituality has been hard for Westerners to recognize and accept. There was also a cultural resistance to it in the Greco-Roman world, where successful devotees were seen as always ascending and continually making progress. The sign of Jonah is at the heart of the matter and, not surprisingly, leads to a short teaching by Jesus on darkness and light (11:33–36). Chapter 11 ends with a condemnation of legalism, which is what always recurs when people fail to follow the sign of Jonah. Opposition to Jesus increases in 11:47–54, for those preoccupied with "orthodoxy" find Jesus' view of discipleship hard to comprehend.

Whereas chapter 11 ends with a diatribe against the scribes and Pharisees, chapter 12 begins by making them an object lesson for the disciples. The entire case against them can be summed up in one word: hypocrisy. While Jesus nowhere said that all Pharisees were hypocrites, nor that all hypocrites were Pharisees, he found more hypocrisy among them than in any other group, and regarded hypocrisy as the natural product of their teaching. Hypocrites are those who sacrifice truth to appearance, who are more taken up with what people think than with their internal spiritual condition. They are so busy living up to their reputation that they have no time to be themselves; they are always justifying themselves to others, to themselves, or to God. The opposite of hypocrisy is repentance, which means accepting the truth about oneself, facing oneself as one really is. To one who has no reverence of God, no appreciation of God's grace and mercy, the presence of God could hardly be other than a consuming fire—and what is that but to be cast into hell? (see 12:5). Every person, then, must be loyal to the truth as it has come to him or her, and for the disciples the truth is embodied in Jesus. The "unpardonable sin," of which Jesus speaks in 12:10, also described as blasphemy against the Holy Spirit, is to treat as false that which one knows to be true. It is unpardonable, not because God is unwilling to pardon, but because an inner dishonesty makes a person incapable of that honest appraisal we call repentance.

In 12:13 Luke tells of two men arguing about property and money, regular themes in Luke's Gospel. Jesus refuses to arbitrate, and responds, in effect, by telling a story. Have you noticed how storytelling seems to be a common approach on the part of Jesus? Why stories? Because they represent creative and healing power. Stories don't avoid questions, they go to the root of a question. Stories are how the great masters of religion have always taught. They do so because telling stories gives the soul room to grow and understand—and rather than ending conversation, they keep dialogue going.

Refusing to answer endless questions and to participate in ongoing controversies, Jesus often tells a story, frequently a parable of the kingdom. Sometimes he answers a question with a question. Perhaps I can do that now. If you knew the world was going to end one month from today, what would you do right now? What would really matter to you? Would you spend the final weeks of your life concerned about success, fame, or status, or would you instead tell as many people as you could one or all of three things: "I'm sorry; I love you; I forgive you"? That's what it means to live as a kingdom person: to live now what matters forever. Jesus' answer to the questions and controversies of all our journeys to Jerusalem is this: Live now what matters in eternity; live on earth what's happening in heaven.

"Stop working for the kingdom," Jesus tells us. "You already have the kingdom. Stop trying to achieve; it is already yours. Stop trying to get saved; you are saved already. Insofar as you accept the kingdom each moment, insofar as you let it invade your reality, you will experience it." That's why the call is to faith—to trust. Such faith is the opposite of anxiety. We have God's approval; we are God's children. God loves us—unconditionally! At this point comes the call to be awake (12:35–48), to live life in the present. Jesus is not calling us to be afraid of God or warning us about God. Rather he is asking us to live fully in the moment. In Catherine of Sienna's words, "It's heaven all the way to heaven, and hell all the way to hell."

The Presence of the Kingdom in Luke's Gospel (Luke 13:10—19:27)

The dominant theme in the preaching of Jesus—indeed the center of his mission and message—is the coming of the kingdom of God. Luke speaks of the kingdom twenty-eight times in his Gospel, but he leaves the concept open and undefined. While the phrase "kingdom of God" is rare in contemporary Jewish writings, it is widely regarded as one of the most distinctive aspects of the preaching of Jesus. Because almost everywhere in the Old Testament the idea of the kingdom is related to the people of Israel and the rule of the house of David in Jerusalem, Jesus is at pains to divest his teaching of this former understanding of the nature of the kingdom. What Jesus proclaims is the immediate sovereignty of God, who will take control of the destinies of all humans, restore humanity to what God had intended it to be, and overthrow the evil powers that had led astray human beings from their proper destiny.

In Mark's Gospel, Jesus' first act upon returning from his sojourn in the wilderness is to proclaim the coming of the kingdom (Mark 1:15; see also Matt. 4:17). There Jesus is picking up where Second Isaiah left off half a millennium earlier. Isaiah had envisioned a day when God would finally bring justice to the world, when the long-suffering faithful could rejoice at the end of oppression. Jesus shared Isaiah's anticipation but was more specific about when this time would come: "Truly I tell you, there are some standing here who will not taste death until they see that the kingdom of God" (Luke 9:27).

Whatever Jesus envisioned in his proclamation about the kingdom, it was going to be on earth. Despite Matthew's preference for the expression, "kingdom of heaven," it is clear that the concept, as Jesus used it, refers to the destiny of people on a new, improved earth. It has nothing to do with the souls of dead people ascending to heaven.

In New Testament teaching the coming of the kingdom is always dependent on divine initiative, never on human achievement. Humans may enter the kingdom; they may proclaim it and inherit it (Matt. 25:34; 7:21), but they can neither earn it nor bring it forth. Because the word "kingdom" in the Gospels suggests a geographical region or realm, which is misleading in this context, scholars prefer the term "kingship" or "kingly rule of God."

The term "kingdom" is complex and paradoxical at its core. In the Synoptic Gospels, the paradoxical nature of the kingdom is manifested in several ways: (a) it is present (Luke 17:21), yet not fully present (Matt. 8:29; 13:30); (b) it is a gift (Luke 12:32), yet it also involves human effort (Luke 12:31); (c) it is an internal reality (Luke 17:20–21), yet it has external implications for the world (Matt. 6:10). Scholars are particularly interested in the first of these, for it addresses the tension between the present time and the future, the "already" and the "not yet." In that regard, they have introduced the term "inaugurated eschatology" to refer to the relation of the present inauguration and the future fulfillment of the kingdom.

There is a present element in the New Testament concept of the kingdom, particularly in the teaching of Jesus, which is colored by a sense of intense urgency. God has already taken the initiative; humans are challenged to recognize the reality of the present situation and to make such decisions as will qualify them to become citizens of the kingdom. The signs of the presence of the kingdom are already present in the ministry of Jesus. When John the Baptist questions the mission of Jesus and asks for signs, he is given clear evidence: "the blind receive their sight, the lame walk, the lepers are cleansed, the deaf hear, the dead are raised, and the poor have good news brought to them" (Luke 7:22). All these are signs that the power of the kingdom is presently at work. Those who refuse to recognize that the power evident in Jesus is a power from God are told: "if it is by the finger of God that I cast out the demons, then the kingdom of God has come to you" (Luke 11:20). When one person, for a period of some thirty-five years, lives in total dependence upon God, with a unique understanding of God's will and in unconditional surrender to it, the kingdom is already present. As Jesus tells the Pharisees in answer to their question about when the kingdom was coming: "the kingdom of God is among you" (Luke 17:21).

According to the New Testament, Christians are kind of hybrid creatures who live in two dimensions. They are citizens of the present age while at the same time living under the dominion of Christ's kingdom. As Paul put it somewhat paradoxically, they live "in the flesh" (human nature) and also "in the Spirit" (the new dimension introduced by Christ). Awareness of this dual citizenship led early Christians to say that they were "strangers" in the historical era on earth (Heb. 11:13). Ever since the New Testament period, Christianity has had to steer between two dangers. On the one hand, Christians have been tempted to withdraw from society on the assumption that Christ's kingdom is not of this world (John 18:36). On the other hand, they have been tempted to make a too easy identification of the kingdom with something in this world, such as the institutional church or the ideal human society. However, the essential message of the New Testament is this: The kingdom is not of this world, yet it has been manifest in this world through the life, death, and resurrection of Christ. Although God's kingdom is a higher order than any political reality or human ideal of the present age, it has influenced and penetrated the kingdoms of this world—not as a tangent touches a circle but as a vertical line intersects a horizontal plane. The task of the church is to bear witness to this "vertical dimension" of history and, in so doing, to seek to leaven and redeem society in the name of Christ (Luke 13:20–21). This attitude toward society is not one of "detachment" but one of "transfiguration," involving a rhythm of withdrawal and return through worship and action, faith and good works.

At the heart of Luke's Sermon on the Plain we find these words: "strive for [God's] kingdom" (Luke 12:31). According to this teaching, the kingdom is to be the believer's first and main concern. It was certainly so for Jesus, who gave up everything for the sake of the kingdom. The theology of Jesus does not admit compromise; there must be a complete break with conventional morality or piety. For example, a rich young man is told by Jesus that he must sell all that he has and give to the poor (Luke 18:18–30). To understand the meaning of such severity, this story must be read contextually. Jesus is on his way to Jerusalem, and the final conflict in which he is to be engaged looms before him. At such a time there can be no hesitation; it must be all or nothing. This is a moment of crisis for those who would follow Jesus. In Luke's travel narrative, when Jesus says, "You cannot serve God or wealth" (Luke 16:13), he is not giving a new commandment. He is simply stating a fact about the choices his followers must make. Before them lie two mutually exclusive worlds. Those who choose to live in one are automatically excluded from the other. When money has priority, God's lordship is compromised: "No one who puts a hand to the plow and looks back is fit for the kingdom of God" (Luke 9:62).

In 14:26–27, Jesus is quoted as saying: "Whoever comes to me and does not hate father and mother, wife and children, brothers and sisters, yes, and even life itself, cannot be my disciple." These powerful and troublesome lines, their rhetoric softened in the Matthean parallel (see Matt. 10:37–38), were not intended to be taken literally (see Mark 7:9–13). They are an example of Middle Eastern hyperbole, so common in the Gospels. Luke's audience was comfortable with extremes—light and darkness, truth and falsehood, love and hate—primary colors with no grey tones or hints of compromise. To say, "I like this and hate that" means "I prefer this to that." For the followers of Jesus, to hate their families meant to give them second place in their affection. However, as the reference to carrying one's cross in 14:27 indicates, there is a cost to discipleship, and that cost often implies relationships, as Paul notes in 2 Corinthians 6:14–16.

These are radical sayings. It is quite plain that if everyone gave away all their possessions to the poor, the only result would be that the rich of today would become the poor of tomorrow and vice versa; the social situation would be neither changed nor improved. Not every command is of equal application to every situation; there must be a measure of adaptation and flexibility. But before we become too easily dismissive of Jesus' radicalism, let us remember that Christian ethics are derived from Christian theology. The central point of that theology is the example of Jesus Christ and his demand that citizens of the kingdom recognize unconditionally the sovereignty of God.

In Luke 13:29 the kingdom of God is shown as a great gathering that includes all humanity. In Luke's version, the gathering takes place from the four points of the compass. This image, like the four-sided cross, is symbolic of the mystery of the kingdom, since its structure suggests the wholeness and harmony of God's kingdom. Its breadth and length, height and depth, embrace what is on the right and left and unite all in Christ, the center. In Ephesians 2:14–16, the reference is to the union, through Christ, of Jew and Gentile, but the image also applies to the union of our personality, the sensual and the intuitive, the spirit and the flesh, the inner and the outward, the knowable and the unknowable, logic and imagination, darkness and light.

We must always remember that the context of Jesus' sayings was the message that God's kingdom was near at hand. Jesus' claims placed persons on the very borderline between the old age and the new. Jesus' perspective made love, not duty, central. However, such love is no natural sentiment or calculated act but is patterned after the love of God. As God's love is bestowed unconditionally upon those least deserving to be loved, so likewise Christians must love even those who seem to be most loveless, including social outcasts or despised enemies. Jesus transforms religious laws by destroying legalism: Christ is the "end of the law" (Rom. 10:4). Rather than setting a standard of perfection that drives us to despair, Christ teachings provide a compass that gives direction to our efforts to improve and transform society. Christian ethics, then, are essentially "resurrection ethics," since they derive their motive and patterns from the love of God manifested in Christ: "Beloved, since God loved us so much, we also ought to love one another" (1 John 4:11).

Despite the emphasis on the present nature of the kingdom, the New Testament also looks forward to the End, to the time when the last enemy has been overthrown and God's absolute sovereignty is established with finality. Thus the expression in the Lord's Prayer: "Your kingdom come" has both a present and a future element, for while it has to do with daily realities, it looks forward to the end of evil on earth, when God's sovereignty is unopposed.

For Jesus, parables are narrated answers to the question, "What is the kingdom of God like?" Luke's travel narrative contains several intriguing parables. In addition to the mustard seed (13:18–19) and the leaven (13:20–21), which speak of the kingdom as present in germinal and dynamic form,

Luke 15 narrates three parables of God's mercy: the lost sheep (15:4–7), the lost coin (15:8–10), and the story of the lost sons, known as the parable of the Prodigal Son (15:11–32). These parables teach about mercy and forgiveness, about God's persistence in seeking what is lost. To call people "lost" is to pay them a compliment, for it means that they are precious in the sight of God. Like God, we, too, should be jubilant when someone's search is successful, when one who is lost is found.

The specific use of the number 100 in the parable of the lost sheep is significant. In biblical times, the number 10, with its multiples of 100 or 1000, was considered perfect or complete. That is why the loss of just one sheep is so important, why one sheep must be found or the one hundred will not be complete. One might as well end up with thirty-seven or forty-five as with ninety-nine as far as completeness is concerned. This also explains the great joy over having found the one lost sheep.

A similar meaning belongs to the parable of the lost coin, which in Greek is about ten drachmas. A drachma is worth about six cents, so it is not a valuable coin. Yet the woman who has lost this coin goes to great efforts to find it because in the Eastern world, a woman was given ten coins by her husband at the time of their betrothal as a pledge of love and loyalty. These coins she was to retain all her life. To lose one was a terrible disgrace and an ominous portent for the marriage. This explains why the woman went to such lengths to find the lost coin and why she called together her friends to celebrate her recovery of the lost piece. We see again the symbolism of completion. As far as their symbolic value is concerned, one might as well lose eight or nine of the coins as to lose one of them.

As Luke 15:11 makes clear, the parable of the Prodigal Son is a story about two sons, both of whom are lost to their father, one in a foreign country, the other to self-righteousness. Both brothers were selfish, though in totally different ways. The selfishness of the younger brother was a reckless love of life, that of the elder to duty. While the elder was devoted to his father's service, never disobeying the rules of society, yet he was the center of his world, unable to enter sympathetically into the joys and sorrows of others. When he hears the merriment caused by the prodigal's return, his impulse is not to join in the revelry but rather to ask for an explanation. The news of his brother's return sets him thinking of his own rights and entitlements, jealously supposing himself to be wronged because his wayward brother is treated with more than justice. He disowns his brother, calling him "this son of yours," painting him in the worst light possible. The father refuses to take sides; with all their shortcomings he loves them both and never ceases to regard them as sons. The moment of redemption occurs when the younger brother "came to himself," or, as the King James

Version states, "came to his senses," that is, confronted himself and his one-sidedness. This self-confrontation must also occur with the older brother.

The parable was told not to offer a generous pardon to the nation's delinquents, but to entreat respectable Jews to rejoice with God over the restoration of sinners, and to warn them that until they learned to do this, they would remain estranged from their heavenly father and pitifully ignorant of God's true character.

In discussing the topic of God's kingdom or rule, we skipped Luke 14, a chapter focused on eating and table-fellowship. The chapter begins with Jesus going for a meal to the house of one of the leading Pharisees. Luke notes that the guests watch Jesus closely. In that hostile setting, Jesus tells three short stories: (1) choosing places at table (14:7-11); (2) choosing guests (14:12-14); and (3) invited guests who make excuses (14:15-24).

As previously noted, in his Gospel, Luke records numerous stories that have something to do with Jesus sitting at a table. For Luke, the table is the place of fellowship and communion. It is also the place where Jesus redefines the social order by doing things differently and challenging those who are in control of the social order—the rich, the elders, the scribes, and the "politically correct." For Luke, the theme of table fellowship seems to be Jesus' unique form of visual sermon, cultural critique, and social protest. When you have a party, Jesus says, "invite the poor, the crippled, the lame, and the blind" (14:13). As Jesus implies, the new order of the kingdom will not simply ignore the status symbols of the world, but reverse them. Human hierarchies mean nothing to God. What matters is our common humanity and the desire to be in fellowship. In his parables and stories, Jesus is empowering the outsider. The apostle Paul also implemented this message in his churches when he declared, in one of his most revolutionaries statements: "There is no longer Jew or Greek . . . slave or free . . . male and female; for you are one in Christ Jesus" (Gal. 3:28).

In 14:33 Luke addresses the renunciation of possessions, an issue that resurfaces often in his writing, as it does in 18:18-30, in the idyllic summaries in Acts 2:44-45 and 4:32-37, as well as in the instructive story of Ananias and Sapphira in 5:1-11.

Among the Jewish people of Jesus' day, wealth was thought of as a sign of God's blessing. Jesus disagreed. Despite the wealth and prosperity gospel many preachers are proclaiming nowadays, power and success are not signs of God's blessing. "It is easier for a camel to go through the eye of a needle," Jesus noted, "than for someone who is rich to enter the kingdom of God" (18:25). Of course, we must not read this as an absolute law, or seek its enforcement, for that is not what Jesus was teaching. He was simply answering a question, discerning insincerity in the ruler's query. He seems to be saying,

"If you want to enter into the freedom I am talking about, if you want to live authentically, here's my answer: Give it away. It will possess you more than you will ever possess it." When the man replies, "I am not ready to live like that," Jesus replies, "Okay, you asked, I answered."

If Americans were to select one book of the Bible and say, "This is going to be our guidebook, our philosophy of life," I doubt it would be Luke's Gospel, because it hits us too deeply in areas where most are quite comfortable. Luke punctuates his discussion on wealth and discipleship with an impossible one-liner: "none of you can become my disciple if you do not give up all your possessions" (14:33).

Luke 16 forms a distinct unit that begins and ends with a parable—the dishonest steward and the rich man and Lazarus—each of which begins, "There was a rich man." Between the two is a collection of sayings that were addressed to "the Pharisees, who were lovers of money" (16:14). The warning that one's wealth must be handled wisely is a recurring theme in Luke's travel narrative. Luke 17 draws together various teachings on discipleship (17:1-10), addressed to the disciples; a transitional healing story, which reintroduces the journey motif while underscoring the theme of gratitude (17:11-19); and a final section on the coming of God's kingdom (17:20-37).

In 18:1-14 Luke provides two transitional parables—the unjust judge and the persistent widow (18:1-8) and the Pharisee and the tax collector (18:9-14)—both organized around the theme of prayer. By reading these parables together, the reader is instructed to pray with the determination of the widow and with the humility of the tax collector. In chapter 18, parallels can be drawn between the Pharisee of 18:9-14 and the rich ruler of 18:18-25 as well as between the humility of the tax collector (18:9-14) and the little children (18:15-17).

In 18:15 Luke returns again to Mark's Gospel, which he has not used since 9:30. He takes over with slight alteration the two stories of the children and the rich man, which Mark had placed side by side because together they describe the conditions of entry into the kingdom of God. The story of the blessing of the children is a rebuke to that adult complacency that regards children as beneath the notice of God. It assures us that children (even infants, according to Luke) whose parents bring them to God in faith belong already to God's family and therefore to God's kingdom (this theme, important to the Synoptic tradition, also appears in 10:21 and 17:2)

Let us be clear, however; Jesus is not asking his disciples to become childish. He commends to them only certain characteristics of childhood, including receptivity—meaning the ability to accept freely what is given— and teachability—the ability to learn and remain open to new and different things.

By contrast with the children, Luke's ruler wished for nothing he could not earn. He supposed that entry into the kingdom was through effort and by accomplishment. He had passed "Intro to Religion 101" to his own satisfaction, and now wished to attempt "Advanced Religion 402." Jesus' response is unexpected: entry into eternal life is a miracle of God's grace, which cannot be earned but only accepted with humility and faith. The peril of possessions is that they stand in the way of this redeeming grace.

Before reaching Jerusalem, Jesus voices the third prediction of his passion (28:31–34), which Luke views as the fulfillment of prophecy. The third prediction is the most detailed, anticipating and foreshadowing the passion narrative, which is about to unfold. The crucifixion was to be the miracle of grace by which God would make it possible for disciples to enter the kingdom, breaking through self-sufficiency with a demonstration of divine love. However, even that event had to occur before Jesus' disciples could understand its meaning (see 19:11).

The long period of journeying toward Jerusalem, which began at 9:51, draws to its close in 18:35, at which point a blind beggar from Jericho (Mark calls him Bartimaeus) addresses Jesus by the title "Son of David." This is the only occasion in the Gospels when Jesus is addressed by this title. With this reference readers are reminded of the Magnificat in the infancy narrative, where Mary announces the widespread popular belief that Jesus was the promised king from the house of David. Almost a year has passed since Peter declared Jesus to be Messiah (Luke 9:20), and Luke reminds us here and in the chanting of the familiar Psalm 118:25–27 during Jesus' triumphal entry into Jerusalem in 19:38 that Jesus is that long awaited messianic king. To the Hallel song sung by pilgrims Luke inserts the word "King," so as to leave no doubt that the crowd believed themselves to be taking part in the coronation procession of the Messiah.

The parable of the pounds (19:11–27), which Jesus tells as he nears Jerusalem, is given as a warning to those who misunderstand his coming to Jerusalem. In light of the third passion prediction in 18:31–34, and the ignorance of the disciples in 18:35 ("But they understood nothing about all these things"), the parable is probably directed to the clueless disciples. The misguided expectation of the disciples is clarified in Matthew' Gospel, where after his encounter with the ruler, Jesus informs his disciples that "after the renewal of all things, when the Son of Man is seated on the throne of his glory, you who have followed me will also sit on twelve thrones, judging the tribes of Israel" (Matt. 19:28). Mark's Gospel does not include this reference and Luke waits until a more opportune moment, as part of the instructions given at the Last Supper, to include it. For the disciples, the consummation of the kingdom was imminent, somehow connected with their journey to Jerusalem.

Throughout the early church there were many who expected an imminent return of Christ, that he would return in glory within a generation. When the first generation had passed, it was natural that there should be some reappraisal of the eschatological hope. Matthew emphasizes the future coming of the kingdom, but Luke adopts a different understanding. He gives prominence to sayings in which the kingdom is a present reality, and tones down the futuristic note in others (9:27; 22:69; see Mark 9:1; 14:62). In Luke's view, the imminent crisis predicted by Jesus was his own death, involving persecution for his followers and judgment for Jerusalem. The final crisis of history would be sudden, but might be indefinitely delayed.

CHAPTER 11

Jesus' Passion, Resurrection, and Ascension (Luke 19:28—24:53)

Assignment: Read chapter 11 of *Power Revealed* and chapters 18:31—24:53 of Luke's Gospel. Answer the following questions, writing the answers in your journal. [If you are in a study group, be prepared to share your views with others in the class.] (1) In your estimation, what role does the crucifixion of Jesus play in God's plan of salvation? Can people be saved apart from the cross? Explain your answer. (2) In your estimation, what role does the resurrection of Jesus play in God's plan of salvation? Can people be saved apart from the risen Christ? Explain your answer.

Outline to Luke 19:28—24:53

   I. Jesus' Final Days 19:28—23:56
      A. Teaching Ministry in Jerusalem 19:28—21:38
         1. Arrival in Jerusalem 19:28-46
         2. Teaching in the Temple 19:47—21:38
      B. The Passion of Jesus 22:1—23:56
         1. The Last Supper 22:1-38
         2. Jesus in Gethsemane 22:39-46
         3. The Arrest of Jesus 22:47-53

4. Peter's Betrayal 22:54–65

5. The Trial of Jesus 22:66—23:25

6. The Crucifixion of Jesus 23:26–49

7. The Burial of Jesus 23:50–56

II. The Resurrection Ministry of Jesus 24:1–53

A. The Empty Tomb 24:1–12

B. The Road to Emmaus 24:13–35

C. Commissioning of the Disciples 24:36–53

Jesus' Teaching Ministry in Jerusalem (19:28—21:38)

The final act of the divine drama of redemption opens with the entry of Jesus into Jerusalem. The account opens with the story of a colt, on which Jesus will ride into Jerusalem. The allusion here is to Zechariah 9:9. If we are right in thinking that Jesus intended to act out the Old Testament prophecy, his purpose must have been not to excite nationalistic fervor. Patriotic feeling was always at its highest at the Passover season, which was the time when the Messiah was expected to appear in Jerusalem.

Jesus wanted to announce that God was now asserting sovereignty over Jerusalem, but he wanted no misapprehension about the nature of this long-promised reign: it was to be a peaceable kingdom (see 19:42). Zechariah 9:10 speaks of peace on earth, but as the crowd chants from Psalm 118:26 (see Luke 19:38), they sing of peace prepared in heaven, a peace God has now achieved by victory over evil (see 10:17–18), so that what remains is for the implications of the heavenly triumph to be worked out on earth, as the angelic host sang at Jesus' birth (see 2:14). The Pharisees, fearful that this outburst of enthusiasm might bring reprisals from the Romans, protest at the exuberance of the disciples. Jesus replies that his coming is the event for which the whole of Israel's history has been a preparation, so that the very stones from which roads and buildings were constructed would cry out in protest if Jesus did not receive his proper welcome (see Hab. 2:11).

The lament that follows shows how little Jesus had counted on earthly success. He came to Jerusalem ready for tragedy, and the heart of the tragedy lay in the word "visitation" (19:44).[1] Luke began his Gospel by declar-

---

1. The term "visitation" reminds readers of the utterance of the prophet Jeremiah against Jerusalem in the time of King Josiah. The Greek version (LXX) of Jeremiah 6:15 reads: "in the time of their visitation they will perish."

ing that God had "visited and redeemed his people" (see 1:68, RSV), and the long central section of his work was designed to lead up to the day when Jerusalem would receive the royal visit. Now, he tells us, the day has come and Jerusalem is not ready for it. Yet the fact remains that God has visited his people either for salvation or for judgment; and, if Jerusalem will not have Jesus as Savior, she will have him as Judge.

When Jesus enters Jerusalem, he goes to the temple, the city's spiritual center, and there he performs a parabolic cleansing (19:45–46).[2] The temple authorities had allowed the establishment of a market in which worshippers could exchange their common currency for the temple coinage in which the annual tax had to be paid, and could buy for sacrifice animals that were guaranteed "without blemish" (Lev. 1:3). Despite the commercialism, which threatened to obscure the purpose of the temple and its worship, Luke connects the cleansing of the temple with Jerusalem's unreadiness for God's visit.

We have reflected elsewhere on the importance of the temple for Luke, the only New Testament writer to view positively this institution. It is no surprise, then, that Luke's account of the cleansing is the briefest of the four Gospels, for in Luke there is no hint that what Jesus did should be seen as a blow announcing the end of the temple and its services. Rather, Jesus purifies the temple in order that it can become the place of his own teaching ministry (19:47; for the sequence of cleansing and ministering, see Mal. 3:1–4). For Luke it is excess, and not the system itself, that comes under Jesus' attack.

When Jesus drove out the moneychangers, such action does not mean that he brought to a halt the lucrative temple industry. This was most likely a limited action, meaning that it was primarily symbolic in nature, demonstrating the need for the cleansing of the temple. Jesus, an outsider to the power structure of the temple, issues a challenge to the authority of the temple that disrupts the temple system during one of the most significant feasts of the year, causing a commotion that culminated in his crucifixion. According to Luke, Jesus returned to the temple daily, teaching the crowds that gathered. His popularity is such that the leaders could neither overlook his influence nor take effective action against him. The only course open to them was to try and trap him into making some statement that would either incriminate him with the Roman government or discredit him with his supporters (20:1–8). If, in answer to the question about his authority, Jesus asserted his messiahship, a charge of sedition could be laid before Pilate. If,

---

2. The quote in Luke 19:46 is taken from Jeremiah's "Temple Sermon" in Jeremiah 7:11.

CHAPTER 11—JESUS' PASSION, RESURRECTION, AND ASCENSION

on the other hand, he declined to make such a claim, he would forfeit the approval of the crowd. But Jesus deftly countered his questioners by inviting them to answer their own question, for which they found no adequate answer.

Jesus way of responding offers a great corrective to much religious debate today, which is often dogmatic, argumentative, and ultimately unproductive. Jesus wishes to show that arguing and debating about scripture and theology often destroys rather than builds faith. According to Luke, the method of Jesus is to bypass theological traps. He knows when he is being manipulated, and he does not take the bait. Often he answers a question with a question, as he does in 20:24-25. Controversy undermines real faith because it destroys relationships and respect between people. In such discussions, people become defensive or offensive. They rarely create a safe or loving atmosphere, but rather a competitive game where battling egos take the place of truth, which is always relational.

Until this time in Luke, Jesus' controversies have been largely with Pharisees over issues having to do with legalism. Now in these last chapters, his controversies are with the priests and the scribes—the religious establishment, who rely on tradition and political correctness. Jesus repeatedly saves his harshest words for such people (see 20:46-47). When Jesus tells the parable of the wicked tenants (20:9-18), he is alluding to Isaiah's parable of the vineyard (Isa. 5:1-7), in which the vineyard represents Israel. It is evident that the Jewish authorities recognized that Jesus told this parable against them. Nevertheless, when the parable was expounded by the early church, it was treated as an allegory. The landlord became identified with God, the servants with the prophets, the son with Jesus, the tenants with the Jewish leaders, and the "others" of verse 16 with the Gentile church. Traces of such allegorizing evidently entered Luke's version of the parable. According to Mark's version (12:1-11), the son was killed inside the vineyard and his body thrown over the wall. Luke, like Matthew, altered this to make the death occur outside the vineyard, thereby applying it to the death of Jesus, who "suffered outside the city gate" (Heb. 13:12). The comment of the bystanders, "Heaven forbid!" (Luke 20:16) is a Lukan addition that makes sense only if we suppose that they were treating the end of the story as an allegorical prediction of the fall of Jerusalem.

The question on the afterlife posed by the Sadduccees in 20:27-40 is crucial in several respects. This is the only place in Luke's Gospel where this Jewish group appears, and there is no explicit reference to an attempt to trap Jesus (as Luke notes in 20:20). Their question does not concern Jesus, but it was an issue on which the Sadducees and the Pharisees disagreed. The problem is theoretical, possibly even a stock question customarily posed by Sadducees to Pharisees. The questioners address Jesus as teacher and ask him how he interprets a regulation in the Mosaic law regarding levirate marriage (the custom of a marriage where a brother-in-law begets children with his brother's wife, to continue his brother's lineage, was practiced not only by Jews but also by Assyrians, Hittites, and Canaanites). The Sadducees, a Jewish group clearly aligned with the aristocratic and priestly classes, rejected the authority of oral tradition, questioned the authority of the prophetic writings, and denied the belief in resurrection. In his answer, Jesus corrects misunderstandings about the afterlife by indicating that earthly institutions such as marriage and childbearing would not continue in the age to come, in part because people will not die, and because the perpetuation of humanity will no longer depend upon procreation and marital union. Being "children of the resurrection" (that is, becoming immortal, like angels), the righteous dead are children of God. Having dismissed the basis for the Sadducees' question, Jesus turns to the root of their question, the doctrine of the resurrection of the dead. By means of midrashic teaching, Jesus grounds the doctrine in the writings accepted as scripture by the Sadducees, namely, the books of Moses. God is Lord of the patriarchs, Jesus notes, citing Exodus 3:6, arguing that the patriarchs must in some sense be alive to God or in God, since only living people can have a god.

The emphasis here is clearly on resurrection, not immortality. Immortality is based on a Greek doctrine of human nature that denies death by making eternal life an attribute of the soul, whereas resurrection is based on a Jewish (and hence a Christian) doctrine of God, which affirms that despite human mortality, God gives life to the dead. The scene concludes with the report that Jesus' opponents, bested in a contest of wits, no longer dared to ask Jesus anything (20:40).

Luke's story of the widow's mite (21:1–4) provides one more example of the social reversal that Jesus brings about. The scribes—those who best know scripture, who occupy places of honor in the synagogues, who make their wealth and gain their prestige at the expense of people like the poor widow—these give out of their surplus, but the widow out of her deficit. In God's sight, her apparently small offering is deemed greater than the seemingly superior donations of the wealthy.

Chapter 21:7–36 is devoted to a series of eschatological announcements and warnings about future events. The setting is the temple, where Jesus has been teaching, and the occasion is its impressive location and design. Jesus comments that the time will come when even the temple will be destroyed, a destruction so thorough that "not one stone will be left upon another" (21:6). The words that follow are known as "the Synoptic Apocalypse" because they appear in all three Synoptic Gospels, and because they describe the future in apocalyptic terms. This passage is susceptible to different interpretations, based on how one answers questions such as whether Jesus is describing the events of the end of history or the events of the immediate future (namely, the fall of Jerusalem in 70 CE), and whether the passage should be read literally or symbolically.

Mark's Gospel understood Jesus' prediction to include the *parousia*. Luke, writing fifteen to twenty years later, understood things differently. His discourse ends with instructions to the disciples to pray that they may have "strength to escape all these things" (21:36), and it is reasonable to assume that for him "all things" in v. 32 covered the same set of events as "all these things" in v. 36. However, from the *parousia* and the final consummation of the kingdom there could be no escape, nor can we imagine the disciples of Jesus being taught to pray for any. In Luke, the disciples are being taught to pray that they might survive the preliminary crises of persecution and the siege of Jerusalem, and these, according to Luke, were the events that Jesus declared would happen before a generation had passed away.

As is typical of the apocalyptic genre, the signs of the *eschaton* (the end of the "old age"; see 21:25–26) are described in traditional terms. The sea that threatens to engulf the world is the turbulent reservoir of evil things (Rev. 13:1), over which God still will secure final conquest. The powers of heaven are the heavenly bodies, identified by apocalyptic writers with the gods of Greco-Roman religion as well as with angelic beings created by God and allowed by God to preside over the destinies of pagan nations (Deut. 32:8; Isa. 24:21; 34:1–4). Thus the shaking of the powers of heaven denotes not so much the ruin of the physical universe as the overthrown of pagan imperial supremacy. Jesus' claims as God's Messiah place persons on the very borderline between the old age and the new.

The key to understanding Luke's perspective is given in 21:31–32: "when you see these things taking place, you know that the kingdom of God is near. Truly I tell you, this generation will not pass away until all things have taken place." When Luke is writing, Jerusalem has already been destroyed, as 21:20 makes clear. What then is his message? It is one he has maintained all along: God's kingdom (rule) is inexorably present, a reign of peace to those who accept it and a sentence of doom to those who do not. Luke and his contemporaries believed they were living in a period of indeterminate length, known as "the times of the Gentiles" (21:24), during which God's judgment on Jerusalem must run its course, and only after that would the *eschaton* come, and with it the consummation of the kingdom. This does not mean, however, that God has abandoned Israel. A door opened to Gentiles does not mean a door closed to Jews, as Jesus reminded listeners in an earlier parable: "a man had two sons" (15:11).

In the meantime, Jesus' followers should take things in stride, facing the future confidently. The destruction of Jerusalem did occur historically, and even the Roman Empire came to an end. For Christians, the ancient destruction of Jerusalem is no longer catastrophic because Jesus, "the Alpha and the Omega, the first and the last, the beginning and the end" (Rev. 22:13), has become both temple and New Jerusalem (Rev. 22:22–26).

The Passion of Jesus (22:1—23:56)

The events described in Luke 22–23 are often called the "passion" of Jesus, for they refer not only to his death by crucifixion but also to what he suffered, allowed, and endured vicariously, for the sake of humanity. For traditional Christians, it is Christ's death, more than his teachings or the events of his ministry, which liberates and redeems human beings.

If we look for a ritualized act that sums the life of Jesus for believers, it is the Last Supper. Hence it functions as the liturgical paradigm and central sacrament for Christians. On the night before Jesus died, he gathered his closest followers and they experienced the sharing of his life and death together. The Eucharist, the name Christians give to the reenactment of the Last Supper, represents not only the essence of Jesus but also the essence of Christianity, the church's life of sharing and communion, its life of surrender and faith. At its core is the notion of grace, that those who receive it receive the gift of life, nourishment both for this life and the life to come. The Eucharist not only defines the church; it also celebrates life, fellowship, and communion with God. In addition, it affirms human fallibility and recognizes human dependence upon God. This is why Luke presents, after the Last Supper, the disciples arguing among themselves about which of them would be regarded as the greatest.

The story of the upper room ends with a passage that shows the depth of misunderstanding that continued to separate the disciples from Jesus (see 19:11). What irony and yet what genius Luke shows in placing this story here (Mark and Matthew placed their version of the story earlier, before Jesus' entry into Jerusalem). In 22:24–26, Jesus reminds his disciples that in God's kingdom, greatness is defined by service. This, too, is the message of the Christian Eucharist. While Jesus goes on to talk of apostles as those who would "sit on thrones judging the twelve tribes of Israel" (22:30), the model for "kingdom authority" would be servanthood, not lordship.

What happened historically in the church, particularly after Constantine and the events of the fourth century CE, is that authority came to be identified with power and hierarchy. Instead of modeling themselves on the example of Jesus, church leaders sold out to the world's model of authority, following the example of the princes and lords of Europe.

The criterion for apostolic ministry, defined in 22:28 as "those who have stood by me in my trials," would be put to the test immediately, and in those tests the disciples would betray, deny, and desert their master. In their failure, they would wrestle with the demons of disillusionment, self-contempt, and despair. Judas, by his betrayal, sank lower than the rest (22:3–6, 42–49), as did Peter by his threefold denial (22:54–62). The rest take Jesus' instruction to sell their coats and buy a sword literally (22:36), but that is not what Jesus had in mind, as his reply to their comment about having two swords make clear. The words, "It is enough" refer not to satisfaction with the disciples' military preparedness, but indicate a sad dismissal of the subject (see 22:51). It was on this verse that another literalist, Pope Boniface VIII, in his 1302 Bull *Unam Sanctam*, based the doctrine that God had entrusted to the church the two swords of civil and spiritual authority.

From this point on Luke's story runs parallel to Mark's, though with considerable divergence. According to Mark, Jesus is taken straight to a midnight session of the Sanhedrin, the Jewish governing body. The mocking of Jesus takes place in the court after the hearing, and at a second session held at daybreak the decision is made to send Jesus to Pilate. According to Luke, Jesus is kept under guard in the high priest's house until the Sanhedrin could be called, and it is during the long night of waiting that the guards amuse themselves at the expense of the prisoner and Peter denies his master.

We should not view Jesus' examination before the Sanhedrin as a regular trial according to legal rules of procedure. The fate of Jesus had been decided at an earlier meeting. The purpose of the present session is to build a case that could be submitted to Pilate. Luke omits the preliminary investigation described by Mark and comes straight to the crucial question, "Are you the Messiah?" At first Jesus declines to answer; "Messiah" is an ambiguous term, and Jesus recognizes that the court is in no mood to discuss definitions. He still prefers the title Son of Man, and he reminds the court that this Son of Man is destined to receive from God the authority both to rule and to judge (see Dan. 7:13). The Sanhedrin think that they are sitting in judgment over Jesus, but in reality the roles are reversed; Jesus has become judge, and from this moment they are on trial before the divine tribunal. Finally, however, Jesus replies to their question with a veiled answer, which his interrogators take as assent. It is all they need to frame their charge.

The charge against Jesus is a deliberate inversion of the truth. The Jewish authorities believe Jesus to be guilty of blasphemy, but no Roman court would take such a case. Therefore, presenting trumped-up charges, they fabricate the charge of sedition, that Jesus is an insurgent leader who has been inciting the people to rebel against Rome (23:2). Pilate, seeing through their duplicity, three times declares Jesus innocent,[3] but when he hears that Jesus comes from Galilee, he tries to shift the responsibility to Herod Antipas. While only Luke mentions the trial before Herod, this trial, too, ends with no verdict. Affronted by Jesus' silence, Herod answers by allowing his soldiers to make sport of Jesus, dressing him in royal robes (23:11).

The Barabbas incident (23:18–19) emphasizes the irony of the accusation against Jesus, for it involves releasing a member of the Jewish resistance movement, one who, unlike Jesus, is truly guilty of sedition against Rome. Verse 17 is not part of the original text of Luke, as the manuscript tradition indicates. Furthermore, there is no historical evidence for the custom of releasing a criminal at a Jewish festival. To compound the irony, the criminal who is released bears the name Barabbas. In rejecting Jesus, the true "son of the Father" (see 22:70), the crowd calls for the release of one whose name means "son of the father."

As we consider the crucifixion, an important question remains, "Who killed Jesus?" Pilate, says Luke, found Jesus innocent and wanted to release him. Some scholars detect here an apologetic purpose, prompted in part by Luke's desire to demonstrate to Roman officials that there was no incompatibility between the church and Rome. One recalls the many occasions in Acts when Paul the Roman citizen received protective custody or where Roman officials found him, like Jesus, to be innocent of false charges. In statements like those found in Acts 2:23, 36, and 3:13–15, Luke not only seems pro-Roman but also anti-Jewish. While some passages in the New Testament can and have been used to promote anti-Semitism (1 Thess. 2:16 and Matt. 27:25 are classic examples), Luke can hardly thus be interpreted. On repeated occasions Luke insists on the continuity between Judaism and Christianity, on the adequacy of the Hebrew scriptures to move their readers to faith in Jesus as Messiah, on the pious Jewish family from which Jesus came, and on the portrayal of Jesus as a true Israelite. How, then, are we to understand Luke's presentation of the involvement of the Jews in the death of Jesus? While Luke tells us in Acts 2:23 that Jesus was "handed over" to the Jews for crucifixion, this passage also indicates that the Romans ("those outside the law") were actually responsible for Jesus' execution. While some of the Jewish leaders in Jerusalem seem to have been in league with the Roman procurator out of fear that Jesus was a threat to their positions of privilege, to say that "the Jews" as a whole crucified Jesus is an exaggeration that is not historically accurate (see Luke 18:32).

---

3. All four evangelists relate the examination of Jesus by Pilate and the pressure put on the governor by the Jews, though the record in John's Gospel (18:28—19:16) is the most extensive.

In the preaching of the early church the crucifixion was declared to be the fulfillment of Old Testament prophecies about the sufferings of the righteous Servant of the Lord (see Isa. 52:13—53:12), and this belief has colored the form and language of the passion narrative. The Gospels at this point insert allusions to Psalm 22 and 69, such as the casting of lots over the clothes (Luke 23:34) and the scoffing (23:35), described in words drawn from Psalm 22:7 and 18, and the offering of sour wine in words drawn from Psalm 69:21.

During the crucifixion scene, Luke tells the story of the penitent criminal, emphasizing again the theme of the merciful Jesus. The generous word of forgiveness from Jesus in the last moments of his life has given hope to many people over the centuries. In that scene, Luke reminds us once again that salvation is not earned by doing good works, but is the result of a love-trust relationship with God by means of the Son.

People's final words are often used to summarize the meaning of their entire life. The four evangelists include among their accounts of the crucifixion seven last words (that is, sentences) that came from Jesus while on the cross. In their traditional order they are:

1. "Father, forgive them, for they do not know what they are doing." This prayer of intercession on behalf of those responsible for his death is found in some but not all manuscripts of Luke 23:34.

2. "Truly, I tell you, today you will be with me in Paradise."[4] This promise, given to one of the two criminals crucified with Jesus, is found in Luke 23:42.

3. "Woman, here is your son . . . Here is your mother." These words of loving concern, spoken to Jesus' mother and to "the disciple whom Jesus loved," are found in John 19:26–27.

4. "My God, my God, why have you forsaken me?" This cry of dereliction, taken from Psalm 22:1, is found in Matthew 27:46 and Mark 15:34.

5. "I am thirsty." This cry of physical anguish is found in John 19:28.

6. "It is finished." This word of accomplishment is found in John 19:30.

7. "Father, into your hands I commend my spirit." This prayer of confidence and trust is found in Luke 23:46.

---

4. Paradise, a Persian work meaning park or garden, was taken over into Greek, then into Hebrew. In the Septuagint it was used to translate "the Garden of Eden." Then, because of the belief that God would bring a restoration of primeval bliss, Paradise became the name of the future home of the righteous. Finally, this earthly Paradise was distinguished from the heavenly one, of which the Garden of Eden was an earthly copy.

According to the Gospels, certain events of great significance took place at the crucifixion, among them a preternatural darkness covering the whole earth and the rending of the temple curtain. An eclipse of the sun while the moon is full (according to the Gospel accounts, the crucifixion coincided with the Jewish Passover, celebrated on the evening of the spring full moon) is an astronomical impossibility, but this would only enhance the value of the story for its earliest readers. The rending of the curtain symbolized the opening of access to the inner presence of God (see Heb. 10:19–22). Pilate and the penitent criminal have declared Jesus innocent; now the Roman centurion adds his testimony (23:47). According to Mark and Matthew, the centurion utters a christological confession (Mark 15:39; Matt. 27:54)); however, Luke's version better fits his apologetic purpose. A fourth event, mentioned only by Matthew, speaks of the crucifixion as a moment in which some who were dead are raised (27:52–53). This would have made sense to those Jews who included the resurrection of the righteous as one of the great events anticipated at the End, something that, according to early Christian teaching, had already begun at Jesus' death. Such a view of Jesus' death would not survive in the main stream of the tradition, since it did not fit what became the basic understanding of Jesus' death and resurrection as the "first fruits of those who have died" (1 Cor. 15:20); the rest of humanity would have to await the general resurrection at the *parousia* (1 Thess. 4:16).

The burial of Jesus provides closure to the account of the crucifixion of Jesus and serves as a transition to the resurrection in chapter 24. Luke 23:50–53 describes Joseph of Arimathea in terms that remind us of the godly company in the infancy narrative (2:25, 38). Matthew and John describe him as a disciple of Jesus, but on this point Mark and Luke are silent. They give the impression that, as a member of the Sanhedrin, he was sympathetic with the mission of Jesus, wishing to dissociate himself from the Jewish council's decision. This passage also reflects Jewish law, which required that an executed criminal should be buried before nightfall, lest the land be defiled by the curse under which he died (Deut. 21:22–23).

The Day of Preparation (23:54) refers to Friday. The sabbath began at sundown, according to the Jewish reckoning that the day begins at sunset. The resurrection took place on the first day of the week, as we read in 24:1, making Sunday morning the third day after Jesus' death.

The Resurrection Ministry of Jesus (24:1–53)

The earliest evidence for the resurrection is provided not by the Gospels but by the epistles of Paul, particularly in 1 Corinthians 15, an early Christian

CHAPTER 11—JESUS' PASSION, RESURRECTION, AND ASCENSION

confession or hymn recorded at least ten years before Mark, the earliest Gospel. In his writings, Paul bases the resurrection faith of the church not on the empty tomb, which he does not mention, but on the appearances of Jesus, among which he includes the appearance to himself. When he speaks of the resurrection body, it is clear he has in mind a spiritual body rather than a body of flesh (see 1 Cor. 15:42–50). However, it is the physical body that puts on immortality, not a disembodied and immortal soul. The spiritual body of which he speaks must be produced out of the physical body by a process of transformation. While Paul does not show any knowledge of the empty tomb tradition, it is assumed, for no Jew would have used the word "resurrection" to describe an afterlife in which the physical body was abandoned to the grave.

The end of Luke's Gospel exerts a powerful influence on our understanding of Luke's themes and theology. Luke's story of the empty tomb runs parallel to Mark's, but differs from it at four points. Where Mark mentions one young man at the tomb, Luke has two (this same number is given in the stories of the transfiguration and the ascension; see Luke 9:30; Acts 1:10), perhaps as a form of cross-reference linking the three events. According to Mark 16:7, the woman are told to tell the disciples that Jesus would meet them in Galilee. Luke's version includes a passing reference to Galilee in 24:6, but in his view, the resurrection appearances occur not in Galilee but only in and around Jerusalem. While the women in Mark, out of fear, fail to deliver their message to the disciples, Luke tells us that the women make a full report to the other disciples. Luke lists the women at the tomb in 24:10, giving Joanna in place of Mark's Salome.

In 24:6–7, Luke assumes that Jesus had told the women that he would be betrayed, crucified, and raised. This information places the women in the inner circle of disciples with whom such a prediction had been shared. As in 8:2–3, Luke is here enlarging the circle of disciples to anticipate Acts, in which the group gathered in prayer to await the Holy Spirit includes women followers (Acts 1:14). In Luke's account of the resurrection, the women are not commanded to go and tell the disciples, as Mark and Matthew tell it. For Luke, the women are not errand runners for the disciples; rather, they are disciples! While it is true that they relate their experience to the apostles, such reporting is no different from other forms of witness.

Some translations omit Luke 24:12 or place it in the footnotes. While the weight of evidence seems to support its inclusion, the questionable status is due to its apparent intrusion in a passage where only female followers are said to be present, coupled with the impression that we have here a direct borrowing from John 20:3–10 (or from a tradition known to John), paving the way for passages such as 24:24 and 24:35. While the lack of agreement in the resurrection narratives of the Gospels is widely attested, it is equally evident that the various resurrection traditions influenced one another during the transmission process.

Later in the day, on the road to Emmaus, about seven miles from Jerusalem,[5] two individuals returning home are joined by a third, and they assume he is a fellow traveler who has overtaken them.[6] The experience of this couple raises interesting questions. Could they have been husband and wife? Since only one is named, could Luke have been the other? However, if Cleopas is the Clopas of John 19:25, then his wife Mary had been one of the group of women at the cross. Might the other traveler have been Mary?

In this story, Jesus is said to have intruded suddenly on the couple's conversation, which was about Jesus and his death by crucifixion. In 24:19 Luke inserts one of his favorite christological titles for Jesus, "a prophet mighty in word and deed." However, Jesus is no longer limited by prophetic terminology, but rather is the subject of biblical prophecy: "Then beginning with Moses and all the prophets, he interpreted to them the things about himself in all the scriptures" (24:27).

Here we find those haunting lines we love so much, "Were not our hearts burning within us while he was talking to us on the road, while he was opening the scriptures to us?" (24:32) and "they told (the other disciples) . . . how [Jesus] had been made known to them in the breaking of the bread" (24:35). In this story, Luke is teaching his community about Christ's presence among them. At least fifty years have passed since Jesus was with them in the flesh, so how is Jesus present now? Luke's response is threefold: Jesus is present (1) in the Eucharist (24:30–31); (2) in the reading of scripture (24:27, 45); and (3) in the promised Spirit (24:49; see 3:17; Acts 2:38; Rom. 8:9). The women could not call back the angels, the two travelers might never meet the stranger again, but it would not matter. Life would never again be the same. For Christians, Easter is not over at sundown on Sunday. It extends into the rest of life.

Jesus finally appears to the Eleven, having appeared earlier to Peter (see 24:34), an interesting confirmation of the tradition preserved by Paul (1 Cor. 15:5). As Luke makes clear, Jesus is no longer subject to limitations of time and place. Like John's Gospel (20:19–29), Luke's narrative notes that

---

5. Because of disagreements in the manuscript tradition, three sites are candidates for the location of Emmaus. The fact that Emmaus cannot be identified with certainty does not diminish the memorable impact of the account. The reference to sixty stadia in 24:13 is not significant. What is important to Luke, however, is that Emmaus is in the vicinity of Jerusalem, and that is what matters.

6. To what degree this account is based on historical fact, we do not know. The story is not found in any other Gospel.

Jesus appeared in a bodily form not subject to ordinary, physical restrictions, while yet having a solidly corporeal nature (capable of eating and drinking with his disciples after he had risen; 24:42; Acts 10:40–41). This perspective is amplified by the failure of the two travelers to recognize Jesus, as well as by his ability to appear and disappear suddenly.

An apologetic motive may underlie Luke's story. Whereas the Greek mind tended to think of reality in terms of abstractions and universal truths, to the Jews reality was always particular and concrete. This means that to a Jew, a disembodied spirit could only seem a ghost, not a living being (24:37). Toward the end of the first century there developed in the church a view called docetism, which denied the reality of Christ's human life and asserted that the divine Christ descended upon the human Jesus at his baptism and withdrew again before his crucifixion. The epistles and Gospel of John contain polemical references to this unorthodox perspective (1 John 2:22; 4:2–3; John 1:14; 6:33; 20:24–29), and it is possible that Luke also wanted, for this reason, to associate the risen Christ with the flesh-and-blood Jesus (see 24:39).

In 24:47–49, the Old Testament instruction given on the road to Emmaus is now carried a stage further. The disciples are formally commissioned to undertake the missionary work of the church (see Mark 16:15; Matt. 28:19–20; John 20:21; Acts 1:8). The stress on witness, the command to remain in Jerusalem (as against the Galilean appearances recorded by Matthew and implied by Mark), the description of the Holy Spirit as power from on high, and the ascension[7] from the Mount of Olives are themes that are taken up and expanded in the early chapters of Acts. The Gospel ends as it began, in the courts of the temple.

The final words of Luke's Gospel lead readers to an appropriate response, to the good news of Jesus' life and message. The disciples receive Jesus' blessing with great joy, and they begin immediately to do as he had instructed. Joy is the natural result of blessing. It is promised to all who study God's Word and seek God's kingdom.

---

7. The ascension of Jesus provides closure to Luke's Gospel. Luke is the only Gospel that narrates the departure of Jesus (see 24:51; also Acts 1:9). Matthew could hardly end with the ascension, since the last words of that Gospel are "I am with you always, to the end of the age" (Matt. 28:20). Paul writes of the exaltation of Jesus (Phil. 2:9), perhaps as synonymous with the resurrection, a concept we find also in other New Testament epistles (see 1 Tim. 3:16; 1 Pet. 3:22). While John does not record an ascension, he speaks instead of the crucifixion as Jesus being "lifted up" (John 3:14; 8:28; 12:32), though in John 20:17 Jesus says to Mary Magdalene, "Do not hold me, because I have not yet ascended to the Father. But go to my brothers and say to them, 'I am ascending to my Father and your Father.'" Luke records two versions of the ascension, one on Easter day, as closing the period of Jesus' ministry, and the other after forty days, which opens the period of the church's mission.

CHAPTER 12

The Christian Mission in Jerusalem (Acts 1:1—6:7)

Assignment: Read chapter 12 of *Power Revealed* and chapters 1:1—6:7 of Acts. Answer the following questions, writing the answers in your journal. [If you are in a study group, be prepared to share your views with others in the class.] 1. What role does Pentecost play in Luke–Acts? In your estimation, would the church have come into existence without Pentecost? 2. What role does the Holy Spirit play in the church today? In your life?

Outline to Acts 1:1—6:7

I. Preface 1:1-14

II. First Panel; Early Episodes in the Jerusalem Church 1:15—6:7

    A. The Restoration of the Twelve 1:15-26

    B. The Mission in Jerusalem 2:1—6:7

        1. The Pentecost Event 2:1-13

        2. Peter's Pentecost Sermon 2:14-41

        3. First Major Summary 2:42-47

        4. The Acts of Peter and John 3:1—4:31

        5. Second Major Summary 4:32-35

6. Life in the Church 4:36—5:11
7. Third Major Summary 5:12–16
8. Persecution 5:17–42
9. The Commission of the Seven 6:1–7

The Ascension of Jesus and the Restoration of the Twelve (1:1–26)

Unlike Luke 1:1–4, the transition between prologue and narrative is very smooth in Acts 1:1–2, and Luke does not need to state again his purpose for writing. Luke tells us a number of things in his opening sentence. First, we learn that Acts is the continuation of a story. Next, we learn that Jesus instructed his followers "through the Holy Spirit." Luke puts it this way because in his account the Spirit will also be the means of instruction in the church: designated individuals will speak through the Holy Spirit. This instruction, Luke emphasizes, is given "to the apostles whom he had chosen." This is a clear link back to the Gospel, where the term "apostles" refers to the Twelve whom Jesus chose and commissioned. Acts 1:21–22 makes clear that the term is used of those who had witnessed the ministry of Jesus up to and including the resurrection appearances. Unless Acts 14:4 and 14 are exceptions, it appears that Luke confines the apostles to the Twelve. It could be, however, that Luke is using the term "apostle" in its general sense, meaning an agent of Jesus ("one who is sent"), in which case Paul and Barnabas are not to be distinguished from the Twelve.

Luke's introduction sets the scene for his opening chapter by recounting the postresurrection appearances of Jesus to his apostles. Scholars have often noted the recapitulative nature of Acts 1:1–14. Whereas Luke 24 serves as a means of closing the first account, Acts 1 serves to initiate what follows. A comparison of these chapters reveals several incongruities. The first concerns the ascension of Jesus. According to Luke 24:51, Jesus was taken up to heaven, yet in the opening chapter of Acts Jesus is back in Jerusalem with his disciples. The overlap, however, is intentional, swinging the spotlight from Jesus to his followers.

Luke is the only evangelist who clearly mentions the ascension, and he does so in both books. The Gentiles in his audience would have been familiar with the idea of gods or semidivine figures materializing on earth in disguise and then returning to the heavens, but they were less familiar with the idea of resurrection, a uniquely Jewish doctrine. Conveying the meaning of resurrection is Luke's task. The ascension, addressed to believers, serves a different function, to make clear to the disciples that Jesus' life on earth had a definite closure.

In Luke 24, the account is telescoped, giving the impression that all took place on one day, whereas in Acts Luke speaks of a forty-day period when Jesus appeared to his disciples before his ascension. The number "forty" is a conventional biblical number, not to be taken literally. It refers to a considerable period of time, but more, its use points to sacred time, alerting the reader to look for the hand of God in history. During the time of Noah, God caused it to rain forty days and nights. The Israelites were supported by God for forty years in the wilderness. David, Israel's ideal king, reigned for forty years. For Luke, forty days has a prophetic focus. In the Bible, there are three individuals who went off by themselves for forty days to discover the will of God. Moses was with God forty days on Mount Sinai, when he received the Ten Commandments (Exod. 34:28). Likewise, the prophet Elijah spent forty days on Mount Horeb, where he heard God's voice (1 Kgs. 19:8–12). Finally, Jesus was led by God's Spirit into the wilderness, where he was tested for forty days (Luke 4:1–2). Now Luke presents a fourth forty-day period. During this sacred time he continued to reinforce his teaching about the kingdom of God—that ultimate sacred time—promising his followers not only the law of God (brought by Moses), nor even the word of God (brought by Elijah), but the very presence of God—the Holy Spirit.

By speaking of the kingdom and of the Spirit, Luke addresses various continuities throughout Acts. First is the continuity between the ministry of Jesus and that of his followers, but perhaps more important to his purpose is the continuity between Judaism and Christianity. This concern is understandable in the first century, because the one thing bound to offend non-Christians in the Roman Empire was a religion that was too new, a religion that could not claim the respect of antiquity.

The promise of the Spirit in 1:5 prompts the question, "Is this the time when you will restore the kingdom to Israel?" It is a natural question, but it reveals the basic misunderstanding that the apostles maintained since their arrival in Jerusalem. The idea of restoration, for Jews, involved home rule, including theocratic rule over the land of Israel (see Luke 24:21). Jesus' reply in 1:7 suggests that God will fulfill this expectation, but, as 1:8 makes clear, a task remains to be completed before "the restoration," namely, witnessing in Jerusalem, in all of Judea and Samaria, and "to the ends of the earth." This verse announces Luke's primary theme in Acts, the empowerment of witnesses to be sent from Jerusalem with a global mission. This focus on salvation history necessarily leads Luke to deemphasize, though not dismiss, future eschatological speculation.

CHAPTER 12—THE CHRISTIAN MISSION IN JERUSALEM (ACTS 1:1—6:7)

Behind the apostles' question is a longing to be part of the sovereign political power structure that they hope Jesus will establish. Surely they recalled Jesus' statement in Luke's account of the Last Supper, that they would "sit on thrones judging the twelve tribes of Israel" (Luke 22:28-30). Jesus' reply in Acts 1:8 does promise them power, not to rule, however, but to witness.

Acts 1:9-11 narrates the events of the ascension. In this passage the reader is once again struck by an allusion to Moses and Elijah. Like the story of Jesus' transfiguration (Luke 9:28-36), when two men—Moses and Elijah—talked with Jesus, two angelic figures appear to the apostles, reassuring the disciples that Jesus would return in the same fashion in which he left.[1]

Acts 1:12-14 is part of the recapitulation and expansion of information already given at the close of Luke 24. The list of disciples differs little from the list in Luke 6:14-16, with two notable exceptions. John is placed in the second spot, presumably because Luke knew some traditions about John (see Acts 3-5) but not about Andrew, and of course Judas is left out of this list. Verse 14 provides a brief glimpse of the inner life of the early Christian community, using a Greek term translated as "united," a typically Lukan word used to describe the spiritual unity of believers (see also 2:46; 4:24; 5:12; 8:6; 15:25). The list of congregants gathered in the upper room of a house in Jerusalem includes women, among them Jesus' mother and brothers. Mary is present only here in Acts, as she was present at the beginning of Luke's Gospel.

Due to the biblical significance of the number twelve, symbolic of the twelve tribes of Israel and of all Israel, Luke narrates the selection of a person to take Judas's place, thus restoring the full complement of the Twelve. According to Luke 6:13, Jesus had more than twelve disciples, but from this group he chose twelve "whom he also named apostles." The selection of Matthias is by prayer and by the casting of lots. This process for determining God's will was traditional in Judaism (see Lev. 16:8; Num. 26:55; Prov. 16:33; the Urim and Thummim in Exod. 28:30 were the priestly lot used to obtain oracular decisions). Clearly Luke thinks the choice here (and presumably also the method) valid for determining God's will. The process was likely the one we find in 1 Chronicles 26:13-14, where stones were placed in a container and shaken until one fell out. In Acts, the stone thus chosen represented Matthias.

The point of this action was that Luke anticipates the Twelve having a role, not in relationship to the church or its later mission to Gentiles,

---

1. Most interpreters view the two "men" symbolically, depicting the Torah's requirement that two witnesses are required to confirm the veracity of an alleged event (see Deut. 19:15).

but rather in relationship to Israel, in particular Jews who lived in Judea, Samaria, and Galilee. Luke knows little about the mission in Galilee, but what he knows about the former two he records in the first eight chapters of Acts. Even so, he makes clear that in Samaria it was Philip, not one of the Twelve, who led the way. For Luke, the role of the Twelve is as witnesses about the risen Jesus to Israel, and at the *parousia*, as Israel's judges (Luke 22:28–30). This role is demonstrated in Acts 2, where Peter with the Eleven (2:14) witnesses to the Jews of Judea and Jerusalem gathered for the festival of Pentecost (see 2:36; 4:10). Luke wishes to narrate the successful growth of the church to Gentiles in Asia Minor and Europe apart from Peter or the Twelve, who seem to play little or no role in this process. Whatever success the Twelve may have had in Israel or points east, their success in Israel was apparently short-lived due to the Jewish war with Rome, which began in the 60s, and the spread of Christianity eastward was apparently unknown to Luke, if such apostolic missionary work ever transpired. Concerning the Gentile mission, Luke chooses to focus on Paul as the one person most responsible for the fulfillment of the commission "to the ends of the earth." Thus, Acts is also a chronicle of a movement toward Paul and his churches and away from Jerusalem, Judaism, and even from Peter, who disappears after the Acts 15 council.

The Mission in Jerusalem (2:1—6:7)

Having accomplished the administrative task of replacing Judas with Matthias, the apostles were ready to begin their mission as Jesus' witnesses. Acts 2 stands at the beginning of a cycle of stories that depicts events in the life of the early church during and following the first Christian Pentecost. The Jewish feast of Pentecost (fifty days after Passover), was also known as the Feast of Weeks, an agricultural festival in which the community celebrated the gathering of the first harvest and offered thanks to God for nature's bounty. During the period of early Judaism (300 BCE–100 CE), as attention focused on preserving the religious heritage of the Hebrew people, Pentecost began to lose its association with agriculture. By the first century CE, Pentecost had become primarily a celebration of God's gift of the law of Moses to Israel. As the fifty-day interval between Passover in Egypt and the giving of the law at Mount Sinai reminded Jews of two significant events in the life of Israel, so the fifty-day interval reminded Christians of the crucifixion of Jesus that occurred at Passover and the giving of the Holy Spirit, which occurred fifty days later at Pentecost.

Pentecost, for Luke, is a paradigmatic episode that, in parallel with Jesus' reception of the Spirit at his baptism, signals conferral of power for and the beginning of the mission and witness to the "ends of the earth." Used thematically by Luke, Pentecost is said to mark critical stages of God's dealings with humanity; to initiate the church's beginnings; to signal the community's growth, unity, and mission; and to bring attention to Luke's "agency" christology, whereby Jesus first receives the Spirit and then "pours out" that Spirit upon all who seek, repent, and are baptized in his name.

Given its importance in the origin, growth, and development of the church, what exactly happened at Pentecost, and what did it mean? According to Luke, this event began in a house where the disciples were "all together in one place" (2:1). In the first verses of Acts 2, Luke uses the principle of analogy to describe what happened. The sound from heaven was like a violent wind, but was not one; the tongues were like fire but were not fire. Divided tongues like fire appeared and rested upon all those present.[2] Each person in the room was filled with the Spirit and began to speak in "other tongues" as the Spirit gave ability.

Acts 2:1–4 is filled with biblical allusions. In the Old Testament, when the law is given to Moses on Mount Sinai, the event is accompanied by fire (Exod. 20:18). Furthermore, the Spirit of God is described as a "wind from God" in Genesis 1:2 (see also John 3:8). Likewise, the verb "filled" is an important one in scripture. Elsewhere in Luke–Acts this verb describes an initial endowment of someone by the Spirit for service (Luke 1:15; Acts 9:17) or when one is inspired to speak God's word (Acts 4:8, 331; 13:9). References such as Luke 4:1; Acts 6:3, 5; 7:55; 11:24 indicate that a person who is filled with the Spirit is equipped for some specific task or proclamation. A great deal of this usage is Old Testamental, as when the Spirit filled the prophets to speak, or enabled them to do a mighty deed. Elsewhere what is here called a "filling" is called a baptizing (Acts 1:5; 11:16; see Luke 3:16). In other words, these terms are used by Luke interchangeably and should not be treated as technical terms for different spiritual experiences.

When Luke states in 2:4 that the apostles are speaking "in other languages," the reference is to other human languages, as the context makes clear (2:7–8, 11). A rabbinic tradition from Luke's time suggests that when the Mosaic law was given by God at Sinai, it was given to all nations in all languages. The Alexandrian Jewish philosopher Philo, writing shortly before the time of Luke, makes an even more intriguing comment about the

---

2. The idea of "tongues" of fire coming to rest on each apostle reminds the reader of Jesus' own baptism. In Luke 3:22 we read that at his baptism the Holy Spirit descended upon Jesus "in bodily form like a dove." There, as here, Luke concretizes an experience that others may present metaphorically.

giving of God's law to Israel: "Then from the midst of the fire that streamed from heaven there sounded forth to their utter amazement a voice, for the flame became the articulate speech in the language familiar to the audience" (*Decal.* 46). In Acts 2, it is quite possible that Luke recasts this tradition in light of the Christian experience at Pentecost. This time, however, it is the gospel that is being given to "Jews from every nation under heaven . . . in the native language of each" (2:5–6).

When reading Acts, one encounters as many as twenty-four speeches or sermons, which together account for about one third of the entire book. Readers wonder if speeches such as Peter's sermon on Pentecost (2:14–41) are verbatim transcriptions, or if Luke has condensed the speeches or possibly even imaginatively constructed them. Scholars note that in creating speeches, Luke is following conventional Greek historiography. Such speeches were never verbatim, but rather contained summaries to cover the main points of what was spoken. Also, it was customary to render speeches in the author's own words and style, a custom Luke attempts to follow, though studies show that much of the speech material in Acts, not just the major speeches, display uniquely Lukan stylistic traits and themes. On occasion Luke is said to write in a "biblical" style of Greek, meaning that his vocabulary and syntax are reminiscent of the Septuagint, the Greek text of the Old Testament. For example, when he presents the words of Jesus and his disciples, he has them speak "biblical Greek," that is, the kind of Greek spoken in the third century BCE. Such stylized language is rather amusing, since the real language of Jesus and his apostles was first-century Aramaic. In addition, as the narrative of Acts moves from Judea to the wider Greek and Roman world, Luke's language shifts from provincial Greek reminiscent of the third century BCE to first-century CE Koine (common) Greek—the official language of the Roman Empire.

Much of the material in Luke's speeches make christological and other sorts of points. This arises out of the profound conviction that the early Christians were living in the age when God was fulfilling the Old Testament promises, and filling out the larger meaning or significance of various portions of the Old Testament that did not specifically speak prophetically about the future. It appears likely that early Christians collected key Old Testament texts know as *testimonia*, which various early Christian preachers used along with the basic kerygma about Jesus' death and resurrection, especially when speaking with Jews about Jesus. It was especially Jesus' death by crucifixion that required scriptural validation if Jews were to accept Jesus, since there is thus far no hard evidence that Jews before or during Jesus' day were looking for a crucified messiah. In this regard, Isaiah's references to a vicarious suffering servant were invaluable. Reliance on such

CHAPTER 12—THE CHRISTIAN MISSION IN JERUSALEM (ACTS 1:1—6:7)

testimonia is particularly evident in the speeches of Peter and Paul in Acts, as well as in the extended speech by Stephen in Acts 7.

As we shall see, Peter basically carries the load of preaching the good news in the first half of Acts, and Paul picks up where Peter leaves off. We will note that James's speech in Acts 15 comes at a crucial juncture in the narrative of Acts, helping set the church off in a new direction. Indeed, the speeches in Acts usually come at crucial junctures and in some cases precipitate the action, in general helping to bind the narrative into a whole.

Luke often uses the speeches as vehicles to present early christological perspectives, often placing such conversations in the mouths of key figures at important moments in the story. As a gifted artist, Luke has conversation partners, including the audience in the narrative and his imaginary reader/auditor. While we do not know how Luke obtained his information for these speeches, some, such as Stephen's speech in Acts 7 or Paul's speech to the Ephesian elders at Miletus in Acts 20:18–36, do not sound Lukan and suggest the use of source material. However produced, the speeches in Acts are masterpieces.

In many respects, Peter's "inaugural address" functions much like Jesus' "keynote address" in Luke 4:16–30. His sermon sets forth the "kerygma," the core proclamation of the Christian church. Taking a midrashic approach, Peter echoes prophecy and then goes on to provide a persuasive commentary on its messianic meaning in order to address the present crisis, namely, ignorance of the importance of the present moment in salvation history. Like many contemporary sermons, Peter's Pentecost sermon is divided into three parts: (1) an introductory section that describes the coming of the Holy Spirit as the fulfillment of a prophecy given by the prophet Joel. This gift from God is a portent of this world's last days (2:14–21); (2) a middle section that professes faith in Jesus as Lord and Messiah (2:22–36); (3) a final section that contains a call to repentance and baptism in the name of Jesus Christ (2:37–42).

While the second section describes Jesus as a human being, it is evident that Peter considers Jesus to be more than an ordinary man. Jesus was attested by God with deeds of power (literally "powers"), "wonders, and signs that God did through him" (2:22). In using these three attributes—powers, wonders, and signs—Peter is looking to Israel's past—to the time of Moses and the exodus from Egypt, when God liberated his people with powerful "signs and wonders." For Luke, the people of God are beginning a new exodus that will lead them from the Promised Land into the wider Hellenistic world. "Powers, signs, and wonders" also draw attention to the apostolic age—for in Luke's day, the phrase had become a standard way of describing life in the early church. Thirty years before Luke wrote Acts, Paul spoke of himself as one who performed "signs, wonders, and powers" (2 Cor. 12:12). This phrase also contains a future dimension, for in Jesus' ministry, healing miracles were believed to be a sign that the end was at hand (see Luke 7:18-22). As we learn in Acts 3, with the advent of the church this power is transferred from Jesus to his disciples.

In spite of these obvious marks of divinity that Jesus possessed, he died a cruel and shameful death. Jesus' death appeared to contradict his life. Therefore, in Luke's apologetic speeches, the "scandal" of the cross must be explained, something Peter apparently does in 2:23, where he presents the death of Jesus as part of God's design for salvation. In 2:37-42 Peter calls his hearers to repentance, which in this context challenges them to change their minds about Jesus, to understand that despite his crucifixion, he is indeed the Messiah. Repentance, Peter notes, should be followed by baptism, which results in forgiveness (2:38).

According to Peter, baptism is to be done "in the name of Jesus Christ," meaning that those who are baptized are brought under the power, authority, and forgiveness of Jesus. Baptism, we are told, also brings the gift of the Holy Spirit. Throughout Acts, the presence of the Spirit is seen as the distinguishing mark of Christianity—it is what makes a person a Christian. Through baptism, Peter's hearers are invited to share the gift just given to the disciples on this first Christian Pentecost.

Luke should not be forced into a stereotypical pattern regarding how and when the Spirit is given. Acts 10:44-48 shows Cornelius and his family receiving the Spirit *before* they are baptized, whereas in Acts 19:5-6 the Spirit comes to the disciples of John the Baptist when Paul lays his hands on them *after* their baptism. As in the rest of scripture, the Spirit blows where it will in Acts, refusing to be bound by later ecclesiastical definitions and conventions. Likewise, we should not single out the pattern in 2:38 and make it the one model for conversion. Nowhere else in Acts in this pattern—repentance, baptism, forgiveness of sins, and reception of the Holy Spirit—mentioned. Luke's account of personal calls, transformations, and conversions—whether of Saul, Cornelius, Peter, or the Ethiopian eunuch—are far too rich, varied, and nuanced to be reduced to one factor, formula, or pattern.[3]

The event recorded in Acts 2 is not about the inauguration of the worldwide Gentile mission. While it is possible that Luke has in mind God's greater mission in the world, the context for the phrase "for all who are far away" in 2:39 suggests that it most like refers to the Jews of the world, not to the world in general.

---

3. See the discussion "Conversion in Acts" in Willimon, *Acts*, 100-105.

Luke records that at Pentecost, "about three thousand persons were added" to the Christian community (2:41). It is difficult to know whether Luke is exaggerating here. He is fond of speaking about mass conversions (see Acts 21:20, where Jewish believers are said to number "many tens of thousands" [literal translation]). Whether Luke is exaggerating the numbers, he certainly looks back in time some fifty years through somewhat nostalgic eyes, as we gather from the idealized portrait of the church in 2:43–47. Just as in his Gospel Luke had rendered Jesus' nativity in glowing terms, so here in his first major summary Luke paints a similar picture of the birth of the church. Like Christ, the church is said to be pure and perfect in its infancy. As in his Gospel, where Luke notes that "Jesus increased in wisdom and in years, and in divine and human favor" (Luke 2:52), Luke indicates that the followers of Jesus had "the goodwill of all the people. And day by day the Lord added to their number those who were being saved" (Acts 2:47). The church, like her founder, was increasing in size and favor. As we learn in Acts 4:32–35, Luke's second major summary, this racially and socially mixed group of believers found ways of living peacefully together, and more than that, they freely shared their individual possessions for the common good. The converts are said to devote themselves to four things: (1) the teaching of the apostles, (2) sharing possessions, (3) eating common meals (including the Lord's Supper), and (4) common worship (including praying together (2:42, 44–47). With this spirit of enthusiasm and sharing came spectacular growth.

Acts 2:43–47 suggest that in the earliest days of the Christian community, the Jewish followers of Jesus did not separate themselves from their Jewish heritage, but rather participated in it fully, going regularly to the temple. The believers are said to be highly esteemed by many of their fellow Jews, both for their piety and their generosity. Verse 44 tells us that this group of Christians shared all things in common. What is suggested here is not what we would call communism, namely, some sort of system where there was no such thing as private property. Rather, what is described here is voluntary sharing to meet communal needs as they arose. Barnabas, the symbol of virtue who later becomes a companion of Paul, sells a field and brings the proceeds to the apostles. The voluntary nature of sharing is reinforced in 4:32—5:11, where Ananias and Sapphira are upbraided not because they did not give all (Peter says it was still theirs to give or not to give), but because they lied about the amount they gave. Their duplicity cost them their lives. Evidently, Luke wished to make the point that lying in the church is tantamount to lying to the Holy Spirit.

The material in chapters 3:1—8:3 has to do with the internal life of the early church in Jerusalem, its external activities, especially preaching and healing, and the public response to these activities. The first story in this unit deals with the subject of a healing and preaching, and how these lead to public censure. The miracle in 3:1–10 has notable parallels with Jesus' healing of the paralytic in Luke 5:16–17. Likewise, parallels can be found between this story and that of Paul's healing of the man lame from birth in Acts 14:8–18.

The miracles the apostles perform are not different in kind from those Jesus performed. Luke records many miracle stories in his writings, including seventeen healing stories in his Gospel, often with considerable detail (so much that some readers discern in these accounts the hand of a physician). In his Gospel, Luke's miracle stories generally follow a set pattern. He begins with (1) a description of the illness, followed by (2) an action of Jesus, and ends with (3) the response of the healed person and bystanders to the miracle. In Acts 3, Luke follows the same narrative pattern. However, what we note in Acts is that Peter and John heal by declaring "the name of Jesus Christ" as a source of healing power.

The association of power with the divine name is deeply rooted in Hebrew tradition, one that can easily be misused. Hence the Third Commandment states, "You shall not make wrongful use of the name of the Lord your God" (Exod. 20:7), or, as the more familiar version reads, "You shall not take the name of the Lord your God in vain." Only after Moses learned the name of God was he able to use the awesome power of that name to perform mighty "signs and wonders." Power, however, does not reside in the name itself. Rather, the name represented the power behind it. Words do have power, as we all know, and once uttered, words cannot be retrieved. Miracles, Luke tells us, have to do with God's power and sovereignty, a power humans can tap into but never control.

Luke offers a picture of an astonished crowd running to Peter and John, a gathering Peter uses for a sermon about Jesus (3:12–26). Notice that Peter begins and ends his sermon with the statement that Jesus is God's servant (3:13, 26; see also 4:27, 30), possibly an understanding of Jesus drawn from Isaiah's Servant Songs (see also Acts 8:26–40). Peter also calls Jesus the Holy and Righteous One, perhaps the earliest titles the followers of Jesus applied to their master after his death (see 7:52; 22:14). The fourth christological title, Author of Life, no doubt comes from Jesus' resurrection, to which Peter and the other disciples are witnesses (3:15). Building on his sermon of Acts 2, Peter further develops the notion that Jesus is God's Messiah, whose future return will bring "universal restoration," involving blessing for "all the families of the earth" (3:25).

The speech material in this section varies little from Peter's speech in Acts 2, though we begin to see an apologetic character to Acts, and why

CHAPTER 12—THE CHRISTIAN MISSION IN JERUSALEM (ACTS 1:1—6:7)

Luke must endeavor to set strait the record concerning the foundational events of Christianity. Hostility to the gospel supplies Acts throughout with a dramatic plot, which moves toward a climax in the death of Stephen and then in the second half of Acts, rises to a second climax in the trial of Paul. A variety of themes and motifs introduced in Peter's speech crop up again in Stephen's speech in Acts 7. For example, some of the same biblical texts are used, and in Acts, the prophetic motif linking Jesus with Moses is prominent only in these two speeches (see 3:22–23 and 8:37).

The results of Peter's speech are seen as successful, but for the first time there is significant opposition involving the Jewish authorities. Since the healing of the lame man and Peter's sermon occur within the temple precincts, those in charge—including the priests, the Sadducees, and the officer in charge of the temple police—take offense and arrest the apostles until the Sanhedrin could convene the following morning. The presence of these individuals signals to the listener that the issue of power and authority is about to be raised. Ultimately, the council is not concerned with the apostles' teaching about the resurrection, but what power or whose authority they follow (4:7). We see here the beginnings of a power struggle for the hearts of the Jewish people. The Sadducees, related to the leading priestly families and the banking industry, were also the landed lay aristocracy who dominated the Jewish power structure in Jerusalem at this time.

While the accusation is for teaching that "in Jesus there is the resurrection of the dead" (4:2), the charge would not be pursued very vigorously, since the Sanhedrin included Pharisees among its membership, who believed there would be a resurrection of the dead at the end of time. The Pharisaic members of the council ae offended not over the resurrection, but because Peter and John are proclaiming that "in Jesus," that is, in a crucified criminal, there is resurrection.

The council is initially amazed by the level of conversation conducted by these "uneducated and ordinary men" (4:13). Obviously the disciples of Jesus had learned from their master some important ways of interpreting scripture. The sermons of Peter indicate that the early church had developed a sophisticated interpretive approach to the law, prophets, and Psalms. Scripture, for the Christian community, was to be read and taught through the experience of Jesus' life, death, and resurrection. The Sanhedrin, now aware of this principle of interpretation, orders the apostles not "to speak or teach at all in the name of Jesus" (4:18).

When Peter and John tell of their experience to the gathered community of Christians, the community responds to persecution in prayer, not for relief or deliverance, but for boldness and power to continue in the midst of such adversity. At the end of the prayer, the building in which the community gathered is shaken, a sign that their prayer had been heard. This is followed by the coming of the Holy Spirit, not so much a "second Pentecost," as some interpreters suggest, intended for those newly brought into the community, but as empowerment of believers to respond to persecution boldly and faithfully (4:29).

In 5:12–16 Luke notes that the apostles continued to gather at the temple, their popularity connected with their healing power. The reference to Peter's shadow possessing healing power may represent a temporary lapse into the realm of magic, for Peter had earlier argued that healing did not come through his own power or piety, but by the name of Jesus (3:12, 16).[4] The focus in the New Testament tradition is miracle, not magic. In 5:17–21, the apostles are again arrested, only to experience a miraculous release by an "angel of the Lord."[5] The word "angel" in Greek means "messenger," and that is the function of angels in Luke–Acts. Although Luke sometimes describes them simply as "men" (Luke 24:4), they occasionally have unusual powers (see Acts 12:7, 10). There is irony in the fact that those who have been jailed by the Sadducees are released by an angel, since Sadducees did not believe in angels. Luke's emphasis, however, is clear. Just as the trial scene with Jesus and his enemies was not the end of the gospel, neither would any trial scenes involving Jesus' followers mean the end of the gospel. The gospel may be opposed, but it cannot be arrested.

Finding the apostles teaching in the temple, the astonished Jewish authorities round them up and ask them to explain why they persist in disobeying the council's orders not to teach about Jesus. The council members are concerned with authority and submission, but Peter addresses the issue of religious and political authority with the response, "We must obey God rather than any human authority" (5:29).[6] For Peter and Luke, all the Jerusalem authorities—Jewish and Gentile—share responsibility for Jesus' death (5:30). Despite Jesus' shameful death, God "exalted him at his right hand as Leader and Savior" (5:31).[7] Therefore, the Christian community

---

4. Luke obviously sees the apostles performing the same sort of works as Jesus, and in effect carrying on his ministry in his name. In antiquity, one's shadow was seen as an extension of the person or personality, perhaps even a manifestation of the soul or spiritual life force of a person. This may have some bearing on how we should read Luke 1:35, where Mary is overshadowed by the most potent of all life forces—God in the person of the Holy Spirit.

5. The expression "angel of the Lord" is mentioned regularly in the Hebrew scriptures (see, for example, Gen. 16:7), and angels play a significant role in Luke–Acts.

6. Readers should note that Peter's expression of civil disobedience is not a form of protest against external authority. His dissent does not serve political but rather missionary ends.

7. This is the first time the title "Savior" is used for Jesus in Acts (see also Luke 2:11;

CHAPTER 12—THE CHRISTIAN MISSION IN JERUSALEM (ACTS 1:1—6:7)

must declare its obedience to God's authority above all! Understandably, the members of the Sanhedrin are "enraged" at the apostles' brazen insolence, particularly their blasphemous belief that this executed criminal is God's Messiah. A man under God's curse could not possibly be God's Messiah.

At this point a surprising figure intervenes, Gamaliel, "a teacher of the law, respected by all the people" (5:34). He may have been the grandson of Hillel—founder of the liberal wing of the Pharisaic party—though his relation to Hillel is not certain. He was clearly a leading figure in Pharisaism at this time, though his voice represented a minority opinion. Verse 34 tells us that he ordered the apostles from the room so a closed session of the council could be held. What follows may be one of those occasions when Luke composes a speech on the basis of what one might think the speaker would say, though it is possible that Saul, said to be Gamaliel's former pupil (see Acts 22:3), was either present or heard a report later from Gamaliel himself.

Gamaliel's advice is that the Sanhedrin act with caution. To support his contention that if a movement be of God it will prosper, and if not, it would not, he cites historical examples of two political figures who intended rebellion against Roman rule in Palestine. As is well known, Luke has the historical order of Judas the Galilean and Theudas reversed. Judas led a tax revolt against the Romans in 6 CE, and in 44 CE, according to Josephus, a Roman squadron routed Theudas and his rebel band. This latter event would have occurred fourteen years after Gamaliel addressed the council. It may be that Luke's source was faulty at this point, since Luke is otherwise a rather careful historian. Even though the Sanhedrin was convinced by Gamaliel's argument, the apostles are still flogged for civil disobedience and ordered not to speak in the name of Jesus.

Luke's first "panel" ends with the election of "the seven," a group of pious Jews chosen by the apostles to assist with duties such as food distribution. As we noticed in Luke's Gospel, so again in Acts we find an emphasis on the biblical injunction to meet the material needs of the community's most vulnerable members—widows, orphans, resident aliens, the destitute, and the powerless. In Acts 6:1–6, Luke distinguishes between the "Hebrews" in the church and the "Hellenists." The "Hebrews" of this community were Aramaic-speaking Jews who had grown up in Palestine, while the "Hellenists" were Greek-speaking Jews who had either moved to Jerusalem or were visiting from the diaspora (that is, from communities outside of Palestine). No doubt many pious Jews from the diaspora settled in Jerusalem in their later years. As the men died off, the number of widows grew and became dependent on public charity. These Greek-speaking widows were in

---

Acts 13:23).

need and apparently were being neglected by the Aramaic-speaking members of the church.

In this passage we can see clearly the distinction Luke makes between "apostles" and "disciples." So that they might continue to lead the community through prayer, preaching, and teaching, the Twelve propose that seven Greek-speaking Christians be chosen to take over emerging temporal needs in the church. The Seven may have been modeled on the town councils established in local Jewish communities, sometimes known as "The Seven of the Town." Luke seems to know very little about these seven men, except for Stephen and Philip, of whose activities we learn more in chapters 6–8. Verse 7 represents another of the summary sentences in Acts, but this one does not effectively join two "panels" together, for the narrative continues in 6:8, building on the list in 6:5.

The reference to the conversion of "many of the priests" in 6:7 is surprising, though not implausible. There were apparently thousands of priests in and around the Jerusalem area, who served the temple one or two months each year (recall the story of Zechariah, the father of John the Baptist, who served his term in Luke 1:5–23).[8] Because this was part-time employment, priests were obliged to maintain a trade for their livelihood. If these priests were distanced from the office of the high priesthood, then it is not surprising that some disaffected priests would be attracted to Christianity, a more egalitarian form of fellowship. By his remark, Luke may well have been attempting to make the point that the church was not outside the mainstream of Judaism.

---

8. Lukan scholar Ernst Haenchen estimates a figure of 18,000 priests living in Jerusalem at this time.

CHAPTER 13

The Christian Mission in Judea, Samaria, and Syria (Acts 6:8—12:24)

Assignment: Read chapter 13 of *Power Revealed* and chapters 6:8—12:24 of Acts. Answer the following questions, writing the answers in your journal. [If you are in a study group, be prepared to share your views with others in the class.] 1. Think about when you met Christ or became his follower. Describe what you were like before you turned your life over to him. Describe what transformation took place in your life, both instantly and over time. Describe what transformation in your life still needs to take place. 2. When has your faith in Jesus Christ been encouraged by others? When has it been discouraged by others? What do these experiences teach you about being an effective witness for Jesus Christ?

Outline to Acts 6:8—12:24

    I. Second Panel: Extension of the Church through Palestine Acts 6:8—9:31

        A. The Testing of Stephen 6:8—8:3

        B. The Acts of Philip in Samaria 8:4-40

        C. The Conversion and Commissioning of Paul 9:1-31

    II. Third Panel: Extension of the Church to Antioch 9:32—12:24

        A. The Mission of Peter 9:32—11:18

1. Peter in Lydda and Joppa 9:32–43
2. The Conversion of Cornelius 10:1—11:18
B. Christians in Antioch 11:19–30
C. Herodian Persecution of the Church 12:1–24

This chapter presents an overview and commentary on Luke's second and third literary panels.

The Extension of the Church through Palestine (6:8—9:31)

The second panel focuses on the events of Stephen and Philip, two of the Seven Hellenists introduced in 6:5, and introduces readers to Saul of Tarsus (7:58; 8:1), focusing on his conversion (9:1–31). The third panel features the mission of Peter in the region of Caesarea, narrating the conversion of Cornelius, the Roman centurion who became the first Gentile convert to Christianity, and the spread of the Christian movement to Antioch, where the followers of Jesus are first called "Christians" (11:26). The spread of Christianity, as we shall see, was aided by persecution and martyrdom (8:1).

Stephen, a Hellenistic Jewish Christian and one of the Seven, is presented as a true hero in the history of the early church. Described as an individual of grace and power (6:8), Stephen, one of those set aside for church administration, found himself driven by the "full gospel," namely, by evangelistic zeal, arguing theology in a synagogue. When those opposing him could not defeat his arguments, they brought false charges against him ("We have heard him speak blasphemous words against Moses and God"; 6:11), dragging him before the council. There he is forced to defend himself. The length of his speech in Acts 7, the longest in a book full of speeches, indicates something of the importance Luke assigned to this episode in the history of earliest Christianity. There is no doubt that Luke sees the death of Stephen as a turning point, not only for the crisis it engendered, but also because it causes fellow Christians to flee Jerusalem, which in turn leads to the evangelizing of other places. The focus of the narrative shifts from Jerusalem after 8:1.

One of the impressions we get from Acts 6:8—8:3 is that Luke is deliberately writing this story to indicate how Stephen's last days and end parallel those of Jesus. Not only so, but Stephen is depicted as standing in an even longer line of outstanding individuals including not only the later prophets but also especially Joseph and Moses. The specific charge about the destruction of the temple in Acts 6:14 is the same one that had been used against Jesus by his accusers (see Matt. 26:61 and Mark 14:58, to which, interestingly, there is no parallel in Luke's Gospel). Of the many parallels between Stephen's passion and that of Jesus, most are not found in Luke's Gospel account, providing compelling evidence that Luke had Acts in mind while writing his Gospel, editing certain items from his Markan source about Jesus' passion for use in his Stephen story.[1]

Stephen's faith, as we discover in his defense, is centered in the promises of the God of Israel. He begins with the start of the salvation story, the call of Abraham. Stephen outlines the story of Abraham and his descendants as found in Genesis 12–50. Thus Stephen's enemies can only agree with everything he says. The story of the Israelites is Stephen's story, as it is the church's story.

In 7:25, however, Stephen puts a "spin" on Moses' story not found in the Exodus 2:11–14 text. He says that Moses supposed that the Israelites would understand his actions on their behalf, but they did not. Drawing parallels between the people's rejection of God's salvation in their rejection of Moses and their current rejection of God's salvation in their rejection of Jesus, Stephen argues that it is not Christians who had changed the "customs of Moses." Rather, rejection of Moses lies deeply embedded in Israel's own history, rejection that continues in those who hear Stephen's speech.

In 7:44–53 Stephen defends the second charge against him: insufficient reverence for the temple. At the time of Moses, Stephen contends, there was no temple. The people had the "tent of testimony" or "tabernacle," which was a portable sanctuary erected by Moses (see Exodus 35–40). This tent was the sacred place of worship until the time of King David, the greatest of Israel's kings. David wanted to build a temple, but God would not allow it. It was David's son Solomon who erected the first temple at Jerusalem. Taking a line from Solomon's own prayer at the dedication of the temple, Stephen reminds his listeners that "the Most High does not dwell in houses made with human hands" (see 1 Kgs. 8:27). He backs this up with a quotation from Isaiah 66:1–2, implying that the people have made too much of the temple.[2]

While some interpreters consider Stephen's speech critical of the temple as an institution, such a view goes against the generally favorable portrayal of the temple elsewhere in Luke–Acts. While Jesus is said to have

1. A list of ten parallels is given by Witherington, *Acts*, 253. Two of the ten items are found only in Luke and Acts ("committal of spirit" in Luke 23:46/Acts 7:59 and "intercession for enemies" in Luke 23:34/Acts 7:60). Five of the ten items are found in Acts and in other Synoptic accounts of Jesus' death, but not in Luke's Gospel.

2. Readers of Stephen's speech must keep in mind that when Luke wrote Acts, the impressive temple structure lay in ruins, as it does to this day.

predicted the dismantling of the Herodian temple in Luke 21:6, Jesus is described shortly thereafter as one who taught regularly in the temple (22:53). Furthermore, worshipping in the temple characterized the early church (Acts 2:46). Stephen's speech affirms that God transcends human structures, not that God's presence cannot be found in temples. As Luke has demonstrated in Acts 2–6, the Holy Spirit is active within the temple precincts. The declaration of God's independence of the Jerusalem temple in Acts 7:48–50 "is also a declaration of God's availability to all with or without a temple."[3]

In a searing attack, Stephen throws Israel's sorry history in the council's face and now accuses them of betraying and murdering "the Righteous One"(7:52), that is, God's Messiah. He concludes with a blistering attack on their failure as those who had been entrusted with the law of God (7:53). The dispute quickly reaches a boiling point. The council is enraged when Stephen describes a theophany he experiences, seeing a vision of the "Son of Man" standing next to God. The term "Son of Man," used frequently of Jesus in the Gospels, occurs outside the Gospels only here and in Revelation 1:13. Stephen's statement in 7:56 reflects Jesus' own words, also spoken before the Sanhedrin (see Luke 22:69). Stephen is dragged out of the city and stoned to death, the first Christian martyr.

Stephen's examination before the Sanhedrin and the stoning that followed may not have been legally executed, for nothing is said in the account about the court offering a verdict or even announcing a formal sentence. What occurs is a lynching, an act of mob violence. Hence the details about whether the Sanhedrin had the legal authority to execute are moot, for there is no talk about a legal action here. The martyrdom of Stephen should not be viewed as an isolated act of violence. Believers are now hunted and scattered across Judea and Samaria. Earlier, Jesus had predicted that the gospel would be taken by witnesses (the word "witness" in Greek means "martyr") into "all Judea and Samaria" (Acts 1:8). Little did his followers know that the impetus for the evangelism would be persecution!

Luke uses this scene to introduce a person who will become a major figure in his narrative. Saul of Tarsus, Gamaliel's rabbinical student, is introduced as one of those leading the attack on the followers of Jesus. Stephen was a Greek-speaking Jew, perhaps a Pharisee, who began to see problems with legalistic religion. Here we meet another Greek-speaking Jew, a Pharisee named Saul (he is not called by his Roman name, Paul, until 13:9).

The peace that the church enjoyed during its early days is suddenly shattered. According to Luke, the martyrdom of Stephen results in a great persecution against the church, forcing all the believers to leave Jerusalem

---

3. Tannehill, *Luke–Acts*, 2:93.

except for the Twelve. Saul takes personal responsibility to uproot this noxious sect, as he confirms in Galatians 1:13 and Philippians 3:6. Luke clearly intends the reader to see the episodes in Acts 8 as part of the fulfillment of Jesus' words that his witnesses would carry out their work "in all Judea and Samaria" (1:8). The material in Acts 8:4–40 chronicles the missionary work of Philip, one of the Seven, in this region.

At this point we begin to see the formation of concentric circles of believers, starting with Aramaic-speaking Christians, with the Twelve as their core, and beyond them Greek-speaking Jewish Christians, with the Seven as leaders. It is premature to talk about the beginnings of the Gentile mission in Acts 8, however, for the Samaritan mission does not lead to the Gentile mission. Luke quite properly sees Samaria as part of the Holy Land, and at least most of its residents as Jews, though on the fringes of Judaism. However, he is aware that most Galilean and Judean Jews viewed Samaritans as at best half-breeds and at worst foreigners, though Luke does see Samaritans as worshipping the same God as Jews (see Luke 17:11–19).

2 Kings 17:24–34 contains a graphic and negative description of Samaritans, who emerged in 721 BCE, after the fall of the Northern Kingdom of Israel to the Assyrians. At this time much of the Israelite population had been deported to the east, and foreigners were relocated to this region. Eventually, intermarriages took place between these foreigners and the Israelites who remained in the land, resulting in a mixed race of people who came to be known as "Samaritans."[4] For Luke, the time for reconciliation is present in the ministry of Philip. As a result of Philip's preaching, many Samaritans became converts (8:12), breaking the important barriers of religion and race. Such a breakthrough apparently caused concern among the Jewish-Christian leaders in Jerusalem, forcing Peter and John to look into the matter (8:14). This results in yet another Pentecost, as Samaritans are included in the blessings of the Holy Spirit (8:17).

Philip's evangelistic ministry involves more than preaching, for he also has the power to exorcise and to heal. Philips's impressive wonder working attracts the attention of Simon, a magician revered by the people of Samaria as "great" (he is remembered in later Christian literature by the name Simon Magus; see 8:9–10). When Peter and John arrived from Jerusalem, they, too, brought with them the power of God, which surpasses all magic. Having seen Peter and John convey the Holy Spirit through the laying on of hands, Simon attempts to purchase the power to do likewise, for which he is reproached and told to repent. One might well speculate that Peter clearly

---

4. Some of the differences between Jews and Samaritans appear in the discussion between Jesus and the Samaritan woman in John's Gospel (see John 4:9, 20).

understood Simon's motive. The medieval term "simony," derived from the name Simon, refers to the buying and selling of church offices (a bishopric might be offered for sale to the highest bidder), just as Simon had tried to purchase the power of the Holy Spirit from Peter. The reader is left uncertain about Simon's ultimate fate.

The narration of Philip's urban mission in Samaria continues with the memorable account of his encounter with an Ethiopian eunuch (8:26–40). In Old Testament fashion, an angel of the Lord comes to Philip with traveling orders, and Philip finds himself transported to a deserted road between Jerusalem and Gaza (see I Kgs. 18:12; 2 Kgs. 2:11). There he encounters an Ethiopian riding in a carriage, returning home by way of Egypt. Philip, seeing the Ethiopian reading from the book of Isaiah, asks if the Ethiopian understands the passage. The passage seems to have been from Isaiah 53, one of the Servant Songs. The identity of this "servant of God" had long been a mystery. Initially, it may have been viewed as a reference to Isaiah himself, a faithful representative of Israel's righteous remnant, though early Christian understood the servant to be Jesus. For the first time in the book of Acts, however, this important Old Testament text is applied directly to Jesus. Philip proclaimed to the Ethiopian that Jesus was the suffering servant of God of whom Isaiah wrote. Perhaps Philip and the eunuch read a bit further in Isaiah's prophecies, discovering the passage that refers to foreigners and eunuchs in Isaiah 56:3–8. The two men came to some water, and the Ethiopian was baptized. Baptism was one of the rites of initiation into Judaism, and now the Ethiopian finds himself joining the Jewish-Christian community, conveying the gospel to Africa. Meanwhile, the Spirit transports Philip to Azotus, where he continues his preaching mission along the Judean seacoast, from Ashdod to Caesarea, the important Palestinian seaport where the Roman procurator had his headquarters.[5]

The story of Saul's "conversion" in Acts 9 is one of the most important events, if not the most important event, that Luke records in Acts.[6] It relates to what has gone before, as the "still" of 9:1 indicates, and yet it points to Acts 10 in that both passages recount a crucial conversion involving two visions and the overcoming of considerable obstacles. The importance of this event in Luke's mind is shown by the fact that Luke gives the story no

---

5. In 63 BCE, Pompey added Caesarea, along with other nearby coastal towns, to the Roman province of Syria. For the next six hundred years, Caesarea is the capital of Roman government in Palestine, seat of the Roman governor and headquarters for the Roman legions stationed in Palestine. It is here that Peter encounters a Gentile centurion named Cornelius (Acts 10).

6. Curiously, Paul never describes a Damascus road experience.

less than three full treatments, the later narrative in Acts 22 and 26 supplementing the basic account in Acts 9.

A variety of scholars find points of agreement and disagreement between Paul's account of his life and conversion (see especially Gal. 1:11–23) and those of Luke. However, the more one presumes that Luke was a companion of Paul, the more one is inclined to believe in the veracity of his portrayal of the apostle to the Gentiles. Despite differences in the three conversion accounts recorded by Luke, some of the differences are likely due to the fact that these accounts serve different purposes and may originally have been meant for different audiences. Their effect is meant to be collective, cumulative, and supplemental to each other. If Luke was present at one of these retellings (the occasion of the testimony before Festus and Agrippa in Acts 26), there is good reason to expect an accurate summary there. The account in Acts 22 represents supplemental information from Paul, and Acts 9 represents Luke's summary in his own words, as he understood the conversion. In any case, we must stress that these accounts are summaries and that Luke has written them in his own style and way. The accounts in Acts 22 and 26 appear to be condensations from speeches made by Paul himself. Paul would be presenting his story to two different audiences there, and wishing to convey different aspects of the account to these two groups. A further complicating factor is that Luke tells us Paul gave the speech we have in Acts 22 not in Greek but "in the Hebrew tongue," which likely means in Aramaic. However, we have this speech in Luke's Greek translation and condensation.

While all three accounts agree in essentials, one of these, that Paul had written authorization from the chief priest in Jerusalem to imprison Christians, is the most contentious. Much ink has been spilled on whether the high priest actually had such a right of extradition during this period. However, our text says nothing about a legal right; the impression is that the high priest was providing letters requesting permission for such actions by Saul. Even if the right of extradition is in view here, we are told by Josephus (*Antiquities* 14.192–95) that Julius Caesar confirmed such right and privileges to the Jewish people and to the high priest in particular, even though Israel was no longer a sovereign or independent state. This privilege may have existed in Saul's day as well. If not, reports of such "letters" may have been part of the pre-Lukan lore about Paul's pre-Christian days, and Luke may simply have been relying on an erroneous tradition.

Another area of controversy involves Paul's upbringing, particularly about his having studied in Jerusalem with Gamaliel. Gamaliel, we learn from Acts 5:18, was a moderate, and if Gamaliel had been his teacher in Jerusalem, Paul seems not to have followed his advice on how to handle dissident Jews. Both Paul and Luke agree that Saul was a zealous student, but Paul never mentions Gamaliel in his letters, probably because Gamaliel and his teaching had become irrelevant in light of Jesus and his teaching. Other differences include Paul's journey to "Arabia" (probably a reference to the Nabatean region east of Damascus) after his conversion, followed by a three-year stay in Damascus (Gal. 1:17–18), which Luke fails to mention. Luke, acting as a salvation historian whose major interest is in the events that caused the spread of the gospel from Jerusalem to Rome, was under no obligation to include episodes that did not contribute significantly to the growth of the church. Both Luke and Paul omit any discussion of the ten-year period during which Paul was in Cilicia and Syria. We must keep in mind that as authors, Luke and Paul present selective accounts.

While such discrepancies may call into question how personally close Luke was to Paul, the core of the Lukan tradition about the apostle conforms with Paul's own account. Luke's concern was to show that a great change had come over Paul—from persecutor of the church to promoter of the gospel. Paul was primarily concerned to show that the gospel came to him through a direct revelation from Jesus, and was not mediated by any human source (Gal. 1:11–12).

By his own admission, Saul's first connection with the emerging Christian movement was as a persecutor (1 Cor. 15:9; Gal. 1:13). According to the testimony of Acts, Saul associated himself with the accusers of the faithful Christian named Stephen, guarding the garments of the witnesses as, in conformity with the ancient law, they threw the first stones at his execution (Acts 7:58—8:1). Then he took part enthusiastically in the campaign of repression against believers in Damascus, intending to make them renounce their faith or face trial and punishment.

If Stephen saw the logic of the situation more clearly than the apostles, the pre-Christian Saul saw it more clearly than the Pharisees. In the eyes of Stephen and Saul alike, the new order and the old were incompatible. Whereas Stephen might have argued, "The new has come; therefore the old must go," Saul for his part argued, "The old must stay; therefore the new must go." Only on one condition could Saul accept that the customs delivered by Moses might be changed. There was an ancient Jewish tradition, possibly predating Saul, which taught that when the Messiah came, he would change the customs or even abrogate the law. But for Saul to believe that Jesus of Nazareth was the expected Messiah was out of the question. It is unlikely that Saul's conception of the status, career, and teaching of the Messiah conformed to that of Jesus. Furthermore, Jesus had been crucified; such a concept contradicted the meaning of the pronouncement in Deuteronomy 21:23 that "anyone that is hung on a tree is under God's curse." Since crucifixion was a Roman form of hanging, although a prolonged and

CHAPTER 13—THE CHRISTIAN MISSION IN JUDEA, SAMARIA, AND SYRIA

more extreme version, it stood to reason that Jesus could not be the Messiah. The Messiah, by definition, was uniquely endowed with the divine blessing ("The Spirit of the Lord shall rest on him," Isa. 11:2), whereas the divine curse explicitly rested on one who was crucified. To the Jews, the very idea of a crucified Messiah was blasphemous (1 Cor. 1:23). Furthermore, it was believed by the Jews that the coming of the messianic age could be delayed by apostasy within the nation. Thus, as Moses took strong action in Numbers 25 when he hanged chiefs and slayed those who worshipped false gods, so Saul believed that in persecuting Christians he was following a righteous path.

With astonishing suddenness, the persecutor of the church became the apostle of Jesus Christ. He was in mid-course as a zealot for the law, bent on exterminating the plague that threatened the life of Israel, when, in his own words, "Christ Jesus made me his own" (Phil. 3:12). What caused this transformation? His own repeated explanation is that he saw the crucified Christ now exalted as the risen Lord: "Have I not seen Jesus our Lord?" he asks when his apostolic credentials are questioned (1 Cor. 9:1), referring to that same occasion later in the same letter where, after listing earlier appearances of Christ in resurrection, he adds, "Last of all, as to one untimely born, he appeared also to me" (1 Cor. 15:8). When, in 2 Corinthians 4:6, he says that "God . . . has shone in our hearts to give the light of the knowledge of the glory of God in the face of Jesus Christ," his language implies a reminiscence of his conversion, described in Acts as having occurred on the way to Damascus, when about midday "a light from heaven flashed around him" and he fell to the ground, hearing a voice say: "Saul, Saul, why do you persecute me?" When Saul asked who was speaking, he heard the reply: "I am Jesus, whom you are persecuting" (Acts 9:3–5). This experience of Jesus had a profound and lasting effect on him. Blinded temporarily by the preternatural light that shone at creation when God said "Let there be light," Saul witnessed Jesus, the likeness of the glory of the God unveiled at last to him. Saul "found himself instantaneously compelled to acknowledge that Jesus of Nazareth, the crucified one, was alive after his passion, vindicated and exalted by God, and was now conscripting him into his service."[7]

Saul's conversion represents a radical shift in his thinking about Jesus and the church. At his conversion Saul learned two things about Jesus: that he was not dead, but alive, and that Jesus was not cursed, but blessed by God. Hence the cross, rather than discrediting Jesus as an imposter, is truly God's provision for humanity and the fulfillment of the promise that through Abraham all nations and peoples would be blessed (Gal. 3:6–9).

---

7. Bruce, *Apostle of the Heart Set Free*, 75.

Jesus was indeed the expected Messiah, but also the "Son of God." This discovery became the subject of his preaching in Damascus (Acts 9:20). As a Christian, he still believed in only one God, but he became convinced that God could only be fully known through Jesus (2 Cor. 4:6). At his conversion he also learned that Christians are not heretics, but God's people. He discovered that in persecuting Christians he had been persecuting Christ (Acts 9:5). That correlation would lead him to one of his most profound insights, that the church was neither a building nor a sect but the "body of Christ" (1 Cor. 12:27). Theologically, the church was a microcosm of the transformation that God's new order would bring for the whole world. To be in the church was to have a foretaste of life in God's kingdom. Socially, the church in the Roman Empire was an alternative society, based on the new freedom and fellowship that Jesus had announced: freedom to love God and to love and serve others (Mark 12:29–31). It must have taken Saul some time to process his new understanding about Jesus and the church, but as far as he was concerned, it was in Damascus that the essential core of his faith as a Christian was first revealed to him.

Acts 9:15 indicates the vocation that God has in mind for Saul: "an instrument I have chosen to bring my name before Gentiles and kings and before the people of Israel." This brings us to an area that has evoked considerable debate. How should we talk about Saul's experience on the Damascus road? Was it a conversion or a call? While Saul was transformed from an adversary to an advocate of Christianity, this change was preliminary to his call from God. His letters nowhere indicate that he ceased to be a Pharisee. In addressing the Sanhedrin, he declared, "I am a Pharisee, a son of Pharisees" (23:6). As he states in Galatians 1:15–16, "God . . . called me through his grace, [and] was pleased to reveal his son to me, so that I might proclaim him among the Gentiles."

The young rabbi Saul now had his true vocation. Ananias, a leader in the Jewish-Christian community of Damascus, was instructed in a vision to go to Judas's house to meet with Saul and heal him of his blindness. An understandably anxious Ananias did as he was told. Saul was healed, he received the Holy Spirit, and he was baptized into the Christian community. At that moment he begins his missionary vocation, entering the synagogues of Damascus to proclaim that Jesus "is the Son of God"[8] and to argue from scripture that Jesus is the Messiah. The structure of the story finds a counterpart in Acts 10, where Peter and Cornelius (like Paul and Ananias) both have visions, and Peter objects.

---

8. Luke's description of Saul's proclamation in Acts 9:20 that Jesus "is the Son of God" (the only time this title occurs in Acts) conforms with Paul's recollection that during his Damascus road experience God revealed "his Son to me" (Gal. 1:16).

After some time had passed, Saul visited Jerusalem, where his reputation as a persecutor of Christians preceded him.[9] There, however, Barnabas becomes his advocate. Barnabas is an important figure in Acts and in Saul's life, yet Barnabas's preaching and teaching are not recorded. What we remember about him is his ability to encourage others. In Acts 11:24 Luke speaks of him with great affection; in that chapter Barnabas travels to Tarsus to find Saul and bring him to Antioch. A priest (Levite; see 4:36) and a diaspora Jew from Cyprus, Barnabas befriends Paul and the two become traveling companions on the first missionary journey. Luke concludes his second panel with an editorial summary (9:31), preparing his audience for the third panel and the extension of the church to Antioch.

The Extension of the Church to Antioch (9:32—12:24)

The material in 9:32-43 brings us back to the subject of Peter's work. The subsection in 9:32-43 is transitional, preparing us for the major narrative about Peter and Cornelius in 10:1—11:18. In this section Peter is portrayed as standing in a long line of great prophetic healers. The entire unit is set in the context of a tour that Peter makes of Christian communities along the Judean seacoast—Lydda, Joppa, and Caesarea. The coastal plain of Sharon extends from Caesarea thirty miles southward to Joppa.

As we noted previously, Luke typically writes double stories in his narrative. In 9:32-43 he chronicles the healing of a paralyzed man and the raising of a dead women. In his writings, Luke frequently deals with pairs that focus on a man and on a woman. By so doing, he is clearly emphasizing that the gospel and all aspects of salvation, including healing, are intended equally for men and women. Both stories have interesting parallels in Luke's Gospel. In the first account, Peter heals a man who had been paralyzed for

---

9. In Galatians 1:17-18, Paul notes that at this time he made a trip to Arabia (probably Syrian Arabia, namely, the Nabatean kingdom east and south of Damascus). Luke omits this three-year sojourn, either because he did not know about it or more likely, because it was irrelevant to his account. A close correspondence, however, does occur between Acts 9:23-25 and 2 Corinthians 11:32-33. The difference in these accounts suggests that rather than slavishly copying material from Paul's letters, Luke is relying on a different source for this information, perhaps Paul himself. We may conclude from 2 Corinthians 11 that Paul had incurred the anger of King Aretas IV (currently ruling the Nabatean kingdom with at least some jurisdiction or influence in Damascus), possibly due to evangelizing activity in the region, perhaps even in its major city, Petra. No doubt, Luke and Paul present selective accounts. Curiously, both omit any discussion of the ten-year-period during which Paul was in Cilicia (including Tarsus) and Syria. Luke leaves Paul in Tarsus in 9:30 only to pick up his story from that location again in 11:25.

eight years. Luke had told a similar story about Jesus who healed a paralytic in Luke 5:24–25, The second story finds Peter at Joppa, called there by members of the church distressed over the death of Tabitha, an important woman in the Christian community, known for her ministry to widows. The name Tabitha is Aramaic, and because his audience does not know this language, Luke gives the Greek equivalent, Dorcas. Luke's account of her raising closely parallels the account of Jesus raising the daughter of Jairus in Luke 8:40–56.

It is important to point out that coastal towns such as Lydda and Joppa, located on an important coastal road, were open to Hellenistic and later to Roman influence. Joppa seems to have been a Greek city during this era, and the port city of Caesarea, to which the narrative takes us next, was thoroughly Hellenized (and Romanized), being the seat of Roman power and the site of the great construction projects of Herod the Great, including the famous theater for Greek drama and the great aqueduct. Because Peter was traveling in increasingly more Hellenized territory, we should not be surprised that it was in this sort of locale that the question of Gentiles and the Christian faith seems to first have arisen in a significant way.

Luke notes that while in Joppa Peter stayed with Simon, a tanner. This detail regarding Simon's trade foreshadows the break Peter will make with more orthodox Judaism. Because of his contact with the hides of dead animals, Simon did work that, according to Jewish law, was considered unclean and therefore defiling. Peter, not known for his consistency (see Galatians 2:11–14), had no problems staying with an unclean Jew, but balked at unclean Gentiles.

Chapter 10 introduces the reader to an important figure in the early church—Cornelius, a Roman centurion. A person of status and rank, he is said to be a "God-fearer," meaning that as a Gentile he had a significant relationship with Judaism, taking part in synagogue services and performing typical duties of a Jew such as prayer, fasting, and almsgiving. This description reminds us of the somewhat similar story involving a centurion who sent messengers to Jesus to come heal his slave. In Luke 7:1–10 we discover this centurion was also highly regarded by the Jews of Capernaum because he generously built a synagogue for them. In accounts such as these we note that Luke makes clear that there is no antagonism between Jesus or his followers toward the Roman presence in Palestine or elsewhere, and that in fact even Roman soldiers found this new movement appealing and worth joining. Passages such as these continue Luke's apologetic purpose on behalf of Christianity.

According to 10:3, Cornelius has a vision at a time when as a devout God-fearer he would be praying. In that vision he was instructed to send men to Joppa to find Peter. At noon Peter went up to the roof of the tanner's house to pray. The normal Palestinian home of this sort would have an outside staircase to the roof where one might go to be alone. Peter, too, has a vision. In the sheet that descended (something like a large four-cornered tablecloth) were all sorts of land and sea creatures, including both clean and unclean animals. Peter is told to "kill and eat" these creatures, clearly a violation of Mosaic law (Leviticus 11 offers a lengthy and detailed list of clean and unclean animals). Peter three times hears a heavenly voice say to him, "What God has made clean, you must not call profane." Readers will note that once again we have Peter denying the Lord three times, only this time in regard to food and table fellowship with Gentiles. Later on, during his imprisonment, Peter will be instructed three times by an angel to do as he is told (12:7–8), much like his threefold commissioning as shepherd of the flock in John 21:15–19, where Jesus' command to Peter, "Follow me," contains an invitation to discipleship as well as to martyrdom and death.

Peter's vision may be important, but he has no idea what it means. It is only when Cornelius's messengers arrive that Peter begins to make sense of what has happened. It is not food that must not be called profane, but the Gentiles. At this point he realizes that the dream of creatures on a four-sided sheet represents all the world's people gathered within the four corners of the earth. That Peter understands this is implied by his offer of hospitality to the Gentiles and his willingness to go with them to Cornelius's house.

The stage is set for Peter's first sermon to a specifically Gentile audience. At this point the story moves progressively into the realm of audacious claims. Peter not only learns that God has changed the rules that determine social interactions between Jews and Gentiles, he also discovers that "God shows no partiality," for "anyone who fears him and does what is right is acceptable to him" (10:34–35). To a first-century Jewish reader, this would have been close to blasphemy, for this message challenges the ancient tradition that God had chosen Israel above all other nations to be his special people (Exod. 19:5–6; Deut. 7:6–8).

The impartiality of which Peter speaks is not the view that all religions are the same to God, or that all human beings are automatically in right relationship with God, but rather closer to the perspective found in Deuteronomy 10:17. There we are told specifically that God's impartiality is the basis for judging human wickedness fairly, whether within or outside of Israel. Acts 10:35 follows naturally from 10:34. Anyone from any nation who fears God and does what is right is acceptable to God. What Peter means is that this statement applies equally to Jews or Gentiles. Being "acceptable" means being in an acceptable state (of repentance) to hear and receive the message of salvation and forgiveness of sins. Luke is not advocating that Cornelius, because of his piety, is already saved, apart from having faith in Christ (see Acts 10:34; also 4:12). Acts 10:37–42 represents the most comprehensive review of the career of Jesus found in any of the sermons in Acts, perhaps because the audience is Gentile. It may also be said that since this is Peter's final sermon, Luke has edited it in such a way that it sums up the early kerygma used by the apostles (especially Peter) in their preaching.

In addition to these insights, Peter is convinced that belief in Jesus brings forgiveness of sins (10:43). This is a quantum leap from the Judaism that Peter had lived and loved. Through this declaration, Peter bluntly challenges the efficacy of the sacrificial system in Jerusalem in which priests offer sacrifices for the forgiveness of sins. Remarkably, such revolutionary thought and language came to Peter in a vision, one that changed the world.

As we discover, Acts 10 is not only the story of the conversion of Cornelius and his household. It is also the story of the ongoing transformation of Peter as new and deeper awareness of what it means to follow Jesus is made clear to him. As with the gospel of Jesus, the message to Peter is inclusive. Jesus is Lord of all, and everyone is under the Lordship of Jesus Christ. And if this be true, then God cannot show preference for one race, gender, nation, or social class, something Luke has been emphasizing all along (see also Paul's similar dramatic pronouncement in Gal. 3:28). Note, however, that Luke does not address the issue of food laws, for they have not yet been abolished. His focus is on purity, and on the fact that persons can no longer be treated as unclean. This judgment certainly has implications for the keeping of food laws, if Jews and Gentiles are to share fellowship in Christ, but that is a secondary issue yet to be worked out, as Acts 11 and 15 demonstrate.

The story concludes with the "Gentile Pentecost," the fourth outpouring of the Holy Spirit in Acts. Like the Jews of Jerusalem who received the Holy Spirit, now these Gentiles of Caesarea have received the same gift and symbol of God's presence and power. Cornelius along with his family and friends are baptized with water, and they constitute the first Gentile-Christian community. Baptism, it seems, will replace circumcision as the rite of initiation into the family of God. Acts 11:1–18 narrates the fallout in Jerusalem for what happened in Caesarea.

The conversion of Cornelius and his family in Acts is second only to the conversion and call of Saul, for it signals the movement of the Christian faith beyond the boundaries of Judaism to the Gentile world. Already Luke has in mind the Jerusalem Council in chapter 15, for which the Cornelius story is designed to function as Exhibit A. There James brings the council to its conclusion with a speech that begins with the conversion of Cornelius (15:14). James's conclusion is based on Peter's presentation to the council, found in 15:7–9, where the allusion to Cornelius is evident, not as an isolated occurrence, but as a generalized principle of basic importance.

Acts 10–15 is a carefully composed unit, devised to present in detail a story that can be validated in miniature in the brief exchange between Peter and the Judaizers (the Jewish Christian traditionalists, sometimes referred to as the "circumcision party") in the mother church in Jerusalem (11:1–18), which concludes with the Lukan principle, "Then God has given even to the Gentiles the repentance that leads to life" (11:18). The Jerusalem Council, in its legitimation of the Gentile mission, becomes the turning point for Luke's conception. As the distinguished Lukan scholar Ernst Haenchen notes, the Jerusalem Council began the shift away from the original organizational structure led by Peter and the apostles to the subsequent structure directed by James "the Just" (the brother of Jesus and early leader of Jerusalem Christianity) and the elders of the mother church in Jerusalem. As early as 12:17 the expression "James and the believers" is used (by Peter) for the Jerusalem authorities.

At the Jerusalem Council, at which James presides, Peter represents only his fellow missionaries. The scene provides a harmonious transition from one system of government to the other, not just the theological point on which they agree. Transition language occurs when the elders are introduced in 11:30 as the recipients of the collection brought by Barnabas and Saul, and when the leadership of the Jerusalem Council is expressed in the phrase "the apostles and the elders" (15:2, 4, 6, 22, 23). The apostles are mentioned for the last time at 16:4, making the Jerusalem Council their swan song. By 21:18 the Jerusalem Church is led only by James and the elders.

The future belongs to this new form of government, presumably including also for Luke's community. On the return trip from the first missionary journey, Barnabas and Paul install elders in each church they have founded (14:23). On his final return to Jerusalem, Paul convenes at Miletus the elders of the Ephesus church (20:17). Thus it is apparent that Luke conceives of this form of church government as standard practice for the Gentile Christianity that he represents.

In 11:1–18 Peter and his fellow travelers return to Jerusalem. News travels fast, so that by the time Peter arrives in Jerusalem he is met by Jewish Christians who are upset by his dealings with Gentiles. They were probably less concerned about Peter's preaching to Gentiles than about his violation of kosher regulation. Peter's explanation is contained in 11:5–17, which is a retelling of his vision, plus the addition of verse 16, one of the few quotes from Jesus found outside the Gospels. It is worth noting that Peter introduces this quote with "I remembered."

The authorization for Peter's action is unmistakable. He had received a vision from God that called him to minister to all people. The words of the risen Jesus, recently spoken to the apostles, provided confirmation that Peter's baptism of these Gentiles was in accordance with the will of God. The Gentiles had also received the Holy Spirit, just as the Jewish Christians in Jerusalem. Peter drew the obvious conclusion: "God gave them the same gift that he gave us when we believed in the Lord Jesus Christ" (11:17). The response of the Jewish Christian hearers was unmistakably enthusiastic: "Then God has given even to the Gentiles the repentance that leads to life" (11:18).

Acts 11:19–26 picks up the story of the spread of the gospel that began in 8:1-4. The disciples who were scattered following the death of Stephen now take the good news to Phoenicia, Cyprus, and the city of Antioch in Syria. The passage focuses on Antioch, the third largest city in the Roman Empire (about a half-million residents) and the capital of the Roman province of Syria, which included Galilee and Judea. The city was predominantly Gentile, though it contained a large Jewish colony. Luke notes that in Antioch the followers of Jesus were first called Christians. Prior to that, early Christians described themselves as being disciples, believers, saints, brothers and sisters, or followers of "the Way," and they are elsewhere called also Nazarenes (Acts 24:5). It does not appear that believers used the term "Christian" of themselves before the second century. Luke's point here is to indicate that the followers of Jesus were first perceived to be a group clearly distinct from Jews in Antioch, a significant fact for a historian presenting an account of early Christian history.

Acts 11:20 notes that some missionaries turned up in Antioch who were from Cyprus and Cyrene (the latter is on the North African Mediterranean coast, west of Egypt). Again, news of a mission to the Gentiles reached the church in Jerusalem, and the leaders there felt the need to investigate. Therefore, Barnabas, a native of Cyprus (see 4:36), was sent to check on work being carried out by his fellow Cypriots. Barnabas was pleased with what he found in Antioch and joined the work among the Gentiles there. This work went so well that he took a trip to Tarsus (just northwest of Antioch) to find Saul and secure his help. The two men worked together for a year.

Acts 11:27–30 speak of Christian prophets coming to Antioch from Jerusalem, including Agabus, whom we see again in 21:10. Prophets appear to have constituted a distinct order of leadership in the early church (see Acts 13:1; 1 Cor. 12:28–29). Among these prophets, Agabus predicts a worldwide famine (this took place during the reign of Claudius, 41–45 CE). We know that an especially severe famine occurred in Palestine between 46 and 48 CE. According to Luke, the famine occasioned a collection among the Christians of Antioch to be sent as relief for the Christian community in Judea.

This story remind us of the reports in 2:44–45 and 4:32–37 that the followers of Christ shared their material possessions. While this sharing in Antioch is less dramatic than earlier reports of commonality, it does indicate that generosity is the hallmark of authentic Christian community. In a few verses, Luke provides a vivid picture of true Christianity. The church is not an aggregate of isolated congregations, each going its own way spiritually and materially, but is a collaboration of congregations,, older ones like Jerusalem giving birth to new ones, and younger congregations like Antioch responding to parishioners in need. Outreach, nurture, and mission are essential yet inseparable. Together, they are driven by philanthropy.

Luke's editorial hand is clearly evident in chapter 12. In the midst of a narrative about the mission in Antioch, he inserts a cycle of stories about Herod Agrippa's persecution, Peter's imprisonment, and Agrippa's death. As Luke indicates, the time of persecution has not passed; in fact it has scarcely begun. The persecutions of the early church would wax and wane for three hundred years, until the time of Emperor Constantine in 313 CE.

The "Herod" of this passage was the grandson of Herod the Great (who ruled Palestine at the time of Jesus' birth) and nephew of Herod Antipas (tetrarch of Galilee during the ministry of Jesus). This Herod is Herod Agrippa I (11–44 CE), who ruled over much of Palestine as a vassal of Rome. As a child he was sent to Rome and received his education there. He was a friend of Caligula and also of Claudius, who was his schoolmate. The Jewish leadership of Jerusalem had great disdain for Herod because of his strong Roman allegiance and his non-Jewish ancestry. Perhaps in order to placate them he attacked a relatively easy target—the Jerusalem church. His attack was aimed at "some" of the Christians, and only James the brother of John and Peter are specifically mentioned. In addition to executing James, Herod had Peter arrested and put in prison, guarded by four squads of soldiers.[10]

The faithful are in prayer during the time of Peter's imprisonment. While Peter is sleeping, a messenger of God awakens him, tells him to get dressed, and escorts him from prison. Peter, alone in the dark streets of the city, heads for the house where church members have gathered. It is the home of Mary, mother of John Mark. Apparently she is a wealthy widow, for she owns a house large enough to host a sizable group, and she has a maid named Rhoda. When Peter knocks, Rhoda goes to the door, but she is so excited she forgets to let him in. The story quickly comes to an end as Peter

---

10. A squad consists of four soldiers; hence, Peter was guarded by sixteen soldiers, their watch limited to three hours per group of four to ensure they remained alert. Under such circumstances, escape would be impossible.

describes his escape and asks that this be told to James (this is the first mention in Acts of Jesus' brother, the new head of the Jerusalem church) and other believers. Luke records that Peter flees to Caesarea, where he probably placed himself under the protection of Cornelius.

This story of deliverance is one of many in Acts. Such accounts, however, must be tempered with realism and humility. A person told by a televangelist that "if you truly have faith, you will be healed" is vulnerable to skepticism or despair if healing does not occur. While Peter did escape Herod's attack and was spared for another day of witness, this would be for a time only. The gospel continues unhindered, even though its messengers may not.

Luke concludes the account with a tale of Herod's death, bringing to an end his third panel and the first half of Acts with the summary verse in 12:24 and an editorial remark about Saul and Barnabas returning from Jerusalem,[11] and John Mark (Barnabas's cousin and supposed author of Mark's Gospel), companions on the first missionary journey narrated in 13:1—14:28.

Scholars ponder the point of chapter 12 in the narrative, since the story could have been left out without harming the flow of Luke's account of early Christianity. While the story further indicates the shift of power in Jerusalem from Peter to James (see 12:17), it also continues the persecution-in-Jerusalem theme, which for Luke helps explain the shift in focus from Jerusalem to Antioch, explaining why the mission to the Gentiles took the course it did at that time, and why Jerusalem would no longer function as the base for missionaries to the Gentiles (see, for example, the hostility of Jerusalem Jews to Paul and the Gentile mission in 21:27–36).

---

11. While the preposition "to" is the best attested rendering of the original Greek, "from" makes the most sense of the plot and is preferred in this case. In 11:30, Barnabas and Saul go to Jerusalem. Now they return, bringing with them John Mark, a resident of Jerusalem.

CHAPTER 14

The Christian Mission in Asia Minor and Europe (Acts 12:25—28:31)

Assignment: Read chapter 14 of *Power Revealed* and chapters 12:25–28:31 of Acts. Answer the following questions, writing the answers in your journal. [If you are in a study group, be prepared to share your views with others in the class.] 1. Think of someone you know who effectively shares the gospel with others. What qualities do you see in that person? What qualities do you have that makes sharing the gospel natural for you? What makes it difficult for you to share your faith? 2. What do you see in Paul that made him effective in his ministry? Which of these qualities do you want God to develop in you to make you more effective in communicating the gospel? Explain your answer. 3. Choose one or two of the most significant conflicts in your life. How did it/they arise and how was it (were they) resolved? Now make a list of the principles you find about conflict resolution in Acts 15:1–35. How can these principles be applied to your situation?

Outline to Acts 12:25—28:31

    I. Fourth Panel: Extension of the Church to Asia Minor 12:25—16:5

        A. The First Missionary Journey of Paul 12:25—14:28

            1. Prelude to the Journey 12:25—13:3

216 UNIT III—EXEGETICAL TOPICS

        2. Paul and his Companions in Cyprus 13:4–12

        3. Mission at Pisidian Antioch 13:13–52

        4. Mission in Central Asia Minor 14:1–28

    B. The Jerusalem Council and Resolution 15:1–35

    C. The Second Missionary Journey of Paul Begins 15:36—16:5

        1. Split with Barnabas 15:36–39

        2. Mission of Paul and Silas: Return to Asia Minor 15:40—16:5

II. Fifth Panel: Extension of the Church to Europe 16:6—19:20 [Continuation of Paul's Second Missionary Journey]

    A. The Call to Macedonia 16:6–10

    B. The Mission in Greece 16:11—18:22

        1. Paul in Philippi 16:11–40

        2. Paul in Thessalonica and Beroea 17:1–15

        3. Paul in Athens 17:16–34

        4. Paul in Corinth 18:1–17

        5. Return to Syria 18:18–22

    C. Paul's Third Missionary Journey 18:23—19:20

        1. The Mission in Ephesus 18:24—19:20

III. Sixth Panel: Extension of the Church to Rome 19:21—28:31

    A. Continuation of the Mission in Ephesus 19:21–40

    B. Final Travels Between Asia and Greece 20:1–12

    C. Farewell at Miletus 20:13–38

    D. Trip to Palestine 21:1—26:32

        1. Return to Caesarea 21:1–14

        2. Paul's Imprisonment and Defense in Jerusalem 21:15—23:22

        3. Paul before Festus and Agrippa II at Caesarea 23:23—26:32

    E. Paul's Journey to Rome 27:1—28:16

    F. Paul in Rome 28:17–31

We have a great deal to cover in this chapter, so we will be limited in what we examine and in the depth of our coverage. As you follow Luke's plot, consider using an atlas of the biblical world or a map of the Mediterranean world that includes the travels of Paul and his companions. We begin in Syrian Antioch, headquarters and sending church for the Christian mission to the Gentiles (see 13:2–3; 14:26; 15:30–35; 18:22–23).

The First Missionary Journey of Paul (12:25–14:28)

A group of prophets and teachers gathered in Antioch, including Barnabas and Saul.[1] Another member, Manaen, had been a member of the court of Herod Antipas, and it is possible that he, together with Joanna, the wife of Herod's steward, Chuza (Luke 8), may have provided special Herodian information used by Luke. The three leaders left behind—Simeon, Lucius, and Manaen—place their hands on the heads of Barnabas and Saul and send them to Cyprus, Barnabas's homeland.[2] John Mark, Barnabas's cousin, accompanies them. He may have resented his assistant role, or else the overpowering role of Paul, but in either case, he leaves mid-journey (13:13). Paul is angry about the situation, refusing to take John Mark on a later journey, and breaks with Barnabas over the matter. From Colossians 4:10 and Philemon 24 it seems that eventually John Mark and Paul are reconciled and reunited.

Luke traces their journey across the island in 13:4–12, beginning with Salamis, a commercial seaport at the eastern end of the island, and ending with the capital city of Paphos, a seaport located ninety miles to the west. Paul and Barnabas begin their work in the synagogues, a practice Paul will continue (13:14; 14:1–2; 17:1–5; 18:5–6; 19:8–9; 28:23–28). For Paul and for Luke the gospel message is the completion of all the promises God made to Israel.

At Paphos the missionaries encounter a Jewish magician named Bar-Jesus. Romans of high status, such as the proconsul Sergius Paulus, often kept astrologers and sorcerers to help them make difficult decisions, and that was the case here. The name Bar-Jesus means "son of Jesus," but Paul calls him "son of the devil," a play on his name. For his deceit, Paul curses him with temporary blindness, a metaphor for blinding people to God's truth. This causes the proconsul to become a believer, not only because

---

1. Because Luke uses Saul's Roman name from Acts 13:13 on, we use the name "Paul" consistently in this chapter.

2. The cultural and social diversity of this leadership in the church at Antioch is startling: "a Levite from Cyprus, a black man, a North African from Cyrene, a boyhood friend of Herod Antipas, and a Pharisee educated under Gamaliel," Krodel, *Acts*, 226.

he saw what happened to Bar-Jesus, but because he was "astonished at the teaching about the Lord" (13:12). Faith and fear make strange bedfellows, and while Luke's conclusion that such a lesson should compel belief seems odd to modern readers, the result brought another high-ranking Roman official to the Christian movement.[3]

From Paphos, the missionaries journey by ship to the mainland, arriving at the Roman province of Pamphylia. After landing, John Mark leaves his companions and returns to Jerusalem. Paul and Barnabas travel one hundred miles northward to the province of Galatia, arriving at another city named Antioch, in the mountainous region known as Pisidia. Scholars speculate that the missionaries sought higher ground for health reasons. There may be some confirmation for this speculation in Paul's letter to the Galatians, where he reminds them that it was because of a physical infirmity that he first visited their region (Gal. 4:13–14). Paul may have contracted a serious fever from the malaria-ridden swampy coast, and then traveled to higher ground in order to seek relief.

On the sabbath they visit the local synagogue. Paul is a respected Pharisaic teacher and Barnabas a Levite qualified to perform priestly duties. They would be highly honored guests of the synagogue and the congregation would wish to hear from them. As usual, Paul preaches. Synagogue worship began with the recital of the creed—the Shema—followed by prescribed prayers. Next came a reading from the Torah and appropriate passages from the prophets. One competent in the interpretation of scripture then offered a sermon. Finally, the leader of the synagogue pronounced a blessing, and the congregation departed. Customarily, when Paul preaches to fellow Jews and converts to Judaism, he appeals to their holy history, as he does on this occasion. We are not certain which biblical passages Paul was interpreting in 13:16–41, though Habakkuk may be a good candidate.

Paul's message in Antioch, his first in Acts, probably represents what Luke considered typical of Paul. Like other messages in Acts, this one can be divided into three sections. The first section is framed in much the same way as Stephen's defense (Acts 7), as a recitation of God's acts in Israel's history (13:16–25). The second section of Paul's speech (13:26–37) provides a powerful statement of the kerygma, the central message of the Christian faith, focusing on the death and resurrection of Jesus, events Paul believes were prophesied in the Jewish scriptures. Paul's christological interpretation of scripture is undoubtedly fueled by various Old Testament *testimonia*,

---

3. In this passage, Luke changes Saul's name to Paul and Bar-Jesus' name to Elymas. In both cases, Jewish names are exchanged for Gentile names to underscore the conversion of the Roman proconsul, a clear indication of the Christian mission's ultimate success in the Roman world.

groups of biblical texts compiled by Christians to help Jews recognize Jesus as Messiah. The third part of Paul's speech (13:38–41) issues an invitation to the hearers to accept the forgiveness of sins of which Jesus' resurrection is the sign and seal. The whole point of this speech is to warn the audience not to be blind or deaf to the gospel but to receive it as a gift from God. In closing Paul quotes the Septuagint version of Habakkuk 1:5, a text he may have read to them at the start.[4]

Paul's message is well received, and he is invited to speak on the next sabbath. However, a heated argument arises, possibly because some of the visitors, among them many Gentiles, responded positively. Scholars estimate that in the first common century, as many as half of the attendees at diaspora synagogues may have been Gentiles. Pagan writers such as Horace spoke of attending the Jewish synagogue as a natural thing. Juvenal asks his friend, "In what synagogue may I find you?" Seneca and Juvenal also spoke of the decadence of Roman customs and of widespread observation of the Jewish sabbath among Gentiles. As a center for worship and instruction, the synagogue was a means of proselytizing, but at Antioch, the effect was quite the opposite. Gentiles in the synagogue were hearing about Jesus, leading to great gains for the Christian movement and to a great turning point for the early Christian mission.

In 13:46 Paul articulates the approach that will guide his missionary activity: "Since you reject [the word of God] and judge yourselves to be unworthy of eternal life, we are now turning to the Gentiles" (see also 18:5–6; 28:25–28; Rom. 1:16; 2:9–10). In 13:47, Paul cites the prophet Isaiah for support (Isa. 49:6), suggesting that Jesus, the Servant of God, was "a light to the Gentiles" (Luke 2:32; Acts 26:23). In 13:47, Paul seemingly applies the text to himself and to those who are part of his mission.

Luke notes that the Jews incite both devout women of high standing and leading men against Paul and Barnabas—city leaders with a close connection to the synagogue. The missionaries move on, but not without leaving behind a community of believers. The next stop is Iconium, about eighty miles southeast of Antioch, also in the province of Galatia. In 14:1 they are back in a synagogue, where the reaction is mixed. Hearing of a plot to stone them, they flee to Lystra and Derbe. In 14:8–10 we read the story of a man, crippled from birth, healed by the missionaries. The account is almost identical with the healing story in Acts 3. The astonished onlookers take Paul and Barnabas to be gods who have come to earth. They identify Barnabas and Paul as Zeus and Hermes respectively.

4. Another possibility is that the Torah reading included Deuteronomy 4:25–26, with 2 Samuel 7:6–16 as the Haftorah (related reading from the biblical literature) reading.

The brief speech of Acts 14:15–17 is quite different from previous speeches in that the missionaries are dealing only with Gentiles in Lystra, Gentiles who apparently have no understanding of Jewish teachings about God. When Paul preaches to Gentiles, he often turns to arguments about the existence of God, as he does in 14:15. Hence, there is no mention of Jesus, Messiah, crucifixion, resurrection, or any other specifically Christian theme. Focusing on idolatry, the final sentence of this short speech is drawn from popular Hellenistic natural theology (14:17). When Luke finally mentions Jews in Lystra, they are identified as outside agitators who have followed Paul and Barnabas from Pisidian Antioch and Iconium, intending on turning the crowds against the Christian missionaries. They stone Paul almost to death, but he is rescued by a group of believers. At that point he could have called it quits, taking the main highway through the Cilician gates back to Tarsus and home. Instead, the next day he and Barnabas proceed to Derbe before returning to Lystra, Iconium, and Antioch, apparently to strengthen the believers and to appoint elders as local church leaders. They had left this region under peril, and they felt the need to reassure themselves that their mission churches had survived.

Retracing their steps back to the Mediterranean coast, Paul and Barnabas sail to Syrian Antioch where their mission began. The first missionary journey ends with a progress report to the church that served as the headquarters of the Gentile mission. According to 14:28, they remain in Antioch for a considerable period. Toward the end of this period, perhaps in 49 CE, Paul probably wrote Galatians from Antioch, shortly before going up to Jerusalem for the council on Gentile membership in the Christian church.

The Jerusalem Council and Resolution (15:1–35)

Acts 15 marks the midpoint of the book of Acts and a great turning point in the life of the early Christian community. The church that began as a small Jewish sect in Jerusalem is growing, not only numerically but also in its Gentile constituency. So successful was the mission to Gentiles that some of the churches in Asia Minor may have been predominantly Gentile. Church leaders in Jerusalem must have felt pressure to come to terms with the impact this phenomenon represented to Jewish Christianity. Important questions arise, such as the status of Gentiles in the church and the church's relationship with Judaism. It is no exaggeration to say that this chapter is the most crucial in Acts. It resolves the issue of Gentile membership in the church while raising key questions about Luke's relationship to Paul, including the relationship between Acts 15 and Pauline autobiographical remarks

CHAPTER 14—THE CHRISTIAN MISSION IN ASIA MINOR AND EUROPE

in Galatians 2, and the nature and reliability of Luke's writings and Paul's letters.

Paul and Barnabas had been in Antioch for some time when they were visited by an independent (unauthorized) group of Jewish Christians from Jerusalem (Acts 15:1, 24), whose mission was to "correct" Paul and bring him into conformity with Jewish tradition. Their view, stated succinctly, was that males couldn't be Christian without also being circumcised, since God had required circumcision as a sign of God's covenant with Israel. Wasn't this sign still required? they argued. Was the Old Testament covenant still in effect, or had God's laws been abolished? This group sounds very much like the Judaizers who followed Paul into the churches of Galatia in order to "bewitch" the Gentile Christians into accepting circumcision as a condition for membership in the body of Christ (Gal. 1:6–9; 3:1; 6:12–16). The Judaizers, in effect, are demanding that Gentiles first become Jews before becoming Christians.

To resolve this issue, Paul and Barnabas are appointed to go to Jerusalem as representatives of the Antioch church, to discuss the problem with both the apostles and the elders there. The procedure followed in decision making here involves a specific process including (1) discernment of God's will, (2) interpreting scripture in such a way as to make sense of what is happening, (3) utilizing debate and dialogue as part of the process of discernment, and (4) obtaining the consent or agreement of the church to the ruling offered by the Jerusalem church leader, in this case James. The report that Luke gives of the council relies overwhelmingly on speeches by Peter and James, as well as on the document that records the final decisions of the council. Curiously, there is no report regarding any debates or disputes, and no space is given to the arguments or rebuttals of the Judaizing party.

At the council, Peter reprises his decisive testimony at the first Jerusalem Council (11:4–17), harkening back to the episode of Cornelius and his household, noting how the Holy Spirit had come upon Gentiles just as it had previously descended upon Jewish Christians. Underlying all debate is Peter's earlier citation of Joel's prophecy at Pentecost, where God declared, "I will pour out my Spirit upon *all flesh*" (Acts 2:17), the circumstances of which had already been ratified by an earlier council to the effect that "God has given even to the Gentiles the repentance that leads to life" (11:18). The assembly's "silence" in 15:12 directs the reader's attention to listen to what comes next, namely, to Barnabas and Paul's mission report of what God was doing through them among the Gentiles (Acts 13–14).

To persist in distinguishing between Jews and Gentiles in the church would be to "put God to the test," Peter argues, borrowing language from the Old Testament (see Exod. 17:2; Deut. 6:16). Peter's message is clear: Do not put God to the test by placing on the Gentiles a burden that even Jews cannot bear, namely, the yoke of legalism from which Jesus had given them rest (Matt. 11:28–30); this would be hypocrisy. In this Peter and Paul agree, that salvation is by grace alone (15:11). Strangely, only one sentence is given to Paul and Barnabas. Luke tells us nothing about the actual content of their statement, which suggests that Luke is not following a Pauline source about the council. Otherwise he would likely have devoted more space to the one he portrays as the main human protagonist in the rest of his narrative.

After Peter, Paul, and Barnabas had finished speaking, James responded with a definite judgment, finding guidance and confirmation that God had foretold the calling of the Gentiles in the scriptural text from Amos 9:11–12.[5] This action suggests that he possessed singular authority in the Christian community. As the brother of Jesus, the mantle of leadership in the family had fallen on James, the next oldest male after Jesus. By the time we reach the end of Acts, James is the undisputed head of the church. In Acts 21:18, Paul reports the results of his missionary journeys to James and the elders. The Twelve drift completely from view after 16:4. In the midpoint of Acts, James takes center stage as leader of the predominantly Jewish-Christian Jerusalem church, while Peter and the apostles step aside. At the same time, Paul emerges as the leader of the Christian mission among the Gentiles.

The verdict that James renders represents both a compromise and a corrective. It accepts the personal testimony of the missionaries yet without discarding the Jewish heritage. While James disagrees with the Pharisaic demands, he also sends a cautionary note to the missionaries to guard against "gentilizing" repentant Jews into facile cultural compromise that makes the Jewish past irrelevant. Disagreements would continue between Paul and the Jerusalem church, yet the exhortation to not cause others to stumble remains (see Paul's discussion in Romans 14:13–23 and 1 Corinthians 8:1–13).

The consensus reached at the council is that Gentile believers not be burdened with keeping the Old Testament law, particularly the requirement of circumcision. Instead of requiring that converts from paganism be circumcised, the council declares that it is the will of God and of themselves to lay nothing further upon Gentile believers than certain minimum restrictions, called "the essentials" in 15:28. Formulated by James, these essentials were had to do with certain practices in contemporary paganism that were abhorrent to Jews. According to 15:20, 29, and 21:25, four restrictions made up the "apostolic decree," a letter sent from the apostles and elders of the

---

5. It seems odd that James would quote Amos 9 from the Septuagint, and that his interpretation depends on the peculiarities of the Greek rather than the Hebrew text. This indicates that the words of James have been reworked.

Jerusalem church addressed to "the believers of Gentile origin in Antioch and Syria and Cilicia" (15:23).

Luke speaks of the essentials as ritual requirements. They include abstaining from things polluted by idols, from fornication, from whatever has been strangled, and from blood. While it is easy to take these four elements separately, which leads to a focus on Jewish rituals, it is better to keep them together, as a common prohibition. In this case, the social setting is idolatry, in particular, rituals celebrated at pagan temple feasts. There are hints in Acts 15 that what is being prohibited is not Jewish kosher ritual but rather the attending of temple feasts. In 15:20 James states clearly that what should be avoided is "things polluted by idols," that is, pollutions resulting from contact with idol worship. The term "fornication" here likely refers to prostitution, specifically "sacred" prostitution. Fornication is precisely the right term to be used if James has in mind the sort of practices that sometimes accompanied pagan rites and feasts in pagan temples. In addition, James says he is not troubling the Gentiles in what he is about to announce. If he was imposing food laws on Gentiles, this would indeed be burdensome to them. The Gentiles have turned to the true God; what they are being asked to turn from is idolatry and the accompanying acts of immorality. There is also evidence that choking the sacrifice, that is strangling it and drinking or tasting its blood, transpired in pagan temples.

If this is the meaning of the decree in Acts 15, we would expect to find traces in the letters Paul wrote soon after the apostolic council, and that is precisely what we find in the next letter Paul wrote, 1 Thessalonians (see 1:9 and 4:1–9), and in another he wrote not long thereafter, 1 Corinthians (see chapters 5–10), where he speaks of meat sacrificed and eaten in the presence of idols. We see the prohibition of immorality already in 1 Cor. 5:1–8, but Paul deals more specifically with the connection of sexual sin and dining in a pagan temple feast in 1 Cor. 10:7–8. For Paul, the issue is clearly one of venue rather than menu, as his advice in 1 Corinthians 10:23–28 shows. He does not forbid eating food sacrificed in a pagan temple at home, however. In short, Paul, like James, insists that pagans flee idolatry and immorality and the temple context where such things are thought to be prevalent.

In today's culture believers no longer live in a world dominated by pagan shrines or temples. Nevertheless, the polluting effect of idolatry continues, as witnessed in the unprincipled acquisition of wealth, the addiction to consumerism, aggressive selfishness, violent behavior, xenophobia, and triumphal nationalism. "Whatever holds primary value in place of God is an idol, and related institutions function as its temples."[6]

6. Wall, "Acts of the Apostles," 222.

The results of the first council of Christianity, known as the Apostolic (or Jerusalem) Council, are significant. The decision was tactful and effective. It granted freedom to Gentile converts from the observance of the Mosaic laws as a requirement for salvation, but the council cautioned converts no to misuse their freedom so as to scandalize their brothers in Christ by participating in pagan customs that were offensive.

If this decision had not been made, all who are Christians today would also be Jewish in practice. The church would have remained a vestibule of the synagogue. By refusing to impose on Gentile converts the ritual act of circumcision, the council opened the way for the establishment of a truly universal Christianity, not tied to any national, social, or ethnic group.

Acts 15:36—28:31: A Brief Summary

The reader is reminded that unit III includes exegetical topics, not exegetical commentary. Hence, this unit treats Luke–Acts textually rather than exegetically. This approach is most evident here, in the second half of Acts.

For Luke, Acts 12:25—28:31 is almost exclusively the story of Paul, covering the years 46–63 CE. In this section Paul travels widely, twice westward as far as Corinth in Greece before reaching Rome. During that period Paul writes his preserved undisputed correspondence, including Galatians, 1 Thessalonians, 1 and 2 Corinthians, Romans, Philippians, and Philemon. The remaining letters attributed to Paul but of disputed authorship include Colossians and Ephesians, 2 Thessalonians, and the Pastoral Letters, some of which may have been written or dictated during his imprisonment in Rome or otherwise penned later by followers and admirers of Paul.

After the council of Jerusalem, Paul takes Silas (a prophet, according to 15:32) and embarks on his second missionary journey, traveling through Syria and Cilicia to Lystra and Derbe, where they are joined by Timothy, whose mother and grandmother were Jewish Christians (see 2 Tim. 1:5). At Troas, a seaport on the Aegean Sea, Paul receives a vision of a man of Macedonia pleading for help, which causes Paul to cross to Greece, thereby extending the Gentile mission to Europe. Some scholars imagine that Luke was the "man" in Paul's dream, a conjecture based on the first-person plural pronoun "we" that occurs for the first time in the book of Acts in this passage (16:10). The "we" passages begin at Troas and continue to Philippi, indicating that the author's personal participation with Paul began at this point. Philippi may well have been Luke's residence, the comment in 16:12 about "a leading city" revealing Luke's pride in his hometown. Philippi was famous for its school of medicine, with graduates throughout the Roman world. If Philippi was Luke's town, it is reasonable to assume that Paul's "loyal companion" in Philippians 4:3 was Luke, who was based at Philippi when the letter was written, though like many doctors in antiquity, he was itinerant. At Philippi (16:11–40), the openness and support of Lydia, a Gentile devotee of Jewish worship, becomes a model for the Christian community. With Lydia's help, Paul establishes at Philippi what will become his model congregation and to whom he later sends the letter to the Philippians, his "Epistle of Joy," likely sent during his third missionary journey while imprisoned in Ephesus.

At Thessalonica (17:1–9) Paul runs into the same kind of Jewish opposition that marred his mission in Asia Minor before the Jerusalem conference, forcing him to push on to Athens (17:15–34), where he shows familiarity with Greek culture. The author knows about the agora and the hill of the Areopagus, and he depicts Paul delivering there an address in Greek that shows an awareness of the city and of Epicurean and Stoic philosophers. The play on the "altar of the unknown god" and the philosophical and poetic quotations in his address depict Paul sounding very much like typical Hellenistic Jewish missionary propagandists, using logic, common sense, and natural theology before speaking of repentance and the resurrection of Jesus. As elsewhere, his message meets with a mixed reaction. According to 1 Corinthians 1:22–23, it is not only the resurrection, but the crucifixion, that sounds like "foolishness" to the Greeks. Whereas some believe, Paul establishes no church in Athens, for unlike converts from synagogues, Paul's Athenian audience did not divide along religious lines but were more committed to broad cultural and philosophical notions. Unwillingness to let go of such assumptions prevented faith from growing.

During his stay in Corinth (Acts 18:1–18), Paul writes 1 Thessalonians. He later directs correspondence to Corinth, causing us to know more about that church than any other. Corinth was not only a provincial capital but also a major commercial seaport, strategically located on an isthmus connecting the Aegean and Adriatic seas. There Paul befriends Aquila and Priscilla, Jewish Christians from Rome with whom Paul shared a tentmaking trade. As a rabbi, Paul was expected to support himself and to offer his teaching without charge (see 1 Cor. 9:18; 1 Thess. 2:9). Luke also mentions Crispus, a leader of the synagogue, whose conversion to Christianity led many to become believers (Acts 18:8). During Paul's eighteen-month stay in Corinth, angry mobs disturbed the peace, provoked by the growing impact of Christianity in their midst. Paul's return to Antioch in 18:23 concludes his second missionary journey.

Shortly thereafter Paul begins his third and final missionary journey, featuring a three-year stay in Ephesus. The third journey will be Paul's most extensive, revisiting churches he had established but spending the bulk of his time in Ephesus, renting a lecture hall that resulted in outreach throughout the province of Asia. Many Asians may have heard Paul at this time, some becoming believers and taking the seeds of Christianity with them to such towns as Smyrna, Pergamum, Thyatira, Sardis, Philadelphia, and Laodicea (see John's letters to seven churches of Asia in Revelation 2–3). Churches at Colossae and Hierapolis may also have been founded during this period.

At this time Paul also wrote a series of letters to the church at Corinth, squeezing in a visit to that community. In that correspondence Paul indicates that he had suffered considerable persecution at Ephesus (1 Cor. 15:32; 2 Cor. 1:8), including imprisonment. During his stay in Ephesus he probably wrote to the church at Philippi as well as the personal letter to Philemon regarding Onesimus, his runaway slave.

Acts 19:21 is the first indication of Paul's ultimate plan to go to Rome, an important anticipation of how the book will end. Luke then recounts Paul's travels through Macedonia to Corinth, where he remains three months and writes his greatest work, the epistle to the Romans. Hastening to be at Jerusalem for Pentecost,[7] Paul sails to Miletus, bypassing Ephesus. At Miletus he gives an eloquent farewell sermon to the elders of the church of Ephesus (20:17–38), ending with a lesson on leadership. Like the farewell speech at the Last Supper, where Jesus contrasts secular leadership with the company of his followers ("the leader [is] one who serves" Luke 22:25–27), Paul makes a similar point about service and love of money by referring not only to his own example (Acts 20:33–35) but by quoting Jesus (with a quote not found elsewhere in the New Testament): "It is more blessed to give than to receive." Modern clergy may be uneasy about offering themselves as models of faithfulness, but Paul had no such hesitation (see 1 Cor. 4:16).

At Tyre, on the Phoenician coast, Paul receives a warning about not going to Jerusalem, which leads to another dramatic farewell, before continuing to Caesarea (21:7–14). There, at the home of Philip and his four daughter-prophets, the prophet Agabus forewarns Paul of imprisonment should he continue to Jerusalem, but Paul is undeterred. With Paul's arrival in Jerusalem in 21:17, the third missionary journey concludes.

---

7. As we learn from Romans 15:25–28, 1 Corinthians 16:1–4, and 2 Corinthians 9:1–15, Paul is eager to arrive in Jerusalem to deliver the monetary collection he has gathered to alleviate the needs of Judean Christians (see also Acts 24:17). Having already celebrated Passover in Philippi (20:6), Paul is eager to celebrate Pentecost in Jerusalem (see 19:21). The Jewish festival has taken an even deeper significance for Paul as an occasion for celebrating the pouring of God's Holy Spirit upon believers to empower their witness to the "ends of the earth."

The last eight chapters of Acts (21–28) constitute the final section of Acts. In this segment Paul endures trials by his own people, by his own government (Jewish and Roman), and even a trial by the forces of nature as he makes a perilous journey to Rome.

Paul's arrival in Jerusalem comes at a turbulent period in Jewish-Roman relations. There had been a period of poor governance in Judea, including the rule of Antoninus Felix (52–59). The judgment of social historian Emil Schürer on the Judean procurators is quite accurate: "It might be thought, from the record of the Roman procurators . . . that they all, as if by secret arrangement, systematically and deliberately set out to drive the people to revolt."[8] The end result of their severe policy was the full-scale rebellion that began in 66 CE and culminated in the fall of Jerusalem four years later. Paul's return to Jerusalem with Gentiles from various parts of the Roman Empire at this xenophobic moment would have led ardent Jews to be more zealous to extinguish any movement that seemed to threaten their survival as a distinct ethnic and religious group. The picture Luke paints in Acts 21 is quite believable. The theme we find introduced in this segment and continuing until the end of the book, namely, Paul's self designation as a loyal Jew and his mission to Gentiles as not anti-Jewish, is essential to Paul's survival as well as to the successful continuation of the Christian movement at this time. In his trial before the Sanhedrin, Paul wisely took note of the sectarian split in that body between the Pharisees and the Sadducees, using their theological disagreement to his advantage (23:6–9).

Paul's trial in Palestine consists of four hearings in which he is required to defend his calling and convictions. He is brought before various rulers, including (1) Claudius Lysias, the Roman tribune (21:40—23:30, including a hearing before the Sanhedrin, 23:1–10); (2) Antoninus Felix, governor of Judea (24:1–27); (3) Porcius Festus, successor to Felix as Roman governor of Judea (25:6–12); and (4) Festus, Herod Agrippa II (nominal king over the Jewish territories), and his sister Bernice (26:1–32).

In Paul's trial by Festus, Luke introduces a Herodian monarch. Readers will recall that Jesus was also brought before a ruler of the Herodian dynasty during his trial (an episode found only in Luke's Gospel). The Roman governor Pilate, discovering that Jesus is from Galilee, sends Jesus to Herod Antipas, tetrarch of Galilee (Luke 23:6–7). Now, in Acts, Paul is brought before Herod Antipas's grandnephew, Herod Agrippa II. The verbal exchange between Paul and Agrippa is fascinating. The one being questioned becomes the questioner: "Do you believe the prophets?" asks Paul. Agrippa

---

8. Schürer, *History of the Jewish People*, 1:455.

responds, almost sarcastically, "Are you so quickly[9] persuading me to become a Christian?" If sarcasm is intended, Paul ignores it, hoping that all who listen become believers. At the end, as Agrippa and Festus depart, Agrippa notes that Paul would have been set free, had he not appealed to the emperor (26:31–32).

Did Paul make a poor decision in appealing to Rome? Whatever our answer, we can only conclude that his appeal guaranteed he would bring the gospel to the heart of the empire, thereby carrying out the will of God.

As we learn of the Jewish charges against Paul in his trial at Jerusalem, Jews from Ephesus recognized Paul and their Gentile townsman, Trophimus, in Jerusalem. This leads them to conclude—falsely—that Paul had brought Gentiles into the temple, thereby desecrating their holy place (21:27–29). Close to being lynched, Paul is saved by Roman soldiers.

We learn of the essential points of the Jewish charge against Paul in 21:28, where Paul is said to be teaching everywhere against the Jewish people, their law, and their temple. Such charges are not new. The same accusations previously brought against Jesus (Acts 6:14) and Stephen (6:11, 13) are now brought against Paul. In statements made at his defense, Paul indicates that as a Christian he has not ceased being a Jew. Consequently, his faith is not significantly different from what he believed as a Pharisee, for what has been added is not foreign or heretical but rather has been caused by his understanding of scriptural promises he believed to have been fulfilled in Christ. Paul revisits this matter in a remark to the Jews in Rome, where he states, "it is for the sake of the hope of Israel that I am bound with this chain" (28:20).

In his trial before Felix and Festus in Caesarea, the Jews bring formal charges against Paul, none of which they can substantiate (25:7, 18–19). The two conspiracies against Paul's life (23:12–15; 25:3) are indicative of doubts among the Jews concerning the outcome at the trial. The meeting before Felix ends with the court's postponement of the case, and nothing happens legally for two years. Felix, who is about to be replaced as governor by Festus, leaves Paul in prison to curry favor with the Jews, who had accused him of misgovernment (24:24–27).

Paul's Jewish identity is of special importance in his trial because it shows that in dealing with Jews and Romans, Paul is anxious to establish his own as well as Christianity's natural position within Judaism. The Roman authorities would have been inclined to dismiss the case as being an internal Jewish concern, as the Roman proconsul Gallio had done earlier at Corinth

---

9. Most commentators think the meaning of this difficult phrase is "in so brief a time," that is, with such brief argumentation.

CHAPTER 14—THE CHRISTIAN MISSION IN ASIA MINOR AND EUROPE   229

(18:12-17). There is no question that Luke's description of Paul's trials is influenced by his conviction of Paul's innocence. Hence, it is with a clear conscience that Paul professes his faith.

As we read about Paul's trials, we are reminded of the trial of Jesus. This is deliberate, for what characterizes Luke's portrayal of Paul during his trial is its similarity to that of Jesus. As the story of Jesus' passion occupies the key position at the end of the Gospel, so does the account of Paul's trial in Acts. And just as the suffering of Jesus is foretold by the prophets, so Paul's imprisonment and hardships are foretold (see Acts 9:6; 20:22-25). Luke's statement that the Jews would "hand [Paul] over to the Gentiles" in Acts 21:11 is practically identical to the pronouncement regarding Jesus in Luke 18:32.

When Paul is asked whether he is willing to stand trial in Jerusalem, he requests that an appeal be made to the court of Caesar in Rome (25:1-12). A visit by King Agrippa results in another meeting with the court in Caesarea, as Festus needs information about the case for a report to be sent along with Paul to the emperor (25:13-27). From Caesarea Paul embarks with other prisoners for Rome. It is late in the sailing season and the voyage is slow and precarious. The ship is wrecked but runs aground on the island of Malta. After a stay of three months, the travelers leave the island and sail for Rome.

In narrating the sea voyage, Luke provides a classic odyssey. The entire scene reminds us of two other biblical stories: Jonah sailing a story sea, and Jesus calming the sea. Like the story of Jonah, Paul's journey to Rome requires divine intervention and results in preaching a message of repentance to unbelievers.

What happened at Rome? According to Luke, Paul spent two full years in Rome, living in a rented house guarded by a soldier (28:16). Paul's arrival in Rome around 61 CE coincided with the early years of the reign of Emperor Nero (54-68 CE). While Nero is infamous for his violent persecution of Roman Christian in 65 CE, the early years of his reign were radically different. He began his imperial rule by establishing an enlightened and tolerant administration. Paul's appeal to Caesar (25:12; see 26:32) was not ill placed. He had every reason to hope for vindication and freedom.

Luke's final statement summarizes Paul's two years in Rome. The great missionary filled his days teaching anyone who came to him, focusing on the kingdom of God[10] and the Lord Jesus Christ (28:31). In these few words Luke summarizes the preaching and teaching of Paul. These concepts might seem ordinary to our ears and not terribly threatening, yet in first-century

10. The kingdom of God, the central theme of Jesus' preaching ministry, is not as prominent in Acts as in Luke's Gospel. Nevertheless, it functions in Acts as a theological "framing device," appearing at the book's beginning (1:3) and also at its end.

Rome, such terms were loaded with political significance. To speak of a kingdom other than Rome and of a Lord other than Caesar was treasonous. Nonetheless, the Roman authorities tolerated Paul's proclamation.

As elsewhere across the Roman Empire, Paul finds a flourishing Jewish community in Rome. Luke uses a well-known formula to describe the division within Judaism provoked by Paul's interpretation of scripture: "some were convinced . . . others refused to believe" (28:24). Paul's parting volley— a citation from Isaiah 6:9–10 (LXX)—is often understood as a sign of resignation leading Paul to abandon the mission to Israel. However, viewed from Luke's perspective, the quote likely addresses the tragic reality, foretold at Jesus' birth, that the word of God concerning Jesus would function as a sword, dividing Israel into a responsive remnant and a hardened opposition (see Luke 2:34–35).

The plotline of Luke–Acts follows the fulfillment of this prophecy. Israel's dilemma would lead to Gentile opportunity. Some would take this gospel and live out its implications as boldly as Paul did. Others, however, would refuse its claims. The choice holds true today and will continue into the future. The outcome depends on God's faithfulness—and ours.

Luke ends his book abruptly. As with every good story, we are left wanting more. What happened to Paul? Did his case come to trial? Did he receive clemency? Ordinarily, after two years of imprisonment, the statute of limitations for a Roman citizen ran out. Was Paul released, we wonder, and did he go on to Spain as he planned (Rom. 15:22–29)? We are left with conjecture. However, concerning what happened to Paul at his trial, it is clear that Luke knew. The evidence of Acts 21–28 suggests that the Roman authorities thought Paul was not guilty of any crime under Roman law, that the charges against him had to do with Jewish law and theology, and that Paul would have been released had he not appealed to Rome. For that reason, Paul appears to have been placed under the most lenient form of military custody, a relaxed form of house arrest with only a single soldier guarding him.

The natural way to read the clues in Acts is to conclude that Paul was acquitted, or that his case was dismissed. The alternative is to imagine that Luke and his audience knew that Paul was martyred at or near the end of the two-year period and that Luke decided not to explain why this happened, in spite of the hints in the narrative, which suggest a different outcome. In 28:21, Luke notes that the Jews in Rome had received no letter about Paul from Judea, suggesting that the Sanhedrin had decided not to pursue the case.

Acts 28:30 indicates that Luke knew that something happened to Paul after the two-year period of house arrest in Rome; otherwise, Luke would not have specified this definite period. Furthermore, Acts 27:24 strongly suggests that Paul would and did appear before the emperor. According to tradition, Paul was released to continue his missionary work temporarily before returning to Rome where he was again arrested, tried, and this time executed by Nero. Clement, the bishop of Rome at the end of the first century, is the first Christian writer to imply that Paul was martyred in Rome (*1 Clement* 5:5–7). If Paul died a martyr's death at Rome, and Luke knew this full well, why did Luke not develop an account of the death of Paul to parallel the death of Jesus? And what of Peter and the other apostles? Luke must have known something about their continuing ministry. Why did he not continue their story?

Perhaps, like a good storyteller, Luke decided to leave matters unresolved. Having drawn us into his story and piqued our interest about the church, he has done his job. Perhaps he did write a third volume and it is now lost. Perhaps Luke's third volume, as we suggested earlier, is an imitation of Paul's letters (the work known as the Pastoral Epistles—1 and 2 Timothy and Titus). Perhaps Luke died before he could finish his work. In any case, the story of Jesus and the kingdom continues, because the Spirit is still active. Luke is not simply writing history. He writes the story of the Spirit, the same Spirit incarnate in believers today.

Luke's church asks, "Lord, will you at this time restore the kingdom to Israel?" (Acts 1:6). Luke gives no answer except that the story continues. We need not be gazing into heaven (1:11) when the Spirit is active here on earth. There is work for the church to do; the period of the world mission of the church continues. Now, two millennia after Luke wrote, Luke–Acts remind us that despite rejection, persecutions, setbacks, and our own lethargy or cowardice, the gospel proclamation continues to the very end of the earth, by God's grace, "unhindered" (28:31). Luke's account remains as relevant today as ever.

Some Unresolved Issues

The narrative in Acts raises a number of questions about the portrayal of Paul by Luke as compared to what we find in Paul's letters. For instance, in Acts we hear very little about Paul being an apostle or being concerned with a collection for the believers in Palestine, but these are clearly important matters in the epistles. Furthermore, Acts tells us a great deal about Paul being a preacher and miracle worker but nothing about his being a letter writer, while the Paul of the letters only rarely mentions his working of miracles but often refers to his letters. While there are problems involved in comparing the Paul of the letters to the Paul of Acts, they can be resolved if we recognize that Paul's letters, like Luke's account, are tendentious and apologetic. If we believe that Luke was acquainted with Paul—indeed knew his mind and perspective—we must admit that both Paul's letters and Luke's account in Acts must be read critically, consulted carefully, and treated as equals.

If we look closely, we can find doctrines such as grace and justification by faith, both central themes in his letters to the Galatians and Romans, in Paul's speech material in Acts 13–14. Luke knows these are important Pauline themes, and he doesn't hesitate to emphasize them near the beginning of his portrait of Paul as a missionary. We must keep in mind that we have only one Pauline speech to Christians recorded by Luke in Acts—the Miletus speech to the Ephesian elders in 20:18–35—and we should not be surprised that this is the one speech that sounds most like the Paul of the letters. Indeed, the speech is a veritable mosaic of major Pauline themes. The reason seems clear: Luke is present on this occasion, as we learn from the "we" passages.

Another complaint by scholars is that Paul in Acts is too Jewish, too Law observant. This, we are told, is not what one finds in the epistles. This complaint is taken from the picture in Acts 15 of a Paul who takes part in the Apostolic Council and agrees to implement the decrees, as well as the Paul who has Timothy circumcised in Acts 16:3, the Paul who acquiesces to go through the rite of purification in the temple (Acts 21:23–24), and perhaps also the Paul who always visits the synagogue first wherever he goes, protesting before Jewish and Roman authorities from Acts 21 on that he is a good Jew.

These matters must be taken individually and can be addressed only briefly.[11] First, it must be admitted that Paul is portrayed as a good Jew in Acts. However, we must also note that if Acts 15 is about Jewish food laws, it appears unlikely Paul complied with or implemented the decree. However, this is likely not the subject matter of the decrees. They seem to apply to Gentiles abstaining from going to pagan temples and attending pagan feasts, where food offered to idols was both sacrificed to pagan gods and eaten, and where sexual immorality was also known to transpire. In short, the decrees are about avoiding active participation in idolatry and immorality. To this stipulation Paul would and did readily agree, and we see his attempt to implement the decree in 1 Corinthians 8–10.

---

11. The following discussion is adapted from Witherington, *Acts*, 434–38.

In regard to Paul engaging in Jewish practices for pragmatic reasons having to do with his missionary work, there is no reason to doubt that he might have done so—indeed 1 Corinthians 9:20 suggests as much. There is no problem with the idea that he might have undertaken an act of purification on one occasion in the temple as a gesture of peace. Acts 21 does not say that Paul came up with this idea, only that it was strongly suggested by others as something he should do. In regard to Paul going to synagogues to preach to a variety of people, Romans 1:16 states that the gospel is for Jews first, and 2 Corinthians 11:24 suggests that Paul repeatedly went to synagogues, on occasions paying a stiff price for his witness there. As for the circumcision of Timothy, this, too, is not unthinkable as a missionary tactic. Timothy, we must remember, was not simply a Gentile, but was partly Jewish through his mother, and Paul wanted him to be in a position to do as he himself was doing, approaching Jews as a Jew and Gentiles as a Gentile. An uncircumcised Jew would send all the wrong signals to Jews in this era.

Perhaps one reason Paul touts his Jewish heritage as something he could boast of (see Phil. 3:5–6; 2 Cor. 11:22–23) is that as a missionary it was useful to him when he spoke in a synagogue. It would have been necessary to indicate his heritage and credentials as a Jew in order to be permitted to speak, even if he would go on to say that these were things he had left behind. The issue here is whether Luke portrays Paul as one who was still under the yoke of the Law, and therefore not free to choose to keep aspects of the Law. In fact, Luke does not portray Paul as a consistently observant Jew after his conversion. Rather, Paul the Christian associates regularly with, has fellowship with, and even on occasion stays in the houses of Gentiles.

The two important speeches in Acts 22 and 26 do not suggest that Paul as a Christian was claiming to keep all of the Law, or was consistently submitting to all the Mosaic requirements. They speak, rather, of Paul's course of life as a zealous and faithful Pharisee before his conversion, but it is a mistake to suggest that Luke portrays Paul as one who continued to submit to the yoke of the Law as a necessary part of his faith in God after his conversion to Christianity.

The issue of Paul's citizenship is also an area of dispute. Whereas Luke insists that Paul was a Roman citizen (Acts 22:25–29; 23:37), Paul never mentions that status and seems even to negate it. "Three times," he claims, "I was beaten with rods" (2 Cor. 11:25)—a Roman punishment forbidden to be used on Roman citizens. If Paul was a citizen, why didn't he use that privilege to his advantage?

To this matter, we offer the two comments. First, there are only two places in Acts where Paul's Roman citizenship is an issue, in Acts 16:37–39 and 22:25–29, and in both cases Paul uses his citizenship for the purpose of influencing the improper conduct of fellow Roman citizens. Note that Paul does not mention his Roman citizenship while within earshot of a Jewish crowd, even when he is addressing the tribune, because such a reference would probably have impeded his cause with the Jewish audience. In other words, in general Luke makes very little of Paul's Roman citizenship, and only in limited settings. When Paul in Acts is addressing either a Jewish or pagan audience, or a Christian audience in a non-Roman nonlegal setting, he never mentions the matter. For Paul, Roman identity was low in order of importance, ahead of which came his identity as a Christian and as a Pharisaic Jew. Since there are no situations in Paul's letters where he either addresses or answers Roman charges against himself, there is no need to boast or speak about such citizenship. The reason there is no direct evidence about Paul's citizenship in his letters is that all are addressed to those who are already Christians. There is nothing in his letters that casts doubt on the evidence of Acts on this matter.

We conclude our discussion with one final concern, Luke's omission of Paul's apostolicity. When Paul does call Paul an apostle, as in Acts 14:4 and 14, it is likely that the term "apostle" there means a missionary agent or emissary of the Antioch church. Why, then, does Luke fail to portray Paul as an apostle "with a capital A"? Because the book of Acts is not a biography of early church leaders. As a missionary document, its focus is less on personal details of people's lives and more with the planting of churches across the eastern Mediterranean part of the Roman Empire. While Paul does consider himself in his letters to be an apostle, he mentions it only when questions of internal authority and control arise. For example, in Philippians Paul does not present himself as an apostle, but rather as a servant of Christ, like Christ himself (see 1:1—2:7). The message is clear: Paul's authority was not in question or being challenged by that congregation, unlike in Galatia or in Corinth. First Thessalonians would be another good example of a letter where Paul doesn't make claims to his apostolic status or power, since it is not disputed or challenged. In Romans, however, Paul is writing to a congregation not his own, with which he must establish rapport and display his credentials. In other words, Paul's apostolic status in Rome is one he must maintain; he cannot take for granted that the Roman Christians know or recognize that status. In his letters, whenever Paul refers to his apostolic status, it has to do with internal matters in which he seeks to exercise authority or influence. If by apostle one means a person who exercises authority over a particular group of people, Paul is not an apostle to the Gentiles; rather, he is an apostle to churches largely made up of Gentiles.

In sum, the Paul we see in Acts is not un-Pauline, as many claim, much less anti-Pauline. In some cases it is a Paul we do not hear about in the epistles, and in other cases it is a familiar Paul, though from a different and fresh perspective. It is, above all, a Paul interpreted through the eyes of admiration and respect.

Epilogue[1]

LUKE DID NOT WRITE his two volumes to be read piecemeal, as we do today in church, in private devotions, and even in our Bible studies. His books involve an overarching argument, a grand narrative that gives meaning to the whole. The chronological dimension of that narrative is obvious. After the story of the birth of Jesus, Luke–Acts grounds Jesus in a genealogy that goes back to Adam, then tells the story of his ministry, death, and resurrection in order to move readers to his second volume, to the continued work of Jesus through the Spirit in the life of the church.

The geographic dimension, though not as obvious, is equally important. The story begins in Galilee, then winds its way to Jerusalem, where it settles for the last chapters of the Gospel and the first chapters of Acts. From Jerusalem, the story extends to Antioch, Asia Minor, Greece, and eventually Rome. Yet neither chronologically nor geographically is the story finished. Chronologically, we are left with Paul under house arrest in Rome, and are told nothing about the final outcome of his appeal to Caesar. Geographically, though Acts 1:8 promises the disciples that they will be witnesses "to the ends of the earth," the narrative takes us only to Rome and there leaves us, with no hint as to how the promise of Acts 1:8 is fulfilled.

On that basis, it might be appropriate to call Luke–Acts the "unfinished Gospel." It is unfinished chronologically, for the narrative has no conclusion. Rather than ending, it simply stops when Paul is in Rome—precisely the point at which the plot is most engrossing. Like a serial in television, where at the end of an episode we are left hanging, waiting for the next, the reader wishes to know more. And the narrative is unfinished geographically, for it leaves us waiting for the story of how the disciples of Jesus became his witnesses "to the ends of the earth."

---

1. The epilogue is adapted from González, *Luke*, 3–4

This is not a flaw in Luke's writing. Interpreters have debated why Luke does not tell us the outcome of Paul's trial, and some have suggested that it is because Luke wishes to present the Gospel to Roman eyes in its best possible light, and he therefore does not wish to tell that Paul was executed by Roman authorities. This is hardly convincing, for at the heart of Luke's narrative is the story of Jesus, condemned to death by Roman authority. Another possibility is that Luke intended to write a trilogy, thereby completing his second volume. More likely, however, is the possibility that Luke–Acts is unfinished because its author was seeking not only to inform but also to invite Theophilus and all subsequent readers to see themselves as the continuation of that story, enacting the missionary mandate to people in their own generation.

Luke's grand narrative is thus an invitation, a reminder to readers of who they are; and within that grand narrative the various smaller units must also be seen as a calling and an invitation. At this point, Luke is close to our own interest in history. We study and write history to invite. Those who see hope in the present, use history to invite others to hope. Those who see doom, invite others to fear. Those who seek guidance and correction, invite others to follow the guidance and correction of history. "For us, as for Luke, history is ongoing, unfinished, an invitation to join what God is doing among us.

But still Luke would insist on the counterpoint to that: this unfinished history is not simply up for grabs. Its end has already been written. It has been written in the life, death, and resurrection of Jesus, and in his final reign. And, because the end has been written, Luke invites us today to join in the grand narrative that begins in his Gospel, continues in Acts, and leads to us."[2]

---

2. Ibid., 4.

APPENDIX A

Lukan Christology

SINCE JESUS FIRST APPEARED, his followers have debated his nature: is he human, divine, or somehow both? When speaking of Jesus, Luke uses many titles, including Son of Man, Savior, Lord, Messiah, Son of God, and Servant. Statistically, his favorite titles for Jesus are "Christ" ("Messiah") and "Lord." He sometimes combines these, as in Luke 2:11 and Acts 2:36, and, in one instance, links them to another, "Savior" (Luke 2:11). This latter term is significant because, aside from a single reference in John's Gospel (John 4:42), Luke is the only Synoptic Gospel to call Jesus "Savior."

We begin, however, with another designation for Jesus, the scriptural role of prophet, which Luke uses frequently when referring to Jesus, for like Israel's prophets, Jesus discloses the character of God's realm and summons God's people to faithfulness. In addition, prophets meet resistance and rejection, as does Jesus.

Prophet

At the start of the first century CE, prophecy as a profession no longer existed in the Jewish world. In fact, Jewish prophecy had died out several centuries earlier, and in Jesus' day, it existed only in the prophetic writings of the Hebrew scriptures. Ideas regarding the exact nature of this prophetic activity were varied, as was the identity of the expected figure. Speculation centered on Elijah as the coming prophet (see Mal. 4:5), while others awaited the return of Enoch, Moses, Ezra, or Jeremiah.

The Gospels reflect these Jewish expectations. Here we find that John the Baptist is viewed as the eschatological prophet, in the sense of being the forerunner not only of the Messiah but also of God. We read in Zechariah's hymn of praise (Luke 1:76) that the Baptist will be called "the prophet of the Most High" [God], for John "will go before the Lord [God] to prepare his ways." The angel's announcement to Zechariah indicates the same conception of the coming prophet: "With the spirit and power of Elijah he will go before him . . . to make ready a people prepared for the Lord" (Luke 1:17). While John did not think of himself as the prophet of the end time in the sense of one preparing the way for God (see Matt. 11:2-6; John 1:19-23; 3:25-30), his disciples clearly saw him in that role. The expectation of such a prophet with a specific task to perform at the end of time was widespread at the time of Jesus. This expectation was associated with the words of Moses in Deuteronomy 18:15: "The Lord your God will raise up for you a prophet like me from among your own people; you shall heed such a prophet." This prophet was expected to bear an intimate relationship to the Messiah or possibly be the Messiah.

When Jesus appeared, the masses immediately placed him in the prophetic category: "A great prophet has arisen among us!" (Luke 7:16; Mark 6:15; 8:28; John 4:19). For Luke, Jesus is "a prophet mighty in word and deed before God and all the people," as the two on the road to Emmaus call him (24:19). Their description is justified by Jesus' having raised a widow's son from death (7:11-17), as Elijah had done (1 Kgs. 17:17-24). Like Elijah, Jesus leaves the world by heavenly ascension, and, also like him, his return at the end of time is expected. Perhaps Jesus is nowhere more Elijah's antitype than in his attempt to bring the nation at large to repent and change its ways. The call to repentance occupies the greater part of Jesus' teaching on the way to Jerusalem in Luke 10-16. He curses unrepentant Jewish towns (10:13-15); he compares this unrepentant generation unfavorably with Jonah's Ninevites (11:29-32); he recalls ominously the murder of prophets (11:47-52); he holds up local disasters as warnings of worse to come if repentance fails (13:1-5); and a series of parables of repentance, beginning with the fig tree at 13:6-9, has its climax with the great parables in chapters 15 and 16, the parable of the Rich Man and Lazarus ending with prophetic indictment: "If they do not hear Moses and the prophets, neither will they be convinced if some one should rise from the dead" (16:31).

As Luke 13:31-35 indicates, not only his life but also his death show Jesus to be a prophet. Luke tells the passion story in such a way that Jesus is seen to be God's rejected prophet. Luke's version of the passion is also a final lesson in discipleship, for it culminates the teaching Jesus has been giving his disciples all along. In going to his death, Jesus shows what it means to be a servant, to face trials, and to take up one's cross.

Whether Jesus ever thought of himself or was considered by others to be *the* eschatological prophet like unto Moses, there can be little doubt that the way Jesus is presented in Acts 3:22 and 7:37 is intended to show that he is the fulfillment of Deuteronomy 18:15–19. Likewise, the opening words of the Epistle to the Hebrews, while not explicitly Mosaic, are clearly based on a view of Jesus as the prophet of eschatological consummation: "Long ago God spoke to our ancestors in many and varied ways by the prophets, but in these last days he has spoken to us by a Son" (Heb. 1:1–2).

Although Jesus speaks, heals, and dies wearing the prophetic mantle, his anointing by the Spirit points at the same time to an even higher messianic vocation. Though repudiated by unbelieving Jews, Jesus brings the promised redemption to Israel, fulfilling the hopes celebrated in Luke's preface (1:5—2:52). By the first century CE, the lack of the prophetic element in Israel was replaced by the expectation that in the messianic age the spirit of prophecy would be restored and the final prophet—the eschatological prophet—would appear to fulfill all prophecy, in preparation for the anticipated Golden Age on earth.

Messiah (Christos)

The single most common descriptive title applied to Jesus in the early years of the Christian movement was the term "Christ." In Greek, the language of the New Testament, the word "Christ" is a title, a translation of the Hebrew word for "messiah." Saying "Jesus Christ" means saying "Jesus is the Messiah." The Greek word "*Christos*" is simply a translation of the Hebrew *mashiah*, meaning "anointed one." In modern parlance the word "messiah" is roughly synonymous with "Savior," though in scholarly usage it is more specific than that. It is used in the Old Testament both for kings and high priests, who were in fact anointed, and metaphorically with reference to prophets. As used in the Hebrew Bible, the title had no future or eschatological connotation.

In the time of Saul and David the word "messiah" was used as a title for the king, designated as "the Lord's anointed" (see 1 Sam. 12:3; 16:6). God had promised to David that one of his descendants would always sit upon his throne and that "I will be a father to him, and he shall be a son to me" (2 Sam. 7:14). When the dynasty of David ended in 586 BCE, this promise gave rise to the hope that God would one day raise up from the royal house a king to sit upon the throne of David, in order to institute an endless reign of peace and justice. This Messiah would be in a special sense the Son of God. In the postexilic period, when there was no longer a king on the throne, the term as applied to a king came to refer to the one who would restore the kingship of David and usher in the eschatological age. In order to grasp the importance that the first Christians attached to "Messiah" as a title, we have only to remember that this word has functioned as *the* christological title for Christians from New Testament times until today.

In Luke's Gospel, "Messiah" is an important title. In the infancy narrative, the angel Gabriel draws on central messianic themes when he tells Mary that Jesus will be given the throne of his ancestor David (1:32; cf. 2 Sam. 7:12–13, 16) and that he will reign forever (Luke 1:33; cf. 2 Sam. 7:13, 16; Ps. 89:4, 29; 132:12; Isa. 9:7). Other messianic themes include that Jesus is born in David's city, Bethlehem (Luke 2:4, 11), thereby fulfilling the messianic prophecy in Micah 5:2. Jesus is introduced as the Messiah by the angels in the field (Luke 2:11) and confessed as such by Peter (Luke 9:20).

According to Luke, it was only after the resurrection that Jesus explained his mission to his disciples in terms of messiahship, clarifying what it meant to be Messiah and why it was necessary for the Messiah to suffer (Luke 24:24, 46). Luke also repeatedly makes use of the messianic theme that Jesus is the son of David (Luke 1:32, 69; 2:4, 11; 18:38, 39). When at his baptism Jesus was addressed as "my Son," this meant that he was being designated and anointed to his office as Messiah (Luke 3:22; see 4:18; Acts 4:27; 10:38). The theme is obviously important to Luke, who includes Jesus' genealogy to establish that Jesus is descended from David (3:23–38).

Luke believed that the cross was part of the divine plan for the Messiah, prefigured in four poetic passages concerning the Suffering Servant in Isaiah (42:1–4; 49:1–6; 50:4–11; 52:13—53:12), to which there are numerous references in Luke's Gospel (2:30–32; 3:22; 22:37). These prophecies contain descriptions of a Servant of the Lord, who is called to carry God's salvation to the nations of the world with the promise that, despite scorn, injury, and death, the Servant would usher in the reign of God. The Servant is Israel (Isa. 49:3), though Isaiah seems to have been in doubt whether his vision would be fulfilled by the whole nation, a remnant, or by one individual. Luke's contention is that Jesus identified the Servant with the Messiah, and thus interpreted his kingly office in terms not of political might and world conquest but of humble service and vicarious suffering.

In his sermon in Acts 3:13–26, Peter uses some interesting christological titles for Jesus. While they might be strange to our ears, they are among the earliest applied to Jesus. In this passage, Jesus is God's Servant, a reference to the suffering figure described in the prophet Isaiah's Servant Songs.

Jesus is also "the Holy and Righteous One . . . the Author of life, whom God raised from the dead" (3:14–15). These might be the earliest titles the followers of Jesus applied to their master after his death. Isaiah had referred to the Servant of God as "the righteous one [who makes] many righteous" (Isa. 53:11). Jesus' followers were convinced that he was legally righteous, even though he had been condemned in a Jewish and Roman court. The title "Author of life" contains an ironic twist, for the one who was put to death is the one whom God raised from the dead. "To this," Peter adds, "we are witnesses" (Acts 3:15).

Lord (Kyrios)

The term Kyrios is the most frequently used christological title in Luke–Acts, used almost twice as frequently as the term Christ. This emphasis stems from Luke's basic stress on God's sovereignty over history, as expressed in God's plan of salvation for the world that comes to fruition through Jesus. Jesus is the one who expresses and executes this salvation plan, both by his life and death and by his acts as the exalted Lord sending the Holy Spirit to work on earth in his behalf.

The expression "Jesus is Lord" belongs to the very earliest stratum of Christianity. This statement, uttered by the first Christians concerning a penniless first-century preacher from Galilee, ranks among the most astounding claims professed by mortals of another mortal. The statement can be understood on two levels, politically and religiously. As *a political claim*, Christians were affirming that their primary allegiance belonged to Jesus and not to the Roman emperor, government officials, tax collectors, bankers, businessmen, traders, the religious elite, or the military establishment. Historians traditionally attribute to Domitian, who ruled Rome from AD 81 to 96, the start of compulsive emperor worship. One of his decrees began: "Our Lord and God commands that this be done."[1] To the early Christians, such lords and gods were false and their worship blasphemous. The author of the book of Revelation implies that Christ, as "King of kings and Lord of lords," is the only emperor whom Christians can recognize. To say "Jesus is Lord" conveyed the notion of loyalty, directly challenging allegiance to Rome and to all temporal authorities. Such a claim had social, political, and economic implications, for it signified disloyalty to the state and to the Roman gods who guaranteed the state's wellbeing.[2]

---

1. Suetonius, *Domitian*, 13.

2. The author of 1 Peter, who is much more friendly to the Roman Empire than the author of Revelation, exhorts his readers to honor the emperor but to fear God (2:17)

As *a religious claim*, Christians were affirming that Jesus Christ was the personification of God, the one in whom heaven and earth met. Looking at him, and contemplating his death and resurrection in particular, they believed they could see directly into God's world, understanding God's purpose in ways previously unimagined.

To ascribe to Jesus the term "Kyrios" as a title involves an almost incredible paradox, both for the Jew trained in the Old Testament and for a Gentile from the Hellenistic world. Why incredible? Because the title "Lord" would bear a precise meaning for a Jew steeped in scripture. In the Septuagint (the Greek) version of the Hebrew Bible, Kyrios is used for Yahweh, the name of God; indeed, it translates several divine names. And in Jewish liturgies, both in Palestine and in the Jewish communities across the Mediterranean world, "kyrios" was a common word referring to God. As it says in Isaiah 42:8, "I am the Lord (Yahweh), that is my name; my glory I give to no other, nor my praise to idols." Any Jew, therefore, examining the Christian claims for Jesus, would interpret the affirmation "Jesus is Lord" to mean that Jesus is for the Christian what God is for the Jew.

In the Hellenistic Gentile world, which did not necessarily know the Septuagint, the word "kyrios" had a different meaning. In the Oriental and Hellenistic religions prevalent in the Roman Empire at the beginning of the Christian movement, lordship—whether ascribed to a deity or to a ruler—meant absolute power and authority.

The quotation from Psalm 110:1 in Acts 2:34, where both God and Jesus are referred to as "kyrios," shows the flexibility Luke was prepared to use. However, it would be wrong to conclude from such a text that Luke saw Jesus as merely the believer's Lord, for in Acts 10:36 Jesus is called "Lord of all." One of the keys to understanding Luke's use of "kyrios" is to recognize the narrative framework, which allows for a progressive understanding of christology. In general, what Luke says about Jesus depends on what point in the trajectory of his career Luke is discussing. In the Gospel narrative, no character calls Jesus "Kyrios" unless it is under inspiration (Luke 1:43, 76). As soon as the narrative progresses beyond Easter, however, various human beings can and do use Kyrios of Jesus (Luke 24:34; Acts 10:36–38).

Such progressive understanding also helps explain Luke's "adoptionist" language in texts like Acts 2:36, "God has made him both Lord and Messiah, this Jesus whom you crucified." Here, as elsewhere in Acts, Luke is using his christological language in a way that suits his narrative. From Luke's point of view, Jesus did not in any full sense assume the roles of Lord and Messiah over all until after the resurrection and ascension. A text like Acts 2:25 may

---

and to sanctify Christ as Lord in their hearts (3:15).

be understood to imply that Luke may have been aware of the concept of the preexistent Lord, well-known to later Christians from christological passages such as John 1:1–2 and Colossians 1:15–20. In any case, Acts indicates that the basic confession of the early church was the acknowledgement that Jesus is the (risen) Lord (Acts 10:40–42; 11:16; 16:31; 20:21). It is Jesus the risen and exalted Lord whom people are called to turn to and believe in. It is this risen Lord who confronts Saul on the Damascus road (9:1–17; 18:9), and to whom believers must remain faithful (20:19).

Son of God

The title Son of God occurs surprisingly seldom in Luke—only six times, once in the annunciation (1:35), twice in the devil's temptations of Jesus (4:3, 9), twice in the outcry of the demons (4:41; 8:28), and once in the accusations of the chief priests, the scribes, and the council (22:70). The disciples never worship Jesus as "Son of God," and where the centurion declares that Jesus was the Son of God in Mark, Luke has altered the statement so that the centurion says instead, "Certainly this man was innocent" (23:47). By attributing these references to the distorted perception of Jesus by the devil, the demons, and Jesus' adversaries, one might conclude that Luke diminishes the significance of this title for Jesus. However, the title appears obliquely in important contexts, such as in the annunciation (1:32, 35), his baptism (3:22), and at the transfiguration (9:35). Thereafter, Jesus appears to adopt the title in his words to the disciples (10:22) and in the parable of the wicked tenants (20:13).

In the Bible, the title Son of God is complex and capable of several meanings. While most people today take it as meaning someone divine, this is at odds with how most Jews in the first century would have understood that expression. In our way of thinking, a "son of God" would be a god and the "Son of God" would be God, but for most first-century Jews the term "Son of God" would have meant someone human. They would have understood divine sonship to mean (1) being related to God in some special way and (2) being commissioned by God to fulfill some vocation (see Luke 6:35; 20:36).

As Messiah, Jesus was also Son of God. However, this meant far more to him than an official title. At least from the age of twelve, Luke informs us, Jesus had a vivid awareness of God's paternal care and authority, which made it natural for him to speak of God as "my Father" (Luke 2:49). To be Son of God meant to live in God's love, by God's power, and for God's purpose. Later, Jesus discovered that he was unique in knowing the Father with intimacy and certitude, and that God had bestowed on him a divine task to lead others into the sonship that he enjoyed (10:21–22; 11:2).

In his genealogy Luke traces the lineage of Jesus back through David to Adam, the "son of God" (3:38), and he clearly means this to be a comment on the story of the baptism that immediately precedes it. Jesus, as Son of God, fulfills not only Israel's destiny but also the destiny of humanity. Humans were created for the kind of relationship to God that Jesus realized in his life and ministry and made possible for others.

As important as specific designations ("titles") for Jesus are in Luke's story, scholars increasingly recognize that one must draw from the entire narrative (from Jesus' acts, speech, and characterization by the narrator and by other characters) in constructing the christological profile of Luke–Acts.

APPENDIX B

Lukan Soteriology

WHEN CONTEMPORARY CHRISTIANS HEAR the word "salvation" proclaimed on television or from the pulpit, they will likely associate the concept with the evangelical notion of obtaining eternal life, meaning gaining entrance to heaven in the afterlife and spending eternity with God. However, much of ancient religion, whether pagan or Jewish, had little or nothing to do with "being saved" in this sense. The salvation most ancients sought was decidedly this-worldly, whether from disease or disaster in this life, and the redemption many desired was freedom from slavery, debt, and other such forms of social bondage. Luke's view of salvation is considerably broader than the usual pagan sense of the term.

The words "Savior" and "salvation" are found eight times in Luke's Gospel and nine times in Acts. God, of course, is sovereign Savior (Luke 1:47), and Luke provides details in 1:69, 71, 77. However, since Jesus is God's primary instrument for effecting salvation, "Savior" is also appropriate in reference to him (Luke 2:11; Acts 5:31; 13:23), and salvation is regularly associated with his person and action (Luke 6:9; 7:50; 8:36, 48, 50; 9:56; 17:19; 18:42; 19:9, 10; Acts 2:1, 40, 47; 4:9, 12; 11:14; 14:9; 15:11; 16:31). Yet, as significant as the characterization of Jesus as the Savior is in Luke, the title occurs only twice in the Gospel, both times in the infancy narrative. In the first instance it is applied to God (1:47), and in the second an angel announces to the shepherds: "To you is born this day in the city of David a Savior, who is the Messiah, the Lord" (2:11).[1]

1. Of the Synoptic writers, only Luke gives Jesus the title "Savior."

In ancient times, heads of state were frequently identified as "saviors" because of their expected or real benefactions. Luke's references to Jesus as a person with royal credentials (Luke 1:33; 19:38; 22:29, 30; 23:42; indirectly in 19:14, 27; 23:2, 3, 37, 38; Acts 17:7) form part of Luke's unified picture of Jesus as the Great Benefactor, whose purpose and mission is to effect salvation for all humanity (see Acts 10:38). In the Greek world, salvation was typically associated with the bestowal of various blessings and gifts, while in the Old Testament salvation was conceived more as deliverance from enemies.

In the Old Testament, salvation assures the individual renewed relationship with God, though it also conveys protection and liberation from foreign powers. For Luke, the concept of salvation also has social, physical, and spiritual dimensions. For example, in the paradigmatic speech of Jesus in Luke 4, salvation is equated with the preaching of good news to the poor, release to the captives, recovery of sight to the blind, and freeing of those oppressed. The social dimension is seen in the concern for the poor and the release of the captives, the latter of which includes release from demonic possession but is not confined to that realm. We see this dimension in the parable of the prodigal son (Luke 15), where family reconciliation is in view; in the story of Zacchaeus in Luke 19, who is being set free from social prejudice against tax collectors; and in the story of the sinner woman of Luke 7 who is freed from social stigma and being an outcast from society. Healing and exorcism are also seen as means or forms of salvation (in Luke 8:48 the text reads literally "your faith has saved [i.e. healed] you"). These same notions of salvation carry over into the book of Acts, though they do not exhaust Luke's concept of salvation.

For example, already in the Gospel we hear of salvation in the form of forgiveness of sins (Luke 5:20), though even there the physical and spiritual concepts are interrelated. The latter, more "spiritual" view of salvation becomes more prominent in the book of Acts, as the paradigmatic speech in Acts 2 makes clear (2:21, 38). Yet the integral connection between healing and salvation continues to be clear in Acts, as chapters 3–4 show. In Acts 4:9–10 the healing of the crippled beggar happens in Jesus' name, which leads Peter to conclude, "There is salvation in no one else, for there is no other name under heaven, given among mortals by which we must be saved" (4:12).

Like the jailor in Acts 16:30–31, who asks Paul and Silas what he must do to be "saved," belief in Jesus is said to be sufficient not only for the jailor but for his household. It is hard to imagine that the jailor's faith would be sufficient to "save" in the spiritual sense his entire household. Surely what is meant here is that the jailor and his family would be spared from calamity if he believes (i.e. "trusts") in Jesus.

Healings and exorcisms are also saving acts because they remove chosen people from the sphere of Satan's power. Likewise, forgiveness of sins brings liberation from bondage, that is, from the servitude people enter when they turn away from God. In the book of Acts, God's divine prerogative is transferred to Jesus. There, divine gifts are received through conversion, that is, through proclamation and repentance. As 2:21 indicates, converting to Jesus means calling him "Lord," and confessing that he is the promised Savior. God has sent Jesus forth into the world to rescue us from our enemies and to forgive our sins (see 2:38; 3:19; 5:31; 13:38–39; 15:9) and thus to liberate us from eternal death (see 13:46). However, salvation also involves healing the sick (3:7–8; 4:8–12; 28:7–9); illuminating the ignorant (see 3:17; 13:27; 17:30); rescuing the vulnerable from political threat (see 12:4–11; 16:30–31), hunger, and material poverty (see 4:33–34); protection against demonic powers (see 5:16; 16:16–18; 19:11–20; 26:17–18); and protection from natural catastrophe (see 27:21–26, 31–44). Each expression of saving grace heralds God's faithfulness to the biblical promise of a "universal restoration" (see 3:21). It is striking that Luke never uses the term "savior" or "salvation" when he writes about the healing of the sick or the raising of the dead, though the verbal form "to save" with the meaning "heal" does appear, as we have mentioned.

One final observation remains. Luke above all other Gospel writers has a sense of and concern about historical development.[2] This affects both his christology and his soteriology. As scholars note, the christology of Acts is not simply identical with that found in Luke's Gospel, but is rather a further development of it, drawing particularly on crucial events at the close of Jesus' earthly life such as his resurrection and ascension. Of the three passages in Luke–Acts where the term Savior is used of Jesus (Luke 2:11; Acts 5:31; 13:23), especially interesting is Acts 5:31. Here Luke's sense of the historical development of faith is clearly evident, for properly speaking, Jesus does not assume the full role of savior and leader prior to God's having raised him from the dead and exalted him to divine authority. It is only then that Jesus sends the Holy Spirit, which in Lukan theology is seen as Christ's agent bringing salvation to the world (Acts 2:33–38, 48). For this reason we find in Luke's Gospel more mundane sense of the words for salvation than we do in Acts. This is because in Luke's way of thinking, salvation in its more spiritual sense comes about because of Christ's death and resurrection.

---

2. The material in the closing portion of this appendix is adapted from Ben Witherington's essay "The Soteriology of Luke–Acts in Its First-Century Setting," *Acts*, 821–43.

Another factor that accounts for a focus on the more spiritual dimension of salvation in Acts is the coming of God's Holy Spirit, who comes at Pentecost as the dispenser of final salvation.

The prophecy of Joel 2:28-32 cited in Acts 2:16-21 ends with the promise that whoever calls on the name of the Lord will be saved. Who this Lord is, is clarified in what immediately follows—Jesus of Nazareth (2:22-24). Since Luke is a monotheist, it is no surprise that we have the exclusive statement in 4:12: "There is salvation in no one else, for there is no other name under heaven given among mortals by which we must be saved." Luke clearly believes in a universal gospel about salvation for all people (see Luke 2:30-32), but the sole means of obtaining this salvation is through Jesus.

The spiritual meaning of God's act of salvation is the forgiveness of sins, a crucial result and benefit of salvation declared by Luke in Zechariah's prophecy (see Luke 1:77). For Luke, salvation at its core has to do with God's gracious act of forgiving sins through Jesus, which results in the moral, mental, emotional, spiritual, and sometimes physical transformation of an individual. We see this clearly in a text like Luke 19:1-10, the story of Zacchaeus. The story climaxes at 19:9-10, where we are told, "Today salvation has come to this house." What is meant is the transformation of someone's character, the recovery of a spiritually lost individual. Evidence of Zacchaeus's change or conversion is shown by his sudden willingness to give to the poor and pay back fourfold to those he had defrauded. Certainly, "salvation" for Luke has social consequences, but equally clearly is a spiritual transformation of human personality that leads a person to see the logical social consequences of receiving Jesus.

Apart from texts that indicate the present dimension of salvation, two texts speak of a future dimension, Acts 2:21 (part of the quote from the prophet Joel) and Acts 15:11. In the first text, which draws on the Old Testament concept of the Day of the Lord, "salvation" in that setting refers to those who escape the judgment and calamity of that day. Interestingly, Peter makes one noteworthy change in the Acts quotation from Joel, calling the day "great and glorious" instead of "great and terrible" (Acts 3:20/Joel 2:31). This may suggest that Peter's emphasis in his sermon is not on the coming judgment but on the coming redemption implied by the concept of salvation. The same may be said about the other future-oriented text, Acts 15:11. While salvation there has a future reference, we are not told what salvation entails, or what its benefits will be. This drives us back to Luke's Gospel. In Luke 18:26-27, "being saved" is equated with entering God's kingdom, a reality present both in this age (see 17:21) and in the age to come. For Luke, the future is already present, yet not fully so.

What we learn from this discussion is that for Luke salvation, in the present, means forgiveness of sins, spiritual regeneration, and transformation of one's character. While it may be accompanied by immediate, temporal, and even physical benefits, "being saved" does not carry with it guarantees of long life, wealth, safety through trials, or even perpetually good health. What it does promise in a more exclusively futuristic or spiritual sense is "eternal life," an indescribable gift not previously available but made possible by the death and resurrection of Jesus. As Witherington notes, "Luke sees the coming of Christ as not just another epoch of history but as the beginning of the eschatological age, when the dominion of God breaks into human history" through the coming of the Spirit at Pentecost to inaugurate the age of salvation for all peoples. For Luke, it is not the Roman emperor or any other political figure but Christ who is the catalyst of this greatest of all blessings, with benefits both temporal and eternal.[3]

Salvation, in the Lukan sense, is something that comes from and properly belongs to God. From the early chapters of the Gospel, where Simeon claims to have seen "your salvation" (2:30), to the end of Acts, where we hear that God's salvation "has been sent to the Gentiles" (28:28), it is clear that God is the ultimate source of salvation. Salvation is something humans can receive, not achieve; it must be given to them by God.

---

3. Ibid, 843.

Bibliography

Anderson, Bernhard W. *Understanding the Old Testament*. 5th ed. Upper Saddle River, NJ: Pearson Prentice Hall, 2007.
Anderson, Richard H. "Theophilus: A Proposal." *EvQ* 69 (1997) 195–215.
Borg, Marcus J. *The Heart of Christianity*. New York: HarperSanFrancisco, 2004.
Bridges, William. *Transitions: Making Sense of Life's Changes*. Reading, MA: Addison-Wesley, 1980.
Brown, Raymond E. *An Introduction to the New Testament*. New York: Doubleday, 1997.
———. *The Birth of the Messiah: A Commentary on the Infancy Narratives in the Gospels of Matthew and Luke*. Rev. ed. New York: Doubleday, 1993.
Bruce, F. F. *The Acts of the Apostles*. Rev. ed. New International Commentary on the New Testament. Grand Rapids, MI: Eerdmans, 1988 (1956).
———. *Paul, Apostle of the Heart Set Free*. Grand Rapids: Eerdmans, 1991.
Burridge, R. *What Are the Gospels?* Cambridge: Cambridge University Press, 1991.
Cadbury, Henry J. *The Making of Luke–Acts*. London: SPCK, 1958 (1927).
Caird, G. B. *The Gospel of St. Luke*. Pelican Gospel Commentaries. New York: Seabury, 1968.
Cassidy, Richard J. *Jesus, Politics, and Society: A Study of Luke's Gospel*. Maryknoll, NY: Orbis, 1978.
Chrupcala, L. Daniel. *Everyone Will See the Salvation of God: Studies in Lukan Theology*. Milan, Italy: Edizioni Terra Santa, 2015.
Conzelmann, Hans. *The Theology of St. Luke*. 2nd ed. Translated by Geoffrey Buswell. Philadelphia: Fortress, 1982.
Craddock, Fred B. *Luke*. Interpretation: A Bible Commentary for Teaching and Preaching. Louisville: John Knox, 1990.
Culpepper. R. Alan. "The Gospel of Luke." In *The New Interpreter's Bible* IX:3–490.
Danker, Frederick W. *Jesus and the New Age: A Commentary on St. Luke's Gospel*. Rev. ed. Philadelphia: Fortress, 1988.
Drane, John. *Introducing the New Testament*. Rev. ed. Minneapolis: Fortress, 2001.
Drury, John. *Tradition and Design in Luke's Gospel: A Study in Early Christian Historiography*. London: Darton, Longman, and Todd, 1976.
Dunn, J. D. G. *The Acts of the Apostles*. Valley Forge, PA: Trinity, 1996.
Fitzmyer, Joseph A. *The Gospel According to Luke*. 2 vols. The Anchor Bible 28, 28A. Garden City, NY: Doubleday, 1981, 1985.

Franklin, Eric. *Christ the Lord: A Study in the Purpose and Theology of Luke–Acts.* Philadelphia: Westminster, 1975.
González, Justo L. *Luke.* Belief: A Theological Commentary on the Bible. Louisville, KY: Westminster John Knox, 2010.
Goodacre, Mark S. *Goulder and the Gospels: An Examination of a New Paradigm.* Sheffield: Sheffield Academic Press, 1996.
Goulder, Michael D. *The Evangelist's Calendar—A Lectionary Explanation of the Development of Scripture.* London: SPCK, 1978.
———. *Luke: A New Paradigm.* 2 vols. Sheffield: Sheffield Academic Press, 1989.
Haenchen, Ernst. *The Acts of the Apostles.* Transl. and rev. by R. McL. Wilson. Philadelphia: Westminster, 1971.
Hahn, Ferdinand. *Mission in the New Testament.* London: SCM, 1965.
Jervell, Jacob. *Luke and the People of God.* Minneapolis: Augsburg, 1972.
Knight, George W., III. *The Pastoral Epistles.* The New International Greek Testament Commentary. Grand Rapids, MI: Eerdmans, 1999.
Krodel, Gerhard. *Acts.* Augsburg Commentaries on the New Testament. Minneapolis: Augsburg, 1986.
Maddox, Robert. *The Purpose of Luke–Acts.* Edinburgh: T & T Clark, 1982.
Marshall, I. H. *Luke: Historian and Theologian.* Grand Rapids: Zondervan, 1970.
Mattill, A. J., Jr. *Luke and the Last Things.* Dillsboro, NC: Western North Carolina Press, 1979.
McLaren, Brian D. *A New Kind of Christian: A Tale of Two Friends on a Spiritual Journey.* San Francisco: Jossey-Bass, 2001.
Metzger, Bruce. *A Textual Commentary on the Greek New Testament.* 2nd ed. Minneapolis: Fortress, 1994.
Minear, Paul. *To Heal and To Reveal: The Prophetic Vocation According to Luke.* New York: Seabury Press, 1976.
Munck, Johannes. *The Acts of the Apostles.* The Anchor Bible 31. Garden City, NY: Doubleday, 1967.
Pilgrim, Walter E. *Good News to the Poor: Wealth and Poverty in Luke–Acts.* Minneapolis: Augsburg, 1981.
Powell, Mark Allan. *What Are They Saying About Luke?* New York: Paulist, 1989
———. *What Are They Saying About Acts?* New York: Paulist, 1991.
Richard, Earl. *New Views on Luke and Acts.* Collegeville, MN: Liturgical, 1990.
Rohr, Richard. *The Good News According to Luke.* New York: Crossroad, 1997.
———. *The Universal Christ.* New York: Convergent, 2019.
Schürer, Emil. *The History of the Jewish People in the Age of Jesus Christ* (175 BC–AD 135). Rev. by Geza Vermes and Fergus Millar. Vol 1. Edinburgh: T. & T. Clark, 1973.
Spencer, F. Scott. *The Gospel of Luke and Acts of the Apostles.* Interpreting Biblical Texts. Nashville: Abingdon, 2008.
Spong, John Shelby. *Born of a Woman.* New York: HarperSanFrancisco, 1992.
———. *Liberating the Gospels: Reading the Bible with Jewish Eyes.* New York: HarperSanFrancisco, 1996.
———. *Why Christianity Must Change or Die.* New York: HarperOne, 1999.
Talbert, Charles H. *Literary Patterns, Theological Themes and the Genre of Luke–Acts.* Society of Biblical Literature Monograph Series 20. Missoula, MT: Scholars, 1974.
———. *Perspectives on Luke–Acts.* Edinburgh: Clark, 1978.

———. *Reading Acts: A Literary and Theological Commentary on the Acts of the Apostles.* New York: Crossroad, 1997.

Tannehill, Robert C. *The Narrative Unity of Luke–Acts: A Literary Interpretation.* 2 vols. Philadelphia: Fortress, 1986, 1990.

Valantasis, Richard, et al. *The Gospels and Christian Life in History and Practice.* Lanham, MD: Rowman & Littlefield, 2009.

Vande Kappelle Sr., Robert P. *The New Creation: Church History Made Accessible, Relevant, and Personal.* Eugene, OR: Wipf & Stock, 2018.

Wall, Robert N. "The Acts of the Apostles." In *The New Interpreter's Bible* X:3–368.

Wenham, John. "The Identification of Luke." *EvQ* 63 (1991) 3–44.

Willimon, William H. *Acts.* Interpretation: A Bible Commentary for Teaching and Preaching. Louisville: John Knox, 1988.

Witherington, Ben, III. *The Acts of the Apostles: A Socio-Rhetorical Commentary.* Grand Rapids, MI: Eerdmans, 1998.

———. *Jesus the Sage: The Pilgrimage of Wisdom.* Minneapolis: Fortress, 1994.

Wright, N. T. *Jesus and the Victory of God.* Minneapolis: Fortress, 1996.

Index

Abraham, 41, 130, 199, 205
Acts, book of, x, xii
    Alexandrian text of, 87n3
    date of, 69
    ending of, 38, 43, 230, 237–38
    as history, 11, 13, 60
    and Paul's letters, 13, 33, 34n2, 41, 48, 69, 203, 207n9, 220–21, 223, 231–35
    plot and structure, 44–45
    as second-hand primary source, 5
    speeches in, 58, 87, 188–89, 198
    use of sources in, 68–69
    Western text of, 87n3
adoptionism/exaltationism, 120, 121
advent, 73
afterlife, 172
Anderson, Richard H., 42n11
angel, 194, 202
Antioch church, 37, 41, 69, 198, 212–13, 214, 217. 220, 234
Anti-Marcionite Prologue to the Gospel of Luke, 36, 41
anti-Semitism, 104, 176
apocryphal gospels, 18
Apollos, 112
apostles, 98, 100, 112, 174, 183, 185, 196, 211, 234
    healing ministry of, 192, 194
apostolic authority, 25
apostolic decree, 222–23, 232
apostolic teaching, 98, 111, 136
Athanasius, 19

atheism, 91

Bacon, B. W., 75. 76
baptism, 137, 190, 202, 210
Barabbas, 176
Barnabas, 107, 108, 183, 191, 207, 211, 212, 214, 217–20, 221, 222
Bartsch, Hans, 96
Baur, Ferdinand Christian, 101, 102
beatitudes, 89
Book of Mormon, 58
Borg, Marcus, 28
Bridges, William, 10
Brown, Raymond, 13, 129
Burridge, Richard, 57

Caesarea, 31, 124n3, 202, 207, 208, 210, 214, 226, 229
Cadbury, Henry, ix, 14
canonical process, 17–19, 20, 22, 28–29
Cassidy, Richard, 14–15
charismatic authority, 25
Christian
    ways of being, 22–25
Christmas, 118
christology. See Luke (biblical writer), christological agenda
Chrysostom, John, 37, 82
church, 100, 191, 212
    charismatic nature of, x–xi
    continuity with Israel, 11, 84, 92, 93, 96, 97, 101, 102, 103, 104, 125, 176, 184, 191

church (*continued*)
  evangelistic task, 98, 100, 112, 200
  expansion of, 100, 102–3
  Gentile constituency, 84, 102, 103
  Gentile governance. *See* elders
  harmony and unity among early
    believers, 11, 101–2, 185, 191
  persecution of, 213, 214
  and Roman state, 90–94, 95, 176
Claudius (emperor) 212, 213
Codex Alexandrinus, 73, 77
conflict resolution 221
Constantine (emperor), 71, 72, 174, 213
Conzelmann, Hans, 14, 94, 95, 96, 97
Cook, Robert, 152
Cornelius, 38, 59, 69, 89, 96, 107, 144, 206, 208, 221
  conversion of, 208–11

Damascus, 107, 204, 205, 206
Dante Alighieri, ix
David (king of Israel), 7, 63, 124, 126, 131, 151, 159, 166, 184, 199, 241, 242, 246
devil, diabolical, 139, 245
discipleship, 48, 109–10, 112, 143, 144, 147, 148, 151, 152, 154, 156–57, 161, 165, 209, 241
docetism, 181
Domitian (emperor), 243
Drury, John, xiii, 66
dualistic thinking, 99
Dunn, James, 62

Easter, 72, 73, 74, 77, 82, 118, 119–21, 180, 244
Eastern Orthodoxy, 153
elders (church governance), 41, 211, 220
Ephesus church, 41, 225–26
Elijah, 64, 65, 133, 145, 148, 150, 152, 184, 240
Elisha, 65, 144. 145, 148, 150
Emmaus narrative, 180–81
Ephesus church, 41, 225–26
Epiphanius, 37
eternal life, 251
Ethiopian eunuch, 47, 89, 202
exodus, the, 86, 189

Farrar, Austin, 76
Fitzmyer, Joseph, 36, 97

Galilee, 69, 90, 104–5, 179, 186, 237
Gamaliel, 11, 195, 200, 203–4
General (Catholic) Epistles, 46, 48
Gentiles, 209–10
  "God-fearers," 38, 78, 84, 109, 125, 208, 219
  Jewish proselytes, 38, 107, 137
  mission to, 94, 96, 103–5, 107–8, 153, 185, 186, 209, 210, 212, 220, 221–22, 224, 225
Gentilizers, 104, 222
Gnostics, Gnosticism, 18
González, Justo, 90
Good Samaritan (parable), 64, 155
Gospels, 76
  as biographies, 56–57
  form criticism of, 68
  as literary genre, 56
  narrative criticism of, 68
  redaction criticism of, 68
  source criticism of, 66–67
Goulder, Michael, xiii, 66, 70, 73, 76, 77, 79, 80, 81, 82, 84
Griesbach, Johannes, 66

Haenchen, Ernst, 196n8, 211
haggadah, 119
Hanukkah, 74
Herodotus, 15
Hillel, 195
Hippocrates, 15
historiography, 4–6
  See also Luke, as historiographer
Holy Spirit, 49, 83, 96, 121, 122, 231, 249, 250
  age of, 100
  baptism with, 137, 187, 190
  blasphemy against, 158
  and early church, xi, 11, 187
  in Acts, x–xi, xii, 44, 55, 81, 87, 183, 187
  and Jesus, x, 87, 96, 132, 138, 140, 180, 187, 194n4, 241
  and prayer, 156

idolatry, 220, 223, 232
immortality, 172, 179
incarnation, 120, 121, 123, 132
infancy narrative, 37, 67, 77, 118–23, 124–28
Intertestamental Literature, 20
intertextuality, 53, 62, 63
Irenaeus, 33, 46
Israel, 103, 137, 153–54, 171, 185, 196, 230
    God's election of, 112, 154, 209
    God's promises to, 42–43, 101, 174, 217
    restoration of, 94, 97, 103, 104, 184, 192, 231

James (the Just), 189, 210, 211, 213, 214, 221, 222, 223
Jerusalem, 150, 198
    apostolic mission in, 186–96
    church at, 41, 212, 213, 214, 222, 223
    Council, 12, 49, 59, 107, 109, 210, 220–24
    as Lukan metaphor, 105, 106, 141, 148, 150, 151, 179, 180n5, 181
    New, 174
    Roman destruction of, 84, 91, 92, 101, 171, 172–73, 174, 227
Jervell, Jacob, 36, 102, 103
Jesus Christ, 9, 12
    ascension of, 94, 120–21, 179, 181, 183–84, 240
    baptism of, 137–38, 242
    crucifixion of, 83, 85–88, 118, 120, 168, 176–78, 194, 242
    Galilean ministry of, 141–48
    genealogy of, 67, 76, 77, 124, 138, 237, 242, 246
    and God's saving activity, xiii, 15, 210, 243
    healing ministry of, 142
    humanity of, 139–41
    passion of, 168, 174–76, 240–41
    resurrection of, 88, 97, 118, 119–21, 168, 178–81, 183
    return of. See parousia
    teaching ministry of, 142–43
    temptation of, 138–41, 184
    transfiguration of, 74, 113, 148, 179, 185, 245
    and women, 110, 143, 146, 155, 179
John, Gospel of, 66, 81, 92, 123, 136n1, 176n3, 201n4, 209
John the Baptist, 65, 67
    birth of, x, 118, 126, 127, 133, 196
    influence of, 125, 128, 190
    and Jesus, 88, 113, 121, 123, 125, 127, 128, 138, 145, 160
    message of, 81, 137
    ministry of, 136–37
    role of, 74, 77n3, 95, 240
Johnson, Luke Timothy, 22
Jonah, sign of, 157
Josephus, 12, 15, 42n11, 57, 130, 195, 203
Joshua, 76
Jubilee, year of, 88, 141
Judaizers, 104, 107, 211, 221
Julius Caesar, 91, 203
Justin Martyr, 81, 86

Käsemann, Ernst, ix
kerygma, 131, 136n1, 188, 189, 210, 218
kingdom of God, 88–89, 138, 151, 152–53, 156, 162, 167, 184, 231
    in Acts, 229n10
    as Banquet feast, 147–48
    children and, 165
    consummation of, 172, 173
    discourse on, 75, 77
    entrance into, 166, 250
    as good news, 88, 89, 95
    nature of, 159–63, 174
    nearness of, 74, 96, 129, 153, 162, 173
    present nature of, 88–89, 154, 158, 159–61, 167, 173, 250–51
    requirements of, 24
    signs of, 90

Last Supper narrative, 87, 148, 166, 174, 185
leadership, 174–75, 226
lectionary, 72–73, 76, 78, 80, 81
Lightfoot, J. B., 13

Lincoln, Abraham, 5
liturgy, 71–72, 73
Livy, 57
Lord's Prayer, 155–56, 162
Luke (biblical writer)
    apologetic intent, 14, 43, 60, 83, 85–88, 92, 178, 181, 190, 192–93, 208
    as author, ix, 54
    christological agenda, xiii, 98, 112–13, 127, 151, 175, 180, 187, 188, 189, 192, 200, 239–46
    disciple of Jesus, 37–38
    and divine necessity, 87
    and doctrine of atonement, 87
    ecclesiastical agenda, 83, 91–94, 185, 190, 191
    eschatological agenda, 83, 94–97
    ethnicity of, 36–38
    as historiographer, ix, xiii, 10–15, 53, 57–59
    intent to write a trilogy, 38–40
    literary approach, 53–63
    liturgical task, 70, 78–82, 84
    missional agenda, 98, 100–108
    pastoral agenda, 98, 108–12, 185
    and Paul, 32–34, 65, 68–69, 203–4, 220–21, 224–25, 231–35
    and role of the resurrection, 88
    social agenda, xiii, 14–15, 34–35, 83, 88–90, 148, 164, 172, 195–96, 210, 248
    soteriological agenda, 247–51
    use of sources, 63–69, 78–79, 124, 141, 165, 189
Luke, Gospel of, ix, 57
    plot and structure, 43–44
    portrayal of Jesus, 112, 113
    prologue of, 13, 15, 32, 37, 55, 57, 65, 67, 85
Luke–Acts, ix, xii, xiv, 3, 10, 12, 31–50, 83, 92
    audience, 40–41, 42–43
    authorship, 32–40
    autographs of, 87n3
    as canon, 46–49
    date of, 41–42
    and Deuteronomy, 64–65, 79, 150

    genres of, 56–60
    geographical inaccuracies, 12
    historical inaccuracies, 11–12, 195
    Jewishness of, xiii, 36, 81, 84, 126, 196, 232
    and Pastoral Epistles, 39–40
    plot, 43
    purpose of, xiii, xiv, 85–86
    reliability of, 3, 10–14, 15, 69

Marcion(ism), 19, 104
Mark, Gospel of, 41, 56, 57, 65, 66, 67, 70, 77, 78, 98, 112–13
    biographical details of Jesus' life, 121–22
    Jewish liturgical framework, 73–75
    mission to the Gentiles, 104–5
Marshall, I. H., 12
Mary (mother of Jesus), 65, 69, 90, 124, 127, 131, 146n6, 185
Matill, A. J., 96
Matthew, Gospel of, 41, 57, 65, 66, 67, 70, 92
    infancy narrative, 118-19, 122
    Jewish liturgical framework, 75–78
McLaren, Brian, 27
Metzger, Bruce, 87n3
midrash, xiii–xiv, 36, 125, 129–30, 172, 189
mimesis, 57–58
Minucius Felix, 86
miracle stories, 12, 23, 56, 60, 146–47, 147–48, 189–90, 192
Moses
    antitype in Jesus, 75–76, 112, 130, 193, 240, 241
    prominence in Luke–Acts, 65, 189, 199
    role of, 7, 64, 153, 240
    and Torah, 72, 75–76, 80, 172, 184, 187
    and transfiguration of Jesus, 64, 148, 185
Muratorian Canon, 19, 33

Nero (emperor), 91, 229, 231

outsider, other, the, 164, 171

parables, 44, 64, 89, 146, 162–64, 171
parousia, 18, 94, 95, 96, 97, 167, 173, 178, 186, 240
Passover, 72, 74, 77, 78–79, 81, 86, 134, 169, 178, 186
Pastoral Epistles
   authorship, 39–40, 231
Paul (apostle), 45, 101–2, 107, 183, 186, 189, 200
   apostleship of, 234
   conversion of, 107, 202–6
   critique of church, 102
   ecclesiology, 205–6
   Eucharistic formula in, 36
   first missionary journey of, 211, 214, 217–20
   at Jerusalem Council, 220–24
   and Judaism, 108–9, 227, 228–29, 232–33
   letters of, 5, 220, 224, 225, 226
   mission in Athens, 59, 225
   mission in Corinth, 225
   as persecutor of Christians, 203, 204–5, 207
   as Pharisee, 206
   preaching to Gentiles, 220
   preaching to Jews, 218–19
   role of Holy Spirit in, x–xi
   Roman citizenship of, 233–34
   at Rome, 229–31
   scandal of the cross in, 85, 87
   second missionary journey of, 224–25
   and spiritual gifts, xi–xii
   third missionary journey of, 225–26
   trials of, 59, 93, 94, 193, 227, 227–29, 230, 231, 238
   view of church and state, 92
   view regarding Easter, 121
   view regarding "Israel," 103–4
   view regarding resurrection, 178–79
   voyage to Rome, 229
Pentecost, xi, 59, 72, 73, 77, 80, 81, 100, 107, 137, 153, 182, 186–91, 194, 201, 210, 226
   Jewish celebration of, 186–87

Peter (apostle), 45, 86, 94, 101–2, 107, 180, 189, 190, 192, 193, 194, 211–12, 213–14, 221, 222, 231, 242–43, 248, 250
   call of, 143
   and Cornelius, 207–11
   denial of Jesus by, 175, 209
   Pentecost sermon of, 186, 189
Pharisees, 17, 26, 36, 86, 89, 113, 145, 157, 164, 165, 169, 171, 171–72, 193, 195, 227
Philip, 196, 198, 201–2
Philo, 130, 187
Plutarch, 60
power, spiritual, x–xi, 192, 194, 201–2
prayer, 111, 155–56, 165, 193–94
Priscilla, 47, 225
prophets (Christian), 212, 217, 226
Proto-Luke Hypothesis, 66–67, 123–24

"Q" source, xiv, 65, 66, 67, 124

Ramsay, William M., 13
Renan, Ernst, ix
repentance, 157–58, 240, 249
reversal, 90
Ricoeur, Paul, 4
Rohr, Richard, 6, 151
Rosh Hashanah, 74

sabbath, 142–43, 178
sacraments, 72, 174
Sadducees, 17, 171–72, 193, 194, 227
salvation, 112n4, 177
   See also Luke (biblical writer), soteriological agenda
salvation history, 95, 108, 184, 189
Samaria, Samaritans, 34–35, 44, 64, 107, 152, 155, 186, 201–2
Sanhedrin, 15, 93, 175, 178, 193–95, 200, 206, 227, 230
Schuller, Robert, 9
Schürer, Emil, 227
scripture
   authority of, 26
   canon of, 17–21, 22, 25
   Christian, 17–18
   definition of, 20

scripture (*continued*)
   Hebrew, 17, 20, 26, 72–73, 75, 77, 79, 86, 103, 106, 126, 129, 132, 176
   interpretation of, 21–22, 25, 26–28, 86, 193
   reading, 25–28, 49
   and tradition, 20–21
Septuagint, 21, 36, 53, 58, 63, 132, 188, 219, 222n5, 244
Sermon on the Mount, 24, 75, 76, 77, 81, 144
Sermon on the Plain, 24, 61, 89, 141, 143, 161
servanthood, 112, 174, 241
signs and wonders, 189–90, 192
Silas, 224, 248
Simon Magus, 201
spiritual gifts, xi–xii
Spong, John, 66, 77n2
Stephen's speech and martyrdom, 59, 64, 69, 107, 189, 193, 198–200, 204, 228
Sukkoth, 74
Synoptic apocalypse, 172–74
Synoptic criticism, xiii–xiv, 66
   See also source criticism
Synoptic tradition, 25, 66, 70, 73, 94

table fellowship, 89, 98, 110, 142, 164, 209, 210
Tacitus, 57, 91
Talbert, Charles, 60, 62
Talmud, 72

temple, 132–33, 170, 172, 181, 191, 194, 196, 198, 199
temptation narrative, 77
ten Boom, Corrie, 9
Tertullian, 33, 38
testimonia, 188, 218–19
theology
   definition of, 99
Theophilus, 32, 42, 85, 92, 238
Thucydides, 15, 60
Torah, 7, 17, 21, 72, 76, 78, 79, 80, 81, 92
travel narrative, xiv, 44, 64, 65, 79, 106, 150–67, 240
truth, 171
Twelve, the (apostolic disciples), 65, 67, 142, 147, 153, 183, 185, 186, 196, 201, 222
two-source theory, 66

Virgin Birth, 131–32

"we" passages, 33–34, 37, 68, 224–25, 232
wealth and poverty, 89–90, 144, 161, 162, 165, 223
Wenham, John, 37n6
Willimon, William, 4
Witherington, Ben, 249n2, 251
witness, 200
Wright, N. T., 140
Wycliffe, John, 128

Yom Kippur, 74, 80

Zacchaeus, 89, 250

www.ingramcontent.com/pod-product-compliance
Lightning Source LLC
Chambersburg PA
CBHW060557230426
43670CB00011B/1860